D1466836

The American Crisis Series

Books on the Civil War Era

Steven E. Woodworth, Associate Professor of History,
Texas Christian University
SERIES EDITOR

≋ The Civil War was the crisis of the Republic's first century —the test, in Abraham Lincoln's words, of whether any free government could long endure. It touched with fire the hearts of a generation, and its story has fired the imaginations of every generation since. This series offers to students of the Civil War, either those continuing or those just beginning their exciting journey into the past, concise overviews of important persons, events, and themes in that remarkable period of America's history.

Volumes Published

James L. Abrahamson. *The Men of Secession and Civil War, 1859–1861* (2000). Cloth ISBN 0-8420-2818-8   Paper ISBN 0-8420-2819-6

Robert G. Tanner. *Retreat to Victory? Confederate Strategy Reconsidered* (2001). Cloth ISBN 0-8420-2881-1 Paper ISBN 0-8420-2882-X

Stephen Davis. *Atlanta Will Fall: Sherman, Joe Johnston, and the Yankee Heavy Battalions* (2001). Cloth ISBN 0-8420-2787-4 Paper ISBN 0-8420-2788-2

Paul Ashdown and Edward Caudill. *The Mosby Myth: A Confederate Hero in Life and Legend* (2002). Cloth ISBN 0-8420-2928-1 Paper ISBN 0-8420-2929-X

Spencer C. Tucker. *A Short History of the Civil War at Sea* (2002). Cloth ISBN 0-8420-2867-6   Paper ISBN 0-8420-2868-4

Richard Bruce Winders. *Crisis in the Southwest: The United States, Mexico, and the Struggle over Texas* (2002). Cloth ISBN 0-8420-2800-5   Paper ISBN 0-8420-2801-3

Ethan S. Rafuse. *A Single Grand Victory: The First Campaign and Battle of Manassas* (2002). Cloth ISBN 0-8420-2875-7 Paper ISBN 0-8420-2876-5

John G. Selby. *Virginians at War: The Civil War Experiences of Seven Young Confederates* (2002). Cloth ISBN 0-8420-5054-X
Paper ISBN 0-8420-5055-8

Edward K. Spann. *Gotham at War: New York City, 1860–1865* (2002). Cloth ISBN 0-8420-5056-6   Paper ISBN 0-8420-5057-4

Anne J. Bailey. *War and Ruin: William T. Sherman and the Savannah Campaign* (2002). Cloth ISBN 0-8420-2850-1
Paper ISBN 0-8420-2851-X

Gary Dillard Joiner. *One Damn Blunder from Beginning to End: The Red River Campaign of 1864* (2003). Cloth ISBN 0-8420-2936-2
Paper ISBN 0-8420-2937-0

Virginians at War

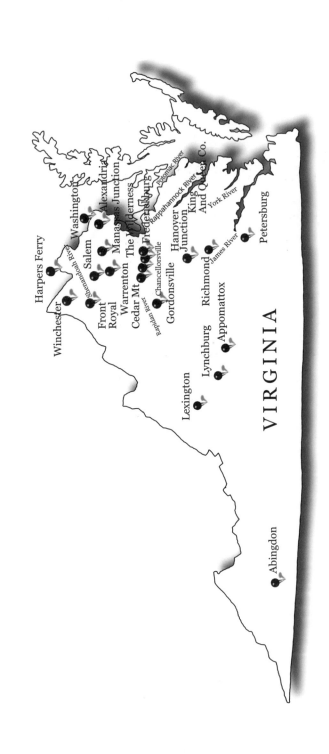

Harpers Ferry

Winchester

Shenandoah River

Washington

Salem

Front Royal

Alexandria

Manassas Junction

Warrenton

Cedar Mt

The Wilderness

Fredericksburg

Potomac River

Rapidan River

Chancellorsville

Gordonsville

Rappahannock River

Hanover Junction

King And Queen River Co.

York River

Richmond

James River

Petersburg

Lynchburg

Appomattox

Lexington

VIRGINIA

Abingdon

Virginians at War
The Civil War Experiences of Seven Young Confederates

The American Crisis Series
BOOKS ON THE CIVIL WAR ERA
NO. 8

John G. Selby

A Scholarly Resources Inc. Imprint
Wilmington, Delaware

Scholarly Resources Inc.
104 Greenhill Avenue
Wilmington, DE 19805-1897
www.scholarly.com

Cover (clockwise):

AMANDA VIRGINIA "TEE" EDMONDS—From Amanda Virginia Edmonds, *Journals of Amanda Virginia Edmonds: Lass of the Mosby Confederacy, 1859–1867*, ed. Nancy Chappelear Baird (1984), xi. *Courtesy of Nancy Chappelear Baird*

LUCY BUCK—From Lucy Buck, *Sad Earth, Sweet Heaven: The Diary of Lucy Rebecca Buck during the War Between the States, December 25, 1861–April 15, 1865*, ed. William P. Buck (1992). *Courtesy of William P. Buck*

ALEXANDER "FRED" FLEET—From the Fleet Family Papers, Charlottesville, Virginia. *Courtesy of William Lankford*

HENRY ROBINSON BERKELEY—*Courtesy of the Virginia Historical Society, Richmond, Virginia*

MAPS ILLUSTRATED BY MICHAEL WAID

Library of Congress Cataloging-in-Publication Data

Selby, John Gregory, 1955–
   Virginians at War : the Civil War experiences of seven young
   Confederates / John G. Selby.
      p. cm. — (The American crisis series ; no. 8)
   Includes bibliographical references and index.
    ISBN 0-8420-5054-X (alk. paper) — ISBN 0-8420-5055-8 (pbk. : alk.
paper)
     1. Virginia—History—Civil War, 1861–1865. I. Titles. II. Series.

E581 .S45 2002
973.7'455—dc21   2002024520

To Deb, Meg, and Jack,
and the memory of
my mother and father

ABOUT THE AUTHOR

John G. Selby received his Ph.D in history from Duke University. He has taught at Guilford College, Duke University, and Roanoke College, where he is currently professor of history. He has published articles and delivered papers on topics ranging from Southern labor history to the Civil War. *Virginians at War* is the first of several books he intends to write on the Civil War.

ACKNOWLEDGMENTS

Let me start by thanking those individuals who shared their family's papers and photographs: Dr. William F. Buck, Nancy Chappelear Baird, William Lankford, and Bell Gale Chevigny. They know and appreciate the historical treasures they guard.

As always, historians are indebted to librarians, in particular, the staffs at the Virginia Historical Society, the Orange County Historical Society, the Virginia Military Institute archives, the Roanoke City Public Library, the Salem Public Library, the Rockbridge County Library, and the Roanoke College Fintel Library. Pat Scott, the inter-library loan coordinator at Roanoke College, ordered over 150 books for me in the process of writing this manuscript and deserves a special commendation.

Several historians have sharpened this work in numerous ways: Michael Chesson, John Mering, William Chafe, and Roberto Rabel. Carol Reardon offered helpful criticism of a paper on some of my subjects, and Steve Woodworth did a yeoman's job in editing the entire manuscript. Anonymous readers at other institutions also helped me immeasurably, and I hope they see that some of their suggestions have been incorporated into this book.

The sharp-eyed editors at Scholarly Resources, Matt Hershey, Linda Pote Musumeci, and Ellen Ellender, improved the manuscript and guided a first-time author through the thicket of publishing. Mike Waid produced some easy-to-read maps on short notice, and although all battles are not mapped, some important ones were included. None of the readers is responsible for any errors found in the book, but they can take credit for making a rough manuscript smoother.

My colleagues in the History Department at Roanoke College encouraged me from start to finish. I thank Gary Gibbs, Michael Hakkenberg, Whitney Leeson, Susan Millinger, Dan Richardson, and Janice Saunders for their continuous support over the years. The former dean at Roanoke College, Ken Garren, took a special interest in this project, and I hope he enjoys the final product. Two grants-in-time and a sabbatical awarded by the college's Faculty Development Committee allowed me to finish this project; I thank the various members of the committee for their support.

Special thanks go to my very good friend from way back, the author John F. Bierlein, whose enthusiasm and confidence in the project never wavered, even during some dark hours. A former colleague at Roanoke College, Roger Hartley, also encouraged me in those lean periods, and his support proved invaluable. My good friend and chairman of the History Department, Mark Miller, has been my principal backer outside my family "from day one," and I cannot measure the debt of gratitude he is owed.

Other friends, colleagues, and students have helped me with this project. Our departmental secretary, Karen Harris, used her wizardry with word processing to shape the unwieldy manuscript into presentable form. At a few critical moments, Amber Proffitt and Samantha Ayers assisted Karen with typing. The index was prepared by my friend and colleague Linda Miller, and readers will benefit from her thoroughness. Webb King did some research in Richmond and Roanoke for me, and Richard Lewis Sanford drove me out to the Orange County cemetery to find the gravestones of Robin and Nan Berkeley. Others helped in more subtle ways, and I apologize in advance for not naming every single one of you, but there are just too many! Within my family, though, I would like to thank Sarah Izzo, Nancy and Kevin Smith, Terry Deaton, Sue Holder, Tom Selby, David Selby, Bill and Peggy Pearson, and Janet Marx for their unending encouragement. My father, John Selby, had more interest in this book at times than I did, and my biggest regret is that he did not live to see its publication.

Nothing would have been accomplished, however, without the love and support of my wife, Deborah. She encouraged me at every stage and made life itself worthwhile, regardless of the status of the project. My daughter, Meg, grew up with this book, and her needs as an infant, toddler, and child kept me firmly planted in the 1990s, no matter how many times my reading took me back to the 1860s. The wonderful care by Meg's primary babysitter, Betty King, helped us raise a fine daughter and gave me the time to work on the book in the summers. Perhaps "it takes a village" to write a book as well as raise a child. Last, our family's newest addition, Jack, knows nothing about this book yet, but someday he will. I hope that he, and others, will be drawn into the drama and passion of history by reading how ordinary people can rise to meet the challenges of extraordinary times.

CONTENTS

INTRODUCTION

THIS BOOK STARTED with a question: What did the Civil War mean to those who fought it? With more reflection on the subject, three related questions arose: Why did people fight? What kept them fighting? And after the war, what meaning did people find in their experiences?

There were several ways to approach these questions. I could look at a single individual, but I wanted something with greater scope than a biography. I could write the history of a single military unit, but I wanted a study that looked closely at the experiences of both men and women. Statistical sampling would produce the most representative cross-section of the population that fought the war, but it would not necessarily offer the revealing personal record I desired. I toyed with the idea of examining a single county or region, as ably done by Wayne K. Durrill, Stephen V. Ash, Daniel T. Sutherland, and William A. Blair, among others.[1] Considering this possibility forced me to define what I really wanted to understand: How did a small group of individuals approach, participate in, and survive the war? If I looked at a county or larger region, I would lose that small-group focus.

My next thought was to look at fifteen to twenty-five persons from a single state. Confining my group to one state would offer a shared political and economic history, while still allowing for the particular contours of individual, family, and community histories to be explored. I chose Virginia, thus limiting this study to the South. Virginia had a number of "mosts" that made it appealing, if not representative of all Confederate states: the most citizens among the Southern states; the most slaves; the most men under arms; the most famous Southern generals; the most fighting within its borders; the most divided by the war (what other Southern state lost a quarter of its territory and saw a new state created out of that former territory?); and the most damaged by the war.

Having decided on the state, the much bigger task of selecting subjects loomed before me. I had three primary considerations.

First, I wanted individuals who had left a rich record, in either letters, diaries, or memoirs, that would allow the reader to follow not only the individual's actions during the war but also, equally important, the individual's thoughts during and, in some cases, after the conflict. Second, I wanted some rough form of balance among the subjects, especially in the number of men and women, the variety of wartime experiences, and representation among some of the different regions of the state. Third, I wanted to unify the subjects by age cohort. Although the entire notion of a generational identity is as contentious as any issue in the social sciences, this study accepts Karl Mannheim's argument that "youth experiencing the same historical problems may be said to be part of the same historical generation." Furthermore, in the years after the war, those who fought became increasingly aware that they were set apart from other generations in American history by this war, thus confirming Mannheim's view that "individual members of a generation become conscious of their common situation and make this consciousness the basis of their group solidarity." I classified those born between 1830 and 1845 as the Civil War generation, subscribing to the 15-year-long life stages described by José Ortega y Gasset and Julian Marias. Additionally, historian Bell Irvin Wiley noted that the "overwhelming bulk" of the men who served in the Confederate military ranged from ages eighteen to thirty-five, which would place most of their births between 1828 and 1845, depending on the years in which they enlisted or were drafted.[2]

After setting out some of the key dimensions of the selection process, I began the search for individual subjects. I examined over 150 diaries, collections of letters, memoirs, and biographies of Virginians, famous and obscure. From that long list I culled twenty persons, whites and blacks, Confederates and Unionists. Then I started researching and writing their stories, striving to describe their common experiences while never losing sight of their individuality.

The more I wrote, however, the more troublesome four facts became. The first fact was that the preponderance of Virginia materials came from Confederates. The second fact was that the Unionist story had its own internal dynamic, one that did not neatly mirror the Confederate story. The third fact was that no individual African Americans had left records as lengthy as many of the Confederate writers. Historian Ervin L. Jordan Jr. has recently demonstrated that the sources do exist to tell the complex history of African Americans in Virginia during the war, but he cast a wide net to find his stories.[3] One can look in vain—as I did—for the collection of 100-plus letters or a 350-page diary from a single African American of the Civil War generation who was born, raised, and remained for his or her entire life in Virginia. The fourth fact was that it was impossible to follow closely the lives of twenty persons without losing track of the individuals and the narrative.

Consequently, I made a difficult but what I felt was a necessary decision: to tell the stories of seven Virginians, instead of twenty. To bring greater cohesion to the task, I further narrowed the group to young white Confederates. Future studies can cover the same ground for Unionists, African Americans, and Northerners.

What emerges from the study of seven young Confederates is a partial picture of a generation struggling to survive the greatest crisis in American history. While only a few of my subjects wanted war, all supported the Confederacy and war after Virginia seceded. They also remained steadfast supporters of the Confederacy until its defeat. Two of them, William T. Poague and Alexander Fleet, were officers in the Army of Northern Virginia, part of what historian Gary Gallagher described as the "emotional core" of the army and, by extension, of Confederate nationalism. The other two soldiers and the three women could also be considered part of this indispensable group of Confederate nationalists. Gallagher wrote in *The Confederate War* that no one had "examined Confederate nationalism from a generational perspective."[4] While seven individuals can hardly represent a generation, their motivations and actions can shed some light on this important subject.

Two themes dominate the lives and experiences of the seven subjects. First, their responses to hardships were shaped primarily by their characters, not their circumstances. Here "character" is defined as the personality, values, virtues, weaknesses, beliefs, fears, and hopes of an individual. It will be seen that character remained fairly constant despite circumstances, showing that what individuals carried into the war they carried through—and out of—the war.

The second theme concerns faith. All of the subjects remained faithful to the cause of Southern independence until its bitter end. Their faith was sustained by their belief in the righteousness of their cause, their desire to protect their homes, community, and comrades in arms, and their strong belief in God and His will. They clearly demonstrate the motivations for fighting and supporting the war that historian James McPherson has identified as "convictions of duty, honor, patriotism, and ideology" as well as "courage, self-respect, and group cohesion" for the combat soldiers and the "firm base of support" from "homes and communities." Two of the soldiers also edge close to historian Peter Carmichael's view that thousands of Confederates saw their cause through a "religious prism" where "duty to God equaled duty to nation."[5]

Other historians have wrestled with the questions of motivation. Bell Wiley emphasized a "desire for adventure" in his pioneering work on the "common" soldiers of the Confederacy, *The Life of Johnny Reb*. Reid Mitchell argued that the Union soldier "fought for home and for Union, for family and honor," and suggested that Confederate soldiers fought for similar reasons. Gerald Linderman found courage to be the "cement" that held armies together, and for the Southerners he added the imperative of defense of their homes. Drew Faust found that in the early days of the war, "Southern ladies struggled to make the Confederacy a common cause with their men, to find a place for themselves in a culture increasingly preoccupied with the quintessentially male concerns of politics and battle." In *The Confederate War*, Gary Gallagher devotes two chapters to exploring the dimensions of "Popular Will" and "Nationalism" that helped sustain the people during their long struggle.[6]

Long before these fine historians debated these questions, the veterans themselves pondered them. Few spoke so eloquently and hauntingly as Joshua Chamberlain, the Bowdoin College classics professor turned general and war hero. In his last work, *The Passing of the Armies*, he tried to describe what kept the Army of the Potomac going in 1864, the worst year of the war: "Things were remnants and reminders. Lines stood thinner; circles ever narrowing . . . [Yet] the strength of great memories, pride of historic continuity, unfailing loyalty of purpose and resolve held these men together in unity of form and spirit."[7] Ultimately, we must turn to the veterans and their peers in the Civil War generation if we are to understand what the war meant to those who fought and survived it. Further, it must be acknowledged that the war's meaning is never static; it changed during the war and afterward, for participants as well as for their descendants.

The seven persons chosen for this study have a central commonality: all were survivors. Historian James I. Robertson Jr. estimates that somewhere between twenty and thirty thousand white males of "fighting age" (eighteen to forty-five), or about 20 percent of that age group in secessionist Virginia, died in the war.[8] The majority of white fighting-age men and women remained as survivors, so the study of seven who lived is not unrepresentative. Moreover, it is necessary to study survivors in order to carry a generational story from youth to old age.

Who, then, are these seven survivors and recorders of their experiences? The women include Amanda "Tee" Edmonds, Lucy Buck, and Susan Caldwell. Tee represents the stereotypical Southern belle, more concerned with affairs of the heart than affairs of state. Born into an upper-middle-class family in upper Fauquier County, Tee would watch the war from a unique vantage point: she was in the very center of Colonel John S. Mosby's "Confederacy." Twenty-one years old when the war began, Tee would endure several Union occupations of her beloved home, Belle Grove, watch two brothers ride off to adventure in Mosby's cavalry, and pursue two romances during the war. She began her first journal in 1857 and ended her journal entries in 1867.[9]

A good counter to the spirited Tee is the sober, more reflective Lucy Buck of Front Royal. Just eighteen years old when the war started, Lucy would experience Union occupation of her home, Bel Air; correspond with two brothers serving in the Army of Tennessee; help bury her favorite cousin, Walter; and constantly pray for victory and greater personal devotion to Christian principles. Her family's fortune would survive the turmoil of war, only to be lost in the financial ruin of the 1870s. Unlike Tee, Lucy had no special suitors or love affairs during the war. She would never marry, but would faithfully record her thoughts in her ever-present journals from Christmas Day 1861 until her death in 1918.[10]

The one outlier in terms of age is Susan Caldwell of Warrenton. Born in 1827, Susan is included in this study because she was a young mother struggling to survive while her husband was gone for four years, thus illuminating the problems faced by a critical segment of the home-front population. Moreover, her family preserved over 100 letters, the majority of them written by Susan to her husband, Lycurgus. The letters are frank and expressive, offering a detailed and poignant view of one family's efforts to support and endure the war. Finally, Lycurgus was employed as a auditor in the Treasury Department in Richmond, thus affording glimpses of the life of a working noncombatant male in the Confederate capital during the war.[11]

The men chosen for the study represent different military ranks and different regions of Virginia. The oldest, William Poague of Rockbridge County, was twenty-six years old when the war began. He had already graduated from Washington College, studied law, and begun working in a law practice in Lexington. He joined the famous 1st Rockbridge Artillery and, through countless acts of bravery and steady leadership, would be promoted through the ranks of artillery officers from lieutenant to lieutenant colonel. He fought in nearly every major battle of the Army of Northern Virginia and would display a precise memory of these battles in his memoir written for his children. His fine memory was constantly tapped by fellow veterans, who wrote to him for his recollections and views from the 1880s until his death in 1914.[12]

The second officer in this study, Alexander "Fred" Fleet of King and Queen County, enlisted as first sergeant of the Jackson Grays in June 1861. He joined the unit after completing his freshman year at the University of Virginia. Just eighteen years old when the war began, Fred spent most of it out of harm's way, stuck in the 26th Virginia, part of General Henry A. Wise's "Legion" that guarded Richmond until early 1864. He would eventually be promoted to first lieutenant, see action defending Petersburg in 1864, and conclude his military service as adjutant to General Wise. Providing a counterpoint to his rather uneventful military service are the dozens of amusing and revealing letters from his family as they describe their troubles with shirkers, runaway slaves, and Union occupiers. At the center of his large family is his mother, Maria Louisa Wacker Fleet, or "Ma" as she was referred to by all, a woman of indomitable courage and strength. She was the backbone of the family, and with her steady hand at the helm, its members survived the war and the tough economic times afterward. The preserved letters of this close family date from 1860 until 1900.[13]

A third young soldier, John Worsham of Richmond, began and ended the war as a sergeant. Along the way he fought in many of the major battles held on Virginia's soil and watched his proud F Company shrink from over 100 men to fewer than ten by January 1863. Recruiting in Richmond refilled the ranks, however, and the company would continue to fight until the end of the war. Worsham's service ended sooner; he was wounded at the Battle of Winchester in September 1864 and spent the remainder of the war at his family's home in Richmond. From there the 26-year-old veteran had a distinct vantage point from which to view the evacuation, destruction, and occupation of Richmond. He pulled together all of his memories and his observations in a manuscript he wrote for publication, *One of Jackson's Foot Cavalry*. Appearing in 1912, the book was reviewed favorably and has stood the test of time by going through several reprints and consistently being cited as one of the best memoirs from Confederate enlisted men. Worsham worked on his manuscript for years, consulting a wartime notebook, some family letters, letters from members of his old unit, and published histories. While flavored by the passage of time and the tides of historical opinion, the manuscript also bears the stamp of authenticity.[14]

The fourth soldier in this study, Henry "Robin" Berkeley of Hanover County, enlisted as a private in the Hanover Artillery in May 1861. He would remain in the remnants of his unit for four years, never rising above the rank of private. A serious and occasionally gloomy young man, Robin managed to keep a detailed diary of both his feelings and movements for four years. Like Fred Fleet, Robin saw minimal action until the last year of the war, when he experienced enough to last a lifetime. He ended his military career in a prison camp, Fort Delaware, on Pea Patch Island in the Delaware River.[15]

A close study of the actions and thoughts of these individuals during the war will provide some glimpses of the turmoil that engulfed the Civil War generation. At the same time, it will be shown that considerable continuity existed side by side with enormous dislocation. Of the seven subjects, only Fred Fleet had his prewar social position significantly altered.[16] All the men followed middle- or upper-middle-class pursuits after the conflict, albeit with fewer opportunities for stable or lucrative employment than in the prewar South. The women either remained with their families or married men of similar means, thus keeping them in the same prewar social class. There was also continuity of character. The war changed lives and brought sudden maturity to these young people, but it did not change their essential natures. Whether serious, lighthearted, resilient, or fretful, they remained the same. The war tested character but did not change it.

Together, the experiences of these seven young people offer a portrait of a segment of a generation confronting challenges greater than those faced by any other generation of Americans, before or since. For better and for worse, the effects of their efforts continue to shape our lives.

NOTES

1. Wayne K. Durrill, *War of Another Kind: A Southern Community in the Great Rebellion* (New York, 1990); Stephen V. Ash, *Middle Tennessee Society Transformed, 1860–1870: War and Peace in the Upper South* (Baton Rouge, 1988); Daniel T. Sutherland, *Seasons of War: The Ordeal of a Confederate Community, 1861–65* (New York, 1995); William A. Blair, *Virginia's Private War: Feeding Body and Soul in the Confederacy, 1861–1865* (New York, 1998).

2. Karl Mannheim, "The Problem of Generations," in *Essays on the Sociology of Knowledge* (London, 1959), 304 and 290; José Ortega y Gasset, *The Modern Theme* (New York, 1961); idem, *Man and Crisis* (New York, 1958); Julian Marias, *Generations: A Historical Method* (Tuscaloosa, AL, 1970); Bell Irvin Wiley, *The Life of Johnny Reb: The Common Soldier of the Confederacy* (Baton Rouge, 1991, reissue of earlier editions), 331. Succinct summaries of the definition and issues surrounding "generations" can be found in articles by Julian Marias, "Generations: The Concept," and Marvin Rintala, "Political Generations," in *International Encyclopedia of the Social Sciences* (New York, 1968), vol. 6 of 18 vols., 88–96. A longer treatment of the problem is found in Alan B. Spitzer, "The Historical Problems of Generations," *American Historical Review* 78 (December 1973): 1353–85. A recent popular book, William Strauss and Neil Howe, *Generations: The History of America's Future, 1584–2069* (New York, 1991), goes much further in the use of generations as a mode of analysis

than does this study. For Strauss and Howe, a generation is approximately twenty-two years long. The authors explain their theory and methodology most comprehensively in their Appendix A, "A Theory of Generations," 433–53.

3. See Stephen V. Ash, *When the Yankees Came: Conflict and Chaos in the Occupied South, 1861–1865* (Chapel Hill, 1995), especially Chapter 4, "Deliverance and Disillusion: The Ordeal of the Unionists," 108–48, for insights into the complexities of the story of Unionists in the South; Ervin L. Jordan Jr., *Black Confederates and Afro-Yankees in Civil War Virginia* (Charlottesville, 1995).

4. Gary W. Gallagher, *The Confederate War: How Popular Will, Nationalism, and Military Strategy Could Not Stave Off Defeat* (Cambridge, MA, 1997), 96. One historian who has begun a generational analysis of young Confederates is Peter S. Carmichael, "The Last Generation: Slaveholders' Sons and Southern Identity, 1850–1865" (Ph.D. diss., Pennsylvania State University, 1996). Three books dip into the generational waters without being as explicitly "generational" in intent: John C. Waugh, *The Class of 1846: From West Point to Appomattox: Stonewall Jackson, George McClellan, and Their Brothers* (New York, 1994); Kevin Conley Ruffner, *Maryland's Blue and Gray: A Border State's Union and Confederate Junior Officer Corps* (Baton Rouge, 1997); and James Lee Conrad, *The Young Lions: Confederate Cadets at War* (Mechanicsburg, PA, 1997).

5. James M. McPherson, *For Cause and Comrades: Why Men Fought in the Civil War* (New York, 1997), 131; Peter S. Carmichael, *Lee's Young Artillerist: William R. J. Pegram* (Charlottesville, 1995), 5. Carmichael incorporates some of his dissertation arguments into his book on Pegram.

6. Wiley, *The Life of Johnny Reb*, 17; Reid Mitchell, *The Vacant Chair: The Northern Soldier Leaves Home* (New York, 1993), 37 and 166. The Southern story is further pursued in Reid Mitchell's essay, "Creation of Confederate Loyalties," in Robert Abzug and Stephen E. Maizlish, eds., *New Perspectives on Race and Slavery in America: Essays in Honor of Kenneth M. Stampp* (Lexington, 1986); Gerald Linderman, "Courage as the Cement of Armies," in *Embattled Courage: The Experience of Combat in the American Civil War* (New York, 1987), Chapters 3 and 81; Drew Gilpin Faust, *Mothers of Invention: Women of the Slaveholding South in the American Civil War* (Chapel Hill, 1996), 10; Gallagher, Chapters 1 and 2 in *The Confederate War*.

7. Joshua L. Chamberlain, *The Passing of the Armies* (1915; reprint, Dayton, OH, 1989), 18–19.

8. James I. Robertson Jr., *Civil War Virginia: Battleground for a Nation* (Charlottesville, 1991), 175 and 15.

9. Amanda Virginia Edmonds Papers, Virginia Historical Society. For ease of reference for writer and reader, I used published, edited versions of diaries or collections of letters when available. I also felt that if a reader wished to know one of these individuals better, it would be convenient to have a published collection to peruse. All references to Edmonds's journals come from Amanda Virginia Edmonds, *Journals of Amanda Virginia Edmonds: Lass of the Mosby Confederacy, 1859–1867*, ed. Nancy Chapplear Baird (Stephens City, VA, 1984).

10. Lucy Buck, *Sad Earth, Sweet Heaven: The Diary of Lucy Rebecca Buck during the War Between the States, December 25, 1861–April 15, 1865*, 2d edition, ed. William P. Buck (Birmingham, 1992). William Buck, a direct descendant of the Bucks of Front Royal, published the first edition of Lucy Buck's diary in 1973. I also consulted another edition of Lucy Buck's diary by Elizabeth Baer, but stuck with the more detailed version produced by William Buck. Elizabeth Baer's edition is based on a privately published version of the diary prepared by a nephew of Lucy in 1940. See Lucy Buck, *Shadows on My Heart: The Civil War Diary of Lucy Rebecca Buck of Virginia*, ed. Elizabeth R. Baer (Athens, GA, 1997). I have also examined the original diaries, still in the possession of Dr. William P. Buck. They are a treasure for those interested in Southern history, stretching from 1861 to Lucy's death in 1918.

11. Susan Caldwell, *"My Heart Is So Rebellious": The Caldwell Letters, 1861–1865*, ed. J. Michael Welton (Warrenton, VA, n.d. [but first available in 1990]). The original letters are in the possession of Bell Gale Chevigny of New York.

12. William Thomas Poague, *Gunner with Stonewall: Reminiscences of William Thomas Poague; A Memoir Written for His Children in 1903*, ed. Monroe F. Cockrell (1957; reprint, Wilmington, NC, 1987). Poague's original, handwritten memoir is housed in the William T. Poague file in the Virginia Military Institute Archives. Here one also finds correspondence with veterans seeking information on battles.

13. Benjamin Robert Fleet, *Green Mount: A Virginia Plantation Family during the Civil War: Being the Journal of Benjamin Robert Fleet and Letters of His Family*, ed. Betsy Fleet and John D. P. Fuller (Lexington, 1962); Maria Louisa Wacker Fleet, *Green Mount after the War: The Correspondence of Maria Louisa Wacker Fleet and Her Family, 1865–1900*, ed. Betsy Fleet (Charlottesville, 1978). The original letters and journal are held by William Lankford.

14. John H. Worsham, *One of Jackson's Foot Cavalry* (1912; reprint, New York, 1992). Bantam Books reprinted Worsham's original book without changes, which is why I used that edition instead of the helpful but slightly altered edition published by McCowat-Mercer Press in 1964 and reprinted by Broadfoot Publishing Company in 1991. See John H. Worsham, *One of Jackson's Foot Cavalry*, ed. James I. Robertson Jr. (1964; reprint, Wilmington, NC, 1991).

15. Henry Robinson Berkeley, *Four Years in the Confederate Artillery: The Diary of Private Henry Robinson Berkeley*, ed. William H. Runge (1961; reprint, Richmond, 1991). The original diary and postwar account book are housed in the Henry Robinson Berkeley Papers in the Virginia Historical Society.

16. The question of how the war affected social position is as old as the war itself. It is one important strand of a long-standing controversy in Southern history: Is the history of the South marked by change or continuity, or by both? C. Vann Woodward spawned dozens of books, articles, and papers by emphasizing change in Southern history, characterizing the postwar generation of leaders in the South as "New Men" in his landmark work, *Origins of the New South, 1877–1913* (Baton Rouge,

1951). While this question no longer occupies center stage in Southern studies, it still has life, as seen in two works on the effect of the Civil War on white Southerners: William G. Thomas, " 'Under Indictment': Thomas Lafayette Rosser and the New South," *Virginia Magazine of History and Biography* 100, no. 2 (April 1992): 207–32; and Fred A. Bailey, *Class and Tennessee's Confederate Generation* (Chapel Hill, 1987).

LIST OF MAPS

Cast of Characters

HENRY ROBINSON BERKELEY

Courtesy of the Virginia Historical Society, Richmond

LUCY BUCK

From Lucy Buck, *Sad Earth, Sweet Heaven: The Diary of Lucy Rebecca Buck during the War Between the States, December 25, 1861–April 15, 1865*, ed. William P. Buck (1992). *Courtesy of William P. Buck*

SUSAN CALDWELL

From *"My Heart Is So Rebellious": The Caldwell Letters, 1861–1865*, ed. J. Michael Welton (n.d.), dust jacket. *Courtesy of Bell Gale Chevigny*

AMANDA VIRGINIA "TEE" EDMONDS

From Amanda Virginia Edmonds, *Journals of Amanda Virginia Edmonds: Lass of the Mosby Confederacy, 1859–1867*, ed. Nancy Chappelear Baird (1984), xi. *Courtesy of Nancy Chappelear Baird*

ALEXANDER "FRED" FLEET

From the Fleet Family Papers, Charlottesville, Virginia. *Courtesy of William Lankford*

WILLIAM T. POAGUE

Courtesy of Virginia Military Institute Archives, Lexington

JOHN H. WORSHAM

From John H. Worsham, *One of Jackson's Foot Cavalry* (1912; reprinted 1992), photo section. *Courtesy of Broadfoot Publishing Company*

PROLOGUE
Virginia on the Eve of
Secession, Winter 1860–61

A DEEP SNOW lay on the ground as the new year began. It was not a remarkable storm, like that of January 1857, when the snow was so deep that it became a benchmark of memory, recalled by over a half-dozen elderly former slaves interviewed in the 1930s. That snowfall had a name and a legend attached to it; a Dr. Cox, "a great drinkin' white man," was on his way back from Petersburg when he froze to death, "sittin' up in his buggy, jes' holdin' de reins lak he was drivin,' " as Sis Shackelford remembered the story.[1] Hence the great snowstorm of 1857 that lasted three days became known as Cox's snow.

There was a storm of a different sort forming in January 1861, one that would make all the snows of the nineteenth century mere footnotes in history. Its signs were everywhere: the fervent editorials in Virginia newspapers, the movement of federal troops in and out of Southern forts, the worried reports from markets in London and New York, and the angry letters printed in the newspapers exhorting Virginians to stand firm against federal interference. Thunder had already been heard from South Carolina, whose secession convention had unanimously passed an ordinance separating itself from the Union on December 20. Similar ordinances were under discussion in every slaveholding state; six more states would pass secession ordinances by February 1.[2] And what of Virginia, the Old Dominion, home to four of America's first five presidents?

Virginians were not immune to the excitement and anxiety of the times. Secession was the chief topic for the extra session of the General Assembly that convened in Richmond on January 7, 1861. According to one pro-secession correspondent, "The very air here is charged with electric thunders of war—on the street, at the capital, in the barroom, at the dinner table nothing is heard but resistance to the General Government, and sympathy with the cause of South Carolina."[3]

To be sure, sympathy and anger abounded in equal measure among the representatives in Richmond, but strong Unionist voices were also heard. In his opening speech to the General Assembly, Governor John Letcher reiterated the proposals he had made after John Brown's raid on the federal armory at Harpers Ferry in 1859—that a convention of all states should be held; and, if differences could not be resolved, peaceful separation should be considered. Furthermore, fugitive slave laws should be enforced and interstate slave trade protected. Letcher did not believe a state convention to consider secession was needed, although he supported the right of a state to secede.[4]

The representatives offered a tepid response. They agreed only that a national convention should be called. They then passed bills closer to their desires: a resolution opposing "coercion" of any state to return to the Union; an appropriation of $1 million to improve Virginia's fortifications and militia; and an act to hold a special election to select delegates to a secession convention.[5] Despite the efforts of former president John Tyler and other prominent Virginians, the compromises discussed at the Washington Peace Conference on February 4 and at subsequent meetings in February came to naught. So did the entreaties of Virginian Wyndham Robertson to the departed states to participate in the Peace Conference.[6]

At the same time that representatives gathered in Washington, one of the most important special elections in Virginia's history was held on February 4. At first blush, the Unionists appeared to have carried the day; one estimate put their number at 120 out of the 152 elected delegates. However, careful investigation showed that the numbers of Unionists were not that solid, and that the key group would be the seventy or so delegates regarded as moderates. For over two months, the Unionists battled the secessionists for the support of the moderates. In the end, events transpiring outside Virginia—the failure of the Peace Conference, Abraham Lincoln's Inaugural Address, the firing on Fort Sumter, and Lincoln's call for volunteers to suppress the "insurrection" in the South—would tilt the scales in favor of the secessionists. That Virginia would hold out so long is not surprising given the electorate's support for John Bell (Constitutional Union Party) and Stephen A. Douglas (Northern Democratic Party) in the 1860 presidential election (Bell carried Virginia). Once the convention passed the secession ordinance on April 17 (by a vote of 88 to 55), there was no turning back. Virginia was about to embark on the most calamitous journey of its long history.[7]

In many ways, the war could not have come at a worse time for Virginia. After nearly half a century of economic and political decline, it appeared to steady itself in the 1850s. With a population of 1,597,000, Virginia retained its place as the most populous of the slaveholding states, a place it had held since it joined the new Union in the late eighteenth century. Population increased by 176,000 persons between 1850 and 1860, the largest absolute decennial increase in the state's history. Still, that increase paled before those of Northern states that had long eclipsed Virginia's 1790 and 1800 rank as the most populous state in the Union: Pennsylvania gained nearly 600,000 persons and New York almost 800,000 during the 1850s. Virginia's problem was that for the first half of the nineteenth century, it had been the source of more emigrants than any other state. Henry Ruffner, president of Washington College in the 1840s, estimated that in the 1830s alone, Virginia had lost 375,000 persons. Modern estimates add support to Ruffner's guess, with some scholars positing that nearly one million people moved out of Virginia in the eighteenth and nineteenth centuries, with the majority emigrating in the latter century.[8]

Emigration implies choice, which the vast majority of blacks did not have. Most were slaves sent south and west at their masters' whim, with the journeys themselves sometimes called another Middle Passage. The most thorough study of interregional slave emigration estimates that over 500,000 slaves left Virginia between 1790 and 1860, making the Old Dominion by far the greatest exporter of slaves, exceeding the *total* number of slaves exported by the next three leading slave-exporting states, Maryland, South Carolina, and North Carolina.[9] Despite this massive exportation, Virginia still had the largest population of slaves and the second-largest population of free blacks in the South; the 1860 census counted 490,865 slaves and 58,042 free blacks in Virginia's 147 counties.[10]

In no way, however, was slavery uniform in the state's counties. Eighty-seven percent of the slaves lived east of the Blue Ridge, with the densest concentrations in the 24-county region known as the Tobacco Belt. Stretching from Albemarle and Louisa counties in the north to Patrick, Henry, Pittsylvania, Halifax, Mecklenburg, and Brunswick counties along the southern border of the state, this region produced 78 percent of Virginia's best cash crop in 1859 (double the amount produced a decade earlier).[11]

With greater use of fertilizer and more diversification of crops in the 1850s, production of wheat, corn, and oats increased, generating almost as much farm income as tobacco by 1860. In a state with 93,000 farms and over 90 percent of the population living in rural areas, these agricultural developments and the corresponding rise in farm income meant that the quality of life improved for many residents.[12] There were new opportunities in the towns and cities, too. By 1860, Virginia boasted 4,890 manufacturing establishments, the most of any state in the South and fifth in the nation. Furthermore, Virginia led the nation in tobacco manufacture and Richmond led the cities of the country in flour milling.[13]

The great boost to agriculture and manufacturing had come with the building of a water and rail network between 1830 and 1860. First came the completion of the James River and Kanawha Canal from Richmond to Lynchburg in 1835 (by 1860 it extended as far west as Buchanan, nearly 200 miles upriver from Richmond); this canal closely tied the Piedmont region with the Tidewater area. Next came a huge spurt of railroad building in the 1850s that gave Virginia the best rail network in the South. Over 1,200 miles of track were added in that decade, the most in any Southern state. No fewer than fourteen railroad companies operated in the state, including such essential wartime lines as the Virginia Central, the Orange and Alexandria, and the South Side.[14]

To a casual observer, all paths, whether by water, rail, or road, seemed to lead to Richmond. Incorporated in 1742, Richmond had long been the largest city in the state, and the capital since 1779. With 37,910 residents in 1860, its population was double that of Petersburg (18,266 residents), the second largest city in Virginia. Other cities with more than 10,000 residents (in descending order from most to least) were Norfolk, Wheeling, and Alexandria. Far more numerous were towns such as Farmville (1,536), Leesburg (1,130), New Market (1,422), Smithfield (777), and Salem (612). While Richmond was large by Virginia standards, it was small compared to the slaveholding South's three largest cities—Baltimore (212,418), New Orleans (168,675), and St. Louis (160,773)—and it was a mere town compared to Northern metropolises such as New York (813,669) and Philadelphia (565,529).[15]

Still, Richmond was a beautiful city, laid out on two plateaus rising above the James River and renowned for its wide streets and fine buildings. Even more important than its architecture was its place in the commerce of Virginia and among its leading citizens. As John S. Wise, son of Governor Henry A. Wise, recalled the Richmond of his youth in the 1850s, "it was the assembling-point of a large class of wealthy persons who resided on their plantations upon the upper and lower James, and in Piedmont, Tidewater, and the South Side." Some had houses in Richmond too, but those who did not never lacked for accommodations. When they came to Richmond, according to Wise, they were "taken in charge by friends and relatives as soon as they reached the city. Everybody was kin to everybody." It was a wonderful time for people of this privileged class, for they were "ushered into vacant chambers that were already yearning for them, attended by the servants that were idle in their absence, furnished with equipages and horses that needed use and work, and fed of an abundance that had been wasted before they came."[16] Such was city life for the wealthy in the Virginia of the 1850s. Overall, the best characterization of towns and cities in antebellum Virginia comes from historian Jack Maddex Jr., who writes that "from the great rural sea of Old Virginia, a few commercial cities stood out as islands."[17]

In virtually every respect, Virginia was a thoroughly Southern state, arguably even the South writ large. At the same time, none of the states that seceded was as deeply tied to the North through commerce, society, polity, and history as Virginia. Although its white residents could largely be described as rural and conservative, almost fiercely loyal and localistic in many cases, this very suspicion of change made most Virginians reluctant to support secession during the tense winter of 1860–61.

As events occurring outside the state gathered a momentum of their own, however, more and more Virginians had to choose, once and for all, between two unpopular alternatives. Few could foresee, in the early bloom of spring in 1861, just how dramatically the ultimate choice of the majority of white Virginians would change their lives, especially the lives of those young adults who would have to fight the war and create a new society out of the wreckage of the old.

NOTES

1. On the deep snow of January 1, 1861, see letter from Louisa County in *Richmond Daily Dispatch*, 2, date mentioned. Charles L. Perdue, Thomas E. Barden, and Robert K. Phillips, eds., *Weevils in the Wheat: Interviews with Virginia Ex-Slaves* (Charlottesville, 1976; citations from the paperback edition, 1992), xl, for explanation of Cox's snow. See also in the same source: James Boatman, interview by Susie R. C. Byrd, 50; Liza Brown, interview by Susie R. C. Byrd, 63; Allen Crawford, interview by Susie R. C. Byrd, 74; Bailey Cunningham, interview by I. M. Warren, 83; Lizzie Hobbs, interviewer unknown, 142; Liza McCoy, interview by Susie R. C. Byrd, 199; Ishrael Massie, interview by Susie R. C. Byrd, 205; Archibald Milteer, interviewer unknown, 213; Jennie Patterson, interview by Susie R. C. Byrd, 219; Sis Shackelford, interview by Claude W. Anderson, 252.

2. James M. McPherson, *Battle Cry of Freedom: The Civil War Era* (New York, 1988), 235.

3. Henry T. Shanks, *The Secession Movement in Virginia, 1847–1861* (Richmond, 1934), 142–45 (quotation on 144).

4. *Journal of the House of Delegates for the State of Virginia for the Extra Session, 1861* (Richmond, 1861), Doc. 1, vi–xxxvi; Shanks, *Secession Movement in Virginia*, 142–43.

5. Shanks, *Secession Movement in Virginia*, 144–50; Daniel M. Crofts, *Reluctant Confederates: Upper South Unionists in the Secession Crisis* (Chapel Hill and London, 1989), 137–38.

6. See David M. Potter, *The Impending Crisis, 1848–1861* (New York, 1976), 545–54, for another thoughtful analysis of why peace efforts failed. Shanks, *Secession Movement in Virginia*, 146–48, covers the Virginia overtures to the Deep South state governments.

7. Crofts, *Reluctant Confederates*, 164–94 and 308–15; Shanks, *Secession Movement in Virginia*, 153–60.

8. *Historical Statistics of the United States: Colonial Times to 1970*, Part 1 (Washington, DC, 1975), 24–37; David Hackett Fischer and James C. Kelly, *Away I'm Bound: Virginia and the Westward Movement* (Richmond, 1993), 66.

Virginia was ranked fifth in population in the 1860 census. New York, with 3.88 million persons, was ranked first—a rank it had held continuously since 1810. Another statistic for measuring influence is proportion of total population. In 1800, Virginia held 15 percent of the residents of the United States; by 1860, it held 5 percent of the residents of the country. New York, on the other hand, had 12 percent of the nation's population in 1860. Somewhat ironically, the two Southern states with the greatest number of Virginia emigrants, Kentucky and Tennessee, were ranked sixth and seventh, respectively, in population in the 1860 census.

9. Michael Tadman, *Speculators and Slaves: Masters, Traders, and Slaves in the Old South* (Madison, 1989), 12.

10. United States Bureau of the Census, *Eighth Census of the United States: Population, 1860*, vol. 1 (Washington, DC: Government Printing Office, 1864), 509 and 513 for Virginia; 355 for Maryland; 102 for comparison to all slaveholding states.

11. Lynda J. Morgan, *Emancipation in Virginia's Tobacco Belt, 1850–1870* (Athens, GA, 1992), 18–32. Morgan's statistics are drawn from the *Seventh Census of the United States, 1850*, and *Eighth Census of the United States: Population, 1860* (vol. 1), *Agriculture, 1860* (vol. 2), and *Manufactures, 1860* (vol. 3).

12. Virginius Dabney, *Virginia: The New Dominion* (Charlottesville, 1971, and second paperback printing, 1989), 279–81; *Historical Statistics of the United States*, part 1, 36 and 459.

13. Dabney, *Virginia: The New Dominion*, 281–83; *Eighth Census of the United States: Manufactures*, 190. Virginia's manufactures were only a fraction of those of the country's leader, New York, which listed 23,236 manufacturing establishments and 221,481 persons employed in them, versus 36,590 Virginians. Moreover, with the exception of Tredegar Iron Works in Richmond, the bulk of Virginia industry focused on the initial processing of its two key agricultural products, tobacco and grains. Perhaps an even more telling statistic is income generated by manufactures. In Virginia in 1860, that figure was $51.3 million; in New York that year, it was $379.6 million.

14. *Eighth Census of the United States: Statistics of the United States (including mortality, property, etc.) in 1860* (Washington, DC: Government Printing Office, 1866), 327–28; John F. Stover, *The Railroads of the South, 1865–1900: A Study in Finance and Control* (Chapel Hill, 1955), 10–11; John W. Barriger, *Railroads in the Civil War* (reprint from the *Bulletin of the National Railway Historical Society*, vol. 31, no. 6, 1966), separate map entitled "Railways of Southeastern United States: April 1861"; John F. Stover, *American Railroads* (Chicago, 1961), 42–46; *Preliminary Report of the Eighth Census*, 234–35. As inspiring as that tremendous growth was to commerce and society, Virginia's track mileage lagged behind some large Northern states: by 1860, Ohio had 2,900 miles of track, Illinois 2,867, and New York 2,701. When the war came, the Union's 21,000 miles of track would give it a significant logistical advantage over the Confederacy's 9,000 miles (see *Eighth Census*).

15. *Eighth Census of the United States: Population*, 519–20; *Eighth Census of the United States: Statistics*, xviii. Richmond was the twenty-fifth largest city in the United States in 1860. Among cities and towns in

Confederate states, it was the second largest. Richmond was a good bit larger than the next three Confederate cities ranked by population: Mobile (29,258), Memphis (22,623), and Savannah (22,292). Of the Confederate states, only Virginia had five cities among the 102 largest cities and towns in the United States (Richmond—twenty-fifth; Petersburg—fiftieth; Norfolk—sixty-third; Wheeling—sixty-fifth; Alexandria—eighty-first).

16. John S. Wise, *The End of an Era* (Boston and New York, 1899), 63 and 65.

17. Jack P. Maddex Jr., *The Virginia Conservatives, 1867–1879: A Study in Reconstruction Politics* (Chapel Hill, 1970), 9.

CHAPTER ONE

"LET US CLOSE UP OUR RANKS," APRIL–MAY 1861

THE RAIN STARTED on Monday and did not let up for a week. In Richmond the James River flowed over its banks, filling some cellars with water, nearly submerging Mayo's Island, and completely covering the wharves at the Rocketts. The river was not close to the high-water mark of 1847, but the flooding still gave cause for concern.[1]

It was much worse elsewhere. The relentless rain caused the greatest flood ever in Augusta County, so severe that on Wednesday the Virginia Central Railroad's daily run from Richmond to Staunton got no further than Charlottesville. Sections of the Parkersburg Turnpike were "literally washed away," while the Rappahannock River rose to record levels, destroying bridges and wharves in Fredericksburg.[2]

It was the dispatch of a "Friend" from Henrico County who put this natural disaster in its most appropriate historical context. He wrote, "Such a fall of water has not been known since 'Gabriel's Insurrection,' which happened in the year 1800."[3] Now, in the year 1861, God's hand had come full circle. The great storm of 1800 had thwarted the largest planned slave insurrection in Virginia's history, yet the effects of that ill-fated rebellion had been felt for three generations. Now nature's storms of April 1861 accompanied a man-made storm so immense in scope, so tragic in effect, that it would transform the nation and sever Virginia from its heroic past and its seemingly timeless way of life.

For many Virginians, though, the military storm that began in Charleston, South Carolina, on April 12, 1861, brought relief to the long-building political crisis. The news of the firing on Fort Sumter came over the telegraph lines in bits and pieces on the evening of Friday the twelfth, with six dispatches published in the *Richmond Daily Dispatch* on the morning of the thirteenth. That shooting commenced was not a surprise; the political jockeying over Fort Sumter and President Lincoln's evolving policies toward secession had been given plenty of attention in the newspapers. What was surprising was the rapidity of the Confederates' success and the paucity of their casualties. When news of the victory arrived on Saturday night (the thirteenth), the editors of the *Daily Dispatch* witnessed "one of the wildest, most enthusiastic and irrepressible expressions of heartfelt and exuberant joy on the part of the people generally, that we have ever known to be the case in Richmond."[4]

Thus began one of the most momentous weeks in American history. On Monday, April 15, Lincoln's swift response to the firing on Fort Sumter was published in the Southern newspapers: he called for 75,000 "volunteers" to suppress the "said combinations" in the South. This appeal was the last straw for many Virginians; Lincoln's policy of "coercion" now directly affected the Old Dominion. Newspapers kept up a steady drumbeat of criticism toward Lincoln and the divided, "do-nothing" State Convention, with the *Richmond Daily Dispatch* urging secession: "Let us close up our ranks, and confide in each other. . . . We have a common foe only six hours' ride from Richmond." Only a little more prodding was needed to force a vote in the State Convention, and that impetus came from Governor John Letcher. On April 16, Letcher officially responded to Lincoln's call for volunteer troops with an emphatic "No." He wrote to the secretary of war, "I have only to say that the Militia of Virginia will not be furnished to the powers of Washington, for any such purpose as they have in view." In Letcher's proclamation of the following day, he went a huge step further, making the reverse of Lincoln's request into law: he ordered "all armed volunteer regiments or companies within this state forthwith to hold themselves in readiness for immediate orders."[5]

On the same day, the seventeenth, that Governor Letcher issued his call-to-arms proclamation, the State Convention passed a secession ordinance by an 88-to-55 vote. The die was cast; Virginia would join the other Southern states in an effort to maintain its "Liberty and Independence," according to the *Richmond Daily Dispatch*. The passage of the secession ordinance was greeted with enthusiasm from every quarter of Virginia. Ben Haley of Danville reported that the "streets ring with applause"; "O.K." of Lynchburg noted that "business is almost entirely suspended"; and even in western Virginia, "Dixie" wrote that "these are stirring times . . . in little Roanoke. We have completed the organization of the Roanoke Flying Artillery, numbering 72 men, and they offer their services to the Governor by to-night's mail."[6]

Nowhere was the celebration grander than in Richmond. Here, in the heart of secession country, the largest parade in living memory took place on Friday evening, April 19. With thousands of men carrying torches and with Roman candles and "sky-rockets" exploding above them, a band led the crowd down a dozen city streets, past houses illuminated with candles, past "ladies who expressed their approbation by waving their handkerchiefs." As one observer noted, "As far as the eye could reach the moving mass of fire surged along and lighted up with its lurid glare every object with almost the brightness of day." Sallie Putnam recorded her impression of the long evening of celebration, insisting that the popular outpouring was not "the result of a sudden ebullition of excitement, but of real emotion, long cherished." While that was undoubtedly true to some degree, it is hard to read anything but excitement in the prediction of a young lawyer to the crowd: "in less than sixty days the flag of the Confederacy will be waving over the White House."[7] The next evening, departing Union forces torched the Navy Yard in Norfolk. War had indeed come to Virginia.

Support for the war probably peaked in May, long before any blood was shed on Virginia's soil. Enthusiasm for war was not limited to Virginia—far from it. "War fever" was a national phenomenon, seen in virtually every crossroads hamlet and metropolitan center from Maine to Texas and commented on by both participants and observers. The firing on Fort Sumter had moved the long-simmering sectional crisis out of the legislative galleries and onto the field of battle, and the American people seemed to respond with a mixture of relief, excitement, and apprehension.

What were Americans really responding to in May 1861? Not to actual war, but to the idea of war, and a particularly romantic idea at that. Soldiers were viewed as knights, freely and willingly offering their lives in defense of their cause. Women were the "ladies" to be protected and the quiet, tireless supporters of the cause. An anonymous female poet from Hanover County captured some of this sentiment in a paean she wrote for a Richmond newspaper, "To My Three Brothers in the Confederate Army":

> For woman's heart will be the shrine
> Where, cherished through all coming time,
> Their memories shall be;
> And towering shafts shall tell to fame
> Each gallant Southron's sacred name
> Whose blood has made us free.[8]

With a push like that from home, and the pull of adventure and camaraderie, it is not surprising that by early June over 40,000 Virginians had volunteered to fight for their state. They came from all parts of the Old Dominion, chasing dreams and trailing memories. From the far southwest corner of the state came the Dare Devils of Grayson County, "deep in leggings, moccasins, and other back-woods appliances." Across the county line two companies were formed in Smythe County, the Marion Rifles, "mostly composed of German citizens," and the Smythe Blues. When the Blues left Marion to the cheers and tears of a huge crowd, an observer saw "strong men . . . unused to 'melting the mood,' weeping like little children."[9]

Up the Valley Road, Rockingham County had offered 800 volunteers, and the women of the county had "six sewing machines at work," making tents and flags. From the Piedmont came the Louisa Grays, each man carrying a Bible given to him "by one of the young ladies in our neighborhood (Miss S.)." The ninety-seven men of the Fluvanna Rifle Guards, "dressed in blue hunting shirts trimmed with red," came with their "muskets."[10] From the Northern Neck came the Essex Light Dragoons, "commanded by Dr. Stark Cauthorn—a man who was *born to rule*." In the same company, former congressman Muscoe Russell Garnett was serving as a *private*. Essex County also raised a company of riflemen and an artillery company.[11]

Southside Virginia produced more than its share of volunteer soldiers. A dozen companies were formed in Petersburg alone. Halifax County saw the president of Hampden-Sydney

College, the Reverend Dr. Atkinson, make up a company from the class rosters, while the permanent residents of the county supported the Brooklyn Greys, fifty-three "all-temperance men." The town of Danville had raised an artillery company of 150 men, outfitted with a "neat gray jacket and pants, trimmed with red," which must have seemed like finery to most of the volunteers, "a majority of them being farmers, who have risen before the sun since they were three years old."

It appeared that every one of Virginia's 152 counties had furnished some troops, and when the *Richmond Daily Dispatch* chided three counties for not doing their share (Franklin, Henry, and Patrick), a correspondent from Patrick County (home of J. E. B. Stuart) was quick to correct the paper's mistaken impression. He wrote that the county had raised three companies but not one had rifles, due to the shortage of firearms. "Patrick is *not* a delinquent," he stated.[12]

Most of the volunteer companies made their way to Richmond. Virtually overnight the city of 38,000 doubled in size, and all day long the shouts of men and the thud of axes could be heard as the men built Camp Lee on the old fairgrounds.[13] Fortunately for Richmond (and us), the soldiers were not confined to camp. Many went into town to have their photographs taken at Rees Gallery for twenty-five or fifty cents. Others went to the Metro Hall to see Turrant's "Dioramas of the Russian War," accompanied by the reading of Tennyson's stirring poem, "The Charge of the Light Brigade"; or, for twenty-five cents, viewed the competing "Colossal Revolving Dioramas of the Russian War and Crimean Scenery" at Mechanic's Hall.[14]

The soldiers brought bustle and cash to the newly designated (May 22) capital of the Confederacy. While the men usually arrived with their own rifles, horses, and home-sewn uniforms, they needed everything else, from caps (30,000) to cigars (500,000). The two major needs were ammunition and tents. The former was put in the hands of the Ordnance Department, while the Quartermaster Department was in charge of the latter. The scarcity of tents quickly became a problem, as this plaintive letter from "Via" at Camp Pickens near Manassas made clear: "[We] are without tents, and we are sleeping with no shelter from the weather but boughs, of which we have constructed rude huts . . . have we any generous friends in Richmond? Do they miss us at home? Or is the old adage true, 'out of sight, out of mind'?" The Quartermaster responded by blaming everyone's favorite scapegoat, Abraham Lincoln: there was an "inadequate supply of tent cloth . . . [because of] Lincoln's blockade, which has cut off the supply of cloth." So unless the soldiers were fortunate enough to come from a community like Salem Church in Hanover County—where women sewed twelve tents, 10 feet long by 10 feet wide, in three days—they would have to rely on the kindness of citizens to buy scarce cloth and sew tents.[15]

For the thousands of soldiers stationed at Camp Lee, the lack of tents was the least of their problems. For many it was the first time away from home and, like countless young men before and since, they had to deal with their homesickness while adapting to the strange, confining rhythms of military life. One volunteer described a typical day: reveille at 5:00 A.M., roll call, then company or squad drill at 7:00 and 9:30. Leisure time until 4:00 P.M., then a one-hour battalion-level drill. Evening brought the regimental dress parade, usually around 7:00 P.M. After the parade there was "tattoo," or roll call, at 9:00 P.M., followed by "taps," or retirement, at 9:30. The much-despised guard duty rotated among the men in the company on a regular basis; usually five men would be on guard for a 24-hour period, each standing watch for two hours at a time. Far more desired were the passes signed by the company captain; typically, six men from each company were allowed into town each day. Conspicuous by its absence was training in the firing of weapons. Some of this can be attributed to the lack of adequate supplies of ammunition in the South and to the confusing array of rifles owned by companies and individuals in both the North and South. Still, practicing with live ammunition was not customary, and the effects of insufficient preparation can be seen in many Civil War battles.[16]

Despite the rigor in some areas and lack of training in others, camp life was not unrelieved drill and tedious housekeeping. There were letters to write, friends to make, religious services to attend, and group amusements. The Lynchburg Home Guard, for example, revived a "Queen of the May" celebration, substituting a hulking 230-pound soldier for a beautiful maiden. For his "coronation" he was led from his berth in a cattle stall to a makeshift throne, where a "wreath of pine tassels" was placed on his head. Another company conducted nightly circuses, calling men into a ring to scamper like animals. This same camp outside Ashland had a glee club, whose singing made the " 'welkin ring' with sweet music . . . [especially] that beautiful melody, 'Home, Sweet Home.' " Some men were engaged in the old boyhood pursuits of fishing and swimming, as Henry Robinson ("Robin") Berkeley noted in his diary. Berkeley also recalled the day that "Edmund Anderson made a kite and sent [it] up by a mile of string, which excited the wonder of the ignorant."[17]

For 21-year-old Robin Berkeley of Hanover County, the Civil War commenced on May 17, 1861, when he and many of his classmates at Hanover Academy enlisted in the Hanover Artillery. Robin was in his second year at the academy when he left. There is no record of his earlier education, but given the quality of his writing and his postwar occupation of teacher, it prepared him well. He came from an old Virginia family, the Berkeleys of Barn Elms. His father, Edmund, was a well-known farmer, active in local politics and owner of a small estate called the White House. His mother, Susan, was also a Berkeley; she and Edmund were first cousins. Although Robin does not discuss his reasons for signing up in his diary, the peer pressure alone must have been enormous: his uncle, Landon Carter Berkeley, had helped form the Patrick Henry Riflemen of Hanover County; a teacher, William Morris Fontaine, enlisted in the Hanover Artillery and was chosen to be third lieutenant; and Robin's older brother, John Hill, enlisted in the same unit, as did his good friend from the academy, Beverley B. Turner.

The closest Robin came to giving an explanation of why he joined the army occurred after the surrender in April 1865. While a prisoner of war at Fort Delaware on Pea Patch Island in the Delaware River, Berkeley discussed his anguish over whether to take the oath of allegiance to the Union. He wrote, "It is a vile piece of tyranny of which they ought to be ashamed." He added, "They pretend to have made war on us to save the Union; but is a Union pinned together by bayonets worth saving?"[18]

Regardless of the motivations for his enlistment, Robin had little time to say farewell to loved ones before his departure. He enlisted on a Saturday, attended church on Sunday, got a uniform on Monday, and left by train for Richmond on Tuesday. When he and his brother went to his Uncle Landon's home, Montout, to eat supper and say good-bye, "sad and anxious-looking faces greeted us; but warm and tender hearts bade us good-by, doubt-less praying that God would watch over us and soon bring us back in peace and safety." Little could anyone dream that the prayers would need to continue for four years.

Far more imaginable was that the young woman who received Robin's badge from the Hanover Literary Society, first cousin Anna Louisa Berkeley, would someday be his wife. The close-ness between the two was already evident. Robin asked her "to keep it and wear it for my sake, and if I never come back, to keep it always in remembrance of me." According to the account of the conversation given in Robin's diary, Anna replied—with tears in her eyes—"You know I will do it." The next day, Robin and John left for Richmond.

The Hanover Artillery was enrolled in the service of Virginia on May 21. It was then sent to Jamestown Island, where the big-gest problem was obtaining provisions and preparing meals. Robin and John formed a mess with their good friend Beverley Turner and five other young men from Hanover County (within a month four more from the same county joined their mess). Af-ter several disastrous attempts, one member of their group "sent home for a cook," and "in a short time we got ourselves fixed up very comfortably."[19]

The unit played no role in the two early engagements of the summer, the battles of Big Bethel and Manassas. When news of the Battle of Manassas reached the camp on July 21, some men in the unit signed a petition "asking the Secretary of War to transfer our company to Manassas." Robin, for unknown reasons, did not sign this petition. His only comment was cryptic: "I, being very satisfied, declined to sign this petition, at which some of the boys became very indignant." His refusal may have stemmed from fear, but that is not likely given his later performance in combat. What-ever the reason, he showed independence, a trait that surfaced from time to time during the war. Moreover, his friends held no grudges over his action; they "soon became reconciled and ev-erything went on quietly and smoothly." This comforting regu-

larity would continue into the fall, when Robin's life took a dras-
tic turn for the worse.[20]

Another 21-year-old, John H. Worsham of Richmond, also
enlisted as a private in those heady days in the spring of 1861.
Son of a merchant tailor, Worsham was working as a clerk at Winston and Peters, commission merchants, during the secession
winter. As tensions mounted, Worsham wasted no time in enlisting, and on April 1, 1861, he signed on with the Richmond militia
unit known affectionately by its members as the "Old F." Worsham only hinted at his reasons in some of the concluding chapters of his memoir. For example, he includes the following poem:

> Furl that banner—softly, slowly;
> Treat it gently—it is holy,
> For it droops above the dead;
> Touch it not—unfold it never,
> Let it droop there, furled forever,
> For its people's hopes are dead.[21]

What is known is that F Company grew rapidly that winter,
swelling from just over 100 to 134 members by May. Its roster
was filled with names from prominent Richmond families, and one
of them would achieve military renown: W. R. J. Pegram, a slight,
bespectacled 19-year-old law student who would rise to the rank
of colonel and command the Purcell Battery for much of the war.

F Company was known as much for its uniform as its per-
sonnel. Members were required to purchase a gray frock coat,
gray pants with black stripes along the outer seam, a gray cap
"trimmed with black braid," a black cloth overcoat, white gloves,
and buttons made of "Virginia fire-gilt." (Much of this uniform
became the standard for the Confederate outfits.) Gear was carried in expensive knapsacks, "imported from Paris, made of
calfskin tanned with hair on, the color being red and white."

The company was one of the first in Virginia to see action—if
that is the proper word. On April 21, F Company was called out
to protect Richmond from the feared attack of the Union gunboat *Pawnee*. Although the *Pawnee* never came close to Richmond,
the townspeople were so grateful for the company's efforts that
the men received an ovation as they marched back into town,

thus concluding what Worsham humorously referred to as the "Pawnee War."[22]

Because it was one of the few older militia companies in Richmond, it was expected that F Company would be dispatched along with the Richmond Light Infantry Blues to Aquia Creek, near Fredericksburg, to prevent Union seizure of the terminus of the Richmond, Fredericksburg, and Potomac Railroad. Arriving there on April 24, the units found that the Union forces had not invaded but just sailed noisily along the river. The units settled into the city fairgrounds, filling their days with drills and the procurement of provisions.

There were lighter moments during this early phase of the war. When the units had dress parades at night, "most of the young ladies of the town" came out to watch, "and they seemed to enjoy it as much as we did their presence." The men formed messes of about ten men each, hiring black cooks to prepare and sometimes procure the food. The only drawback to this simple life was the lodging: F Company had been assigned to the horse sheds, three men to a stall! F Company stayed at the fairgrounds, renamed Camp Mercer, for about three weeks. When the unit left to set up camp closer to Aquia Creek, the men moved out with "sad hearts." The mature Worsham reflected on this first posting: "This was the most comfortable camp we had during the war, but at the time we thought it was execrable."

It was while camped near the creek that F Company had its first exposure to battle. On May 29 a gunboat fired randomly at the camp. A greater exchange took place on June 7, when three gunboats fired at the earthworks near the wharf. F Company responded with shells from 3-inch rifled cannon, apparently hitting several of the gunboats. The bombardment resumed the next day, with as little effect as before. In fact, the only casualty was a chicken coop "knocked to pieces." On June 9 the gunboats departed. Having emerged unscathed from their "baptism of fire," the men happily returned to their drilling and leisure-time pursuits of "fishing on the wharf, bathing in the river, taking rambles through the woods, having on one of the hills in the neighborhood a fine and extensive view of the Potomac."

This extended "summer camp" came to an end on June 14, when the company was ordered back to Richmond. Stationed at

Camp Lee, the unit was formally mustered into service on June 28. It formed part of the new 21st Virginia Regiment, commanded by a former professor at the Virginia Military Institute, Colonel William Gilham. Joined by eight other companies drawn largely from Southside Virginia but including another urban contingent of young men, Company B of Baltimore, the regiment had approximately 850 men on the rolls. Each carrying a Bible, a rifle, and a knapsack filled with clothing and paraphernalia that weighed up to forty pounds, the men of Company F marched out of Camp Lee on July 18, heading down Broad Street, "amidst the inspiring cheers of the multitude that bade us good-bye," to the train station. There they boarded the "cars" for the long overnight trip to Staunton, where they camped for a night before marching off to Buffalo Gap, en route to Huntersville in Pocahontas County, to join General Robert E. Lee's Army of the Northwest.[23]

NOTES

1. *Richmond Daily Dispatch*, April 11, 12, and 15, 1861 (hereafter cited as *RDD*).

2. Ibid., April 18 and 15, 1861. Dates of events often appear out of chronological order in newspaper citations of this time because the newspapers relied on local correspondents to mail them reports. These reports might be published a week after they were written or, if the distances were short and the mail moving quickly, the day after.

3. Ibid., April 11, 1861. See Douglas R. Egerton, *Gabriel's Rebellion: The Virginia Slave Conspiracies of 1800 and 1802* (Chapel Hill, 1993), for the best work on this subject.

4. *RDD*, April 12, 13, and 15, 1861. A casual glance at the articles in the *Richmond Daily Dispatch* and other Southern newspapers during the secession winter of 1860–61 would show extensive coverage and analysis of the deepening sectional crisis. For the editors of the pro-secession *Daily Dispatch*, the question was not would there be war, but when would it start. An article on April 8, for instance, was entitled "The Approaching Civil War."

Casualties were very light on both sides at Fort Sumter; after thirty-four hours of firing and 4,000 shells, no one was killed or seriously wounded. The first fatalities occurred at the surrender ceremony, when two Union soldiers were killed when a pile of cartridges accidently exploded. For the briefest of coverage, see E. B. Long and Barbara Long, *The Civil War Day by Day: An Almanac, 1861–1865* (New York, 1971), 56–59.

5. *RDD*, April 15 and 18, 1861. The War Department specifically requested 2,340 volunteer troops from Virginia. *RDD*, April 17, 1861.

Formerly a staunch Unionist, Letcher was clever enough to see which way popular sentiment was moving. In another section of his April 16 letter to Secretary of War Simon Cameron, he placed the blame for war entirely on the Lincoln administration: "You have chosen to inaugurate civil war, and having done so, we will meet it, in a spirit as determined as the administration has exhibited toward us." *RDD*, April 18, 1861.

6. Ibid., April 19 and 20, 1861. Henry Shanks has a map of the secession vote by county at the State Convention on April 17. As might be expected, fifty-five of the eighty-eight pro-secession votes came from east of the Blue Ridge, while twenty-five of the fifty-five anti-secession votes came from northwest Virginia. (In what would become West Virginia, thirty-one votes were cast against secession, twelve and two-thirds for secession.) After the vote on the seventeenth, some members absent on that day voted for secession, while others conveniently changed their votes, rendering an "official" count of 103 for and forty-six against. Shanks, *Secession Movement in Virginia*, 204–8.

7. *RDD*, April 20, 1861; Sallie Brock Putnam, *Richmond during the War: Four Years of Personal Observation* (1867; reprint, New York, 1983), 21.

8. Linderman in Chapters 1–4 of *Embattled Courage* has an excellent discussion of the key values for soldiers of this era: manliness, godliness, duty, honor, knightliness, and, above all, courage; George C. Rable provides an overview of white Southern women's support for the war in Chapter 2 of *Civil Wars: Women and the Crisis of Southern Nationalism* (Urbana, IL, 1989, and paperback edition, 1991); McPherson, *For Cause and Comrades*, tackles the subject of eagerness for war in Chapters 1–2; see *RDD*, May 20, 1861, for the full text of the poem.

9. Robertson, *Civil War Virginia*, 23; *RDD*, May 4 and April 29, 1861.

10. *RDD*, May 25 and May 13, 1861.

11. Ibid., May 13, 1861.

12. Ibid., May 11, April 19, and May 22, 16, 9, and 20, 1861.

13. Robertson, *Civil War Virginia*, 23.

14. *RDD*, April 15, 20, and 24, 1861.

15. Ibid., May 22, 4, 25, and 10; and June 4, 11, 15, and 10, 1861. Newspaper editors exhorted the wealthier citizens of the city to do their share. Maintaining that just $12 could buy enough cloth to make a tent to accommodate ten men, the editors asked, "Will not our wealthy and patriotic citizens come forward and contribute for the equipment of our own regiments? If our worthy Mayor would call a meeting of the citizens, the requisite funds could be raised in a single day." *RDD*, June 10, 1861.

16. Ibid., July 10, 1861; Paddy Griffith, *Battle Tactics of the Civil War* (Cambridge, 1987), Chapter 5, discusses these problems in detail.

17. *RDD*, May 21, 1861, mentions religious services at Camp Lee (as do scattered references in other news stories throughout this period); *RDD*, May 7 and 13, 1861; Berkeley, *Diary*, May 27, 1861, 8.

18. Berkeley, *Diary*, footnotes 5–7 on p. 4; xv; footnote 12 on p. 5; xvi; and April 26, 1865, 135.

19. Ibid., May 17, 18, 19, 21, 23, 24, 25, and 27, 1861, 4–7.

20. Ibid., May 27, 1861, 7–8. This entry actually covers events of the whole summer. When Berkeley wrote the text in the 1890s, he relied on notes taken during the war and on memory. He lost one book of notes, which covered the period from May 27, 1861, to March 1862. Hence, numerous events are compressed into a single entry (ibid., xxiv).

21. Worsham, *One of Jackson's Foot Cavalry*, xiv, xv, 1, 265 (page references are from the Broadfoot reprint edition).

22. Worsham, *One of Jackson's Foot Cavalry*, 1–4 (Bantam reprint edition). All future references will be to the Bantam edition, unless otherwise noted.

23. Ibid., 5, 6, 9, 11, 12, 13–23, 24, and 25–27; Susan A. Riggs, *21st Virginia Infantry* (Lynchburg, 1991), 2–3.

Chapter Two

They Also Serve
The Home Front, June 1861

SOON AFTER VIRGINIA seceded, six women showed their support by sending a signed, published appeal to the other women of the state, urging them to volunteer their services to the new Confederate States of America. They had formed their own society, "consisting of delegates from the different churches," to unify their supply and aid efforts. The editors of the *Richmond Daily Dispatch* praised them in a story entitled "The Patriotism of the Ladies," and encouraged more women to do the same. Many did, following a well-trod path of political participation through "legislative petitions, voluntary associations, political campaigns, and published reports, appeals, essays, and novels" described by Elizabeth R. Varon in her groundbreaking work on the roles of white women in antebellum Virginia politics. This new situation, however, demanded sacrifices, and people would have to add more responsibilities to their lives.[1]

No group was more affected by these new responsibilities than white women in the South. From plowing to powder-making, they would need to take over many of the tasks previously done by men while still tending to their own domestic and religious duties. It was a burden that most took up willingly, especially young, single women.[2]

A good representative of this group is Amanda Virginia "Tee" Edmonds. Just twenty-two years old when the war broke out, Tee's remarkably candid diary from 1857 to 1867 recounts a busy whirl of outings, visits, and parties—the graceful, sometimes giddy social life that popular culture associates with young, upper-class white women in the antebellum South. The seventh of ten children born to Lewis and Elizabeth "Betsy" Settle Edmonds, Tee appears to have had a solid education (given the quality of the writing in her diary) and a strong sense of self-worth. She was, in the words of her descendant and the editor of her diary, Nancy Chappelear Baird, "spirited, restless, romantic and a lover of excitement." Her family had one of the finest houses in Fauquier County, Belle Grove, near the town of Paris, with another fine house also "in the family," Mount Bleak, which was owned by Tee's uncle, Abner Humphrey Settle. The entire Belle Grove estate encompassed 1,000 acres.[3]

Tee began keeping a diary in June 1857. Her entries of the next three years provide many glimpses of the lives and views of her class, but for reasons of economy, only a few major developments will be described. Amid the constant visiting of friends and family, camp meetings, sewing parties, and occasional formal parties, sadness and tragedy always lurked. For example, on August 14, 1857, her father took sick with a fever, soon followed by a sore throat, an intense pain in his side, then a burning fever again. For ten nights his wife was at his bedside, and he was seen daily by his son-in-law, Dr. Albin Payne, and later by Dr. James C. Brown, who "applied blisters" to her father's breast. The next day, August 27, he died. He was fifty-seven years old.

He left not only a grieving family but also a mountain of debts. An obituary blamed the debts on a "misplaced confidence in the world around him," which the editor of Tee's diary narrows down to "signing notes for friends, which they did not make good." Whatever the reasons for his debt, it had to be paid, and within two years Lewis Edmonds's personal possessions and at least seven of his slaves had been sold, and Belle Grove itself had been put up for public auction (but not purchased, perhaps out of kindness or reluctance to take on its debts). Each sale hit Tee hard, though she qualified her crying over the sale of the slaves with these thoughts: "I am glad they got good homes, and would they all had. . . . I know servants are aggravating sometimes and wish they were in Georgia, but when I see the poor ignorant, and sometimes faithful, ones torn away so, I cannot help feeling for them." Her greatest sadness, of course, came with the death of her father, and it hit her especially hard at Christmas, when she "could not choke the memory as it rushed upward, that Pa, he that was ever here on that occasion, was now so keenly missing from the group that were 'round the table pouring glass after glass." Like most people, however, she dealt with the initial loss by noting its unreality: "It is all over and he is gone, but I cannot realize the awful truth, it seems but a dream."[4]

There were other developments that saddened Tee, but more in keeping with the heartbreaks and disappointments of the young. Every few months one of her close friends would get married, and although she might worry about the match, she worried more that her special man might be too hard to find. As she wrote on her twentieth birthday, "I feel like I was just emerging into sweet girlhood, instead of a lass of twenty. I have a young and blooming heart nevertheless that may yet be caught by a true, noble, generous soul that may ever beat responsive to mine." For nearly three years, Tee carried the torch for a young minister, George Leech. She survived the heartbreak of seeing his engagement to another woman, who soon broke it off. Gingerly, Tee made overtures to him again, even giving him a cigar case as a token of her friendship. While she waited for his response (he was in another town), she met Wirt Lemert of Ohio, who was visiting Paris on business. Lemert quickly fell in love with the petite, attractive Tee, and he told a friend that he most admired her "black eyes . . . [and] intellectual looking face." She sent him "her respects," thinking "it would be sufficient to keep alive the little flame that had been kindled." But her true love was still "Brother" George Leech, and when he wrote a sweet thank-you note for her gift, she wrote, "Did there ever as bright a day of happiness penetrate this heart?" That note and some occasional glimpses or news of him were all that Tee received for the next two years, until she read of his wedding in the *Methodist Sentinel*. As for Wirt Lemert, he was not heard from after he returned to Ohio.[5]

For Tee, then, there were still the occasional parties that lasted until dawn, the excitement of the camp meetings, and the thrill of watching mock medieval tournaments, but no beau, despite the shared efforts of a friend. One night they each wrote the name of their "sweethearts" on a piece of gilt paper, folded it into the shape of a heart, dipped it in red wine, drank the wine, then put the pieces of paper under their pillows, saying that "if we dream of that one, [we] will marry him." Poor Tee not only dreamt of the wrong man, she never grew half as close as she desired to "the only one of whom my heart throbs wildly," George Leech.[6]

Of course, even a romantic like Tee was not immune to the political events undermining her world. Although she rarely mentioned politics or political figures, two major exceptions were her descriptions of John Brown's raid and Virginia's secession. She had nothing but hatred and contempt for Brown, writing in her diary on the day of his hanging, "This day will long, long be remembered, as the one that witnessed old Brown—the villain, murderer, and destroyer of our Virgin peace—swinging from the gallows. O! how many are the rejoicings at his end." As for the execution itself, Tee wrote, "I almost wish I was a man, so that I could have been there to look upon it." Part of Tee's intense loathing sprang from her great fear that the insurrection would spread to Paris. She wrote, "The Negroes have threatened what they intended doing and indeed have put some of their vile threats into execution by burning wheat stacks near Charlestown." Frightened, the members of the household looked to their brothers for protection; Jack even "set up two nights watching with his arms should anything disturb us." Nothing did, and the fear of insurrection faded with the death of John Brown. The fear of war apparently passed, too, for nothing was mentioned of the secession crisis until Virginia seceded. Even then, the entry was short: "Virginia today is numbered with her Southern Sister States."

The sewing of uniforms, the arrangement of a bouquet of flowers, the mustering in of some local men into Captain Richard H. Carter's Piedmont Rifle Company: none of these actions brought home the full import of the war. It took the presentation of the new Confederate flag to the company, sewed by some of the women of Paris, to make people realize that war was truly coming—whatever that might mean. Tee wrote, "The solemn stillness was marred by the manifestation of deep emotion throughout the assembled crowd, tears were seen in the eye of every soldier, and indeed it appeared to me more like the burying of some dear one. Truly, too truly I fear [it] *will* prove the burying of some, if not all." Indeed, Tee would not have been true to herself if she had not taken notice of one of the handsome young men in the company, even on that gloomiest of days. As she told her friend Mel, "I just fell in love and the ideal was taking his departure—what a deplorable condition. . . . [The] little fellow was a great nephew of General Washington; rather small in stature, but good looking. . . . I hope he may prove a General Washington and returned crowned with laurels of honour and victory."[7]

For young women like Tee, war in the early summer of 1861 was exciting and romantic. It was not so for most Southern wives and mothers. As George Rable has written in his book on Southern women during the Civil War, "Mothers especially doubted that secession could take place peacefully or that a civil war would be short and painless."[8] This statement accurately reflects the worries and fears of Susan Emeline Jeffords Caldwell of Warrenton.

Susan Caldwell was thirty-four years old in 1861. Mother of three and pregnant with her fourth child, she had only resided in Warrenton for two years when Virginia seceded. Her husband, Lycurgus, set off for Richmond in June to find a government job. He had four years of experience as an auditor in the Treasury Department, and a friend from those days, Harvel Harris Goodloe, was working on his behalf. That was enough; within a week Lycurgus found a position in the newly created Confederate Treasury Department.[9]

Susan was left at home with the three children, ages one to six; her sister-in-law, Lucy Caldwell Finks; Lucy's husband, John William Finks; and six black slaves she referred to as "servants": Lucy, Harriet, John, Cinda, Susa, and Alice.[10] Though Susan tried to remain cheerful about the separation, her brave mask came down suddenly toward the end of a long letter she wrote to her husband on July 20, 1861: "I long to see you. It seems as if it has been the longest 4 weeks I have ever spent and yet I know not when to look for you."[11]

Apparently, their separations before had been shorter. They had met in 1851 when Lycurgus was a boarder in the home of Susan's parents, John H. and Mary Humbert Jeffords of Charleston, South Carolina. Placed in charge of the telegraph office there by the inventor of the machine, Samuel F. B. Morse, Lycurgus (age twenty-eight) was smitten by the Jeffordses' daughter, Susan (age twenty-four). The slender, dark-haired young woman with piercing brown eyes was the third of five children born to the Jeffordses. The attraction was mutual; the couple was married on October 1, 1851. Lycurgus continued working for Morse in Charleston until late 1854, at which time he and Susan moved to Washington, where Lycurgus obtained a position as an auditor in the Treasury Department. In Washington their first child, William, was born on January 10, 1855, and their second child, Frank H., on May 24, 1857. Their daughter, Jessie, was born in Warrenton on September 2, 1859.

In Warrenton they lived in one of the finest residences in town, a "large fieldstone house" built by Lycurgus's father, James, in 1831 in the "prevailing Federal style . . . [with a] five-bay front wall." After James's sudden death in 1832, his widow, Frances Pattie, continued to live in the house with her three children. Her daughter Lucy married local businessman John W. Finks in 1840, and the Finkses lived in the Caldwell house. It soon became their house in fact as well as deed; Frank Caldwell, eldest son of James and Frances, sold them his share of the property given to him by his father (Lycurgus retained a one-third share in the house). The Finkses added a carriage house, stable, meat house, dairy, icehouse, and a portico with a room above it. Although they had no children of their own, they had adopted a daughter (she died in 1853) and served as guardians to other young women from time to time. Thus, the good-sized house was usually filled with the sound of children and adults bustling about their daily activities.[12]

Susan Caldwell's views of the war are not entirely clear from her letters. She seemed quite happy that her husband was working for the government instead of serving in the military. For instance, when it appeared that John Finks would be "called up" (even though he was forty-three years old in 1861), Lycurgus offered to go in his place. Susan's response was quick and emphatic: "Now Mr. C. I see no reason why you should leave your office in which you are serving your Country and sufficient salary given you to support your family and assist Mr. F. all you can during these perilous times." Health was also a concern of hers. "If you were of a hearty robust nature perhaps I would feel differently in hearing you speak of living in the Camp." A reasonable interpretation of Susan's feelings is that she feared that her husband's sensible response to secession—to work for the new Confederate government in a safe but vital position in the Treasury—was about to be superseded by some latent boyish impulse or an overzealous sense of duty. If Lycurgus made the leap from civilian to military duty, then the worst could happen: he could be wounded or killed. These were the thoughts that Susan could not bear. In this realm, she fits firmly with the majority of white Southern women who, according to Rable, filtered everything through the prism of the family. "Their obsession with the local and the particular—a narrowness but at the same time an acuteness of vision—made their fears especially vivid and realistic." Imagine Susan's relief, then, when Finks was appointed commissary for Warrenton, thus sparing both him and Lycurgus from military service.[13]

Susan was usually careful to couch her wishes in the language of deferential concern. When she urged Lycurgus not to join the military, she tried to soften her request with flattery: "I think you are wrong in so doing while at the same time I admire you for your true nobleness of soul and strong feeling of devotion you bear towards Mr. F. in offering to go in his stead." In case that was not enough, she closed the letter with a plea and some guilt thrown in for good measure:

> My mind is kept too much excited for my situation—you must try and resolve upon your remaining in Richmond and allow my mind to grow quiet. I have not been well for several days. If you were in Warrenton of course I could not say as much—but you are away and relieved from Military duty and that should reconcile you to remain, for you are not fitted for to undertake the hardships of a Soldier's life.[14]

Susan's relief was undisguised in her next letter, after learning that Lycurgus would not be joining the army: "I beg of you to make yourself happy during your stay from us in Richmond. I am glad you are there." She thought he was safer in Richmond than in Warrenton, which was close to the Union lines. Secure in her new knowledge that her husband would not be in uniform in the immediate future, she could freely support his desire to be brave and loyal, upholding his sense of "manhood." She wrote, "In case Richmond should be attacked tho', I will coincide with all your wishes. As dear as your life is to me and I feel at present as if I could not live without you I would not have you act the *Coward* you may rely upon it."[15]

Some of Susan's sensitive personality shows through these brief extracts. For the most part, an assessment of her personality must be inferred from her letters and actions; no thorough biography of her exists. Although her education is not described, it must have been equivalent to that of other young women of her class, given her clear, thoughtful, virtually error-free prose. Perhaps her native intelligence is the source of her good letter writing; she not only reports on what has happened, but tries numerous stratagems to influence her husband. On one hand, one could argue that her extensive effort to shape her husband's actions through tactful phrases and outright emotional appeals is a measure of her powerlessness. On the other hand, those placed in a subordinate position by law and custom must use every wile at their command to sway their superiors. Whether or not Susan's efforts in that regard were successful, through careful reading of her letters one can watch a master diplomat at work. To be fair, Susan seems deeply attached to Lycurgus, if the statements in her first few letters about the great difficulty of operating a household without her husband reflect her actual feelings. She regularly addressed him as "Dearest Papa" and he addressed her as "Dear Daughter." Both terms may seem odd to modern readers, but were not unusual forms of address in Victorian-era letters. Still, only four years separated the two in age. Overall, there is more equality in their relationship than the endearing titles suggest, within a context of "separate spheres" for men and women.[16]

The chief concerns of Susan were her children, Lycurgus, her in-laws, friends, family in Charleston, the household, and the war—in that order. Almost every letter contains some news about the children, much of it poignant. For example, in her very first letter to Lycurgus in Richmond, she wrote that 2-year-old Jessie had "inquired for Papa—. . . insists you are up street at Daddy's store." A week later, she wrote that Jessie had been "taken with something like Diarrhea and sick stomach—and I feared Cholera Infantum so I sent this afternoon for him [the doctor] to see her again. . . . He has left powders for her if she continues to have sick stomach." Jessie's 4-year-old brother was also quite concerned about the illness. Susan wrote, "Frank said prayers for her—and he puts great faith in his asking the Good Lord for any one." Jessie soon recovered, but then it was Frank's turn to get sick. After Lycurgus had visited the family in early July, Susan wrote:

I have had Frank sick for two days like he was when you were
with him. He had eaten too many gooseberries again—that with
the hot weather made the little fellow very sick, he had burning fevers—I had to give him a Calomel powder—which made
him very sick until the medicine operated—he threw off some
bile. . . . He wants to see Papa very much—and would sleep
with you very willingly at night.

As for the oldest brother, 6-year-old Willie, Susan wrote, "He
says a lesson regularly every day of his own accord—he is very anxious to make a visit to Richmond." Susan's letters are also peppered
with news of "Grand Ma" (Lycurgus's mother), "Sister" (Lucy Finks,
her sister-in-law), and "Mr. F." (John Finks, called "Daddy" by the
Caldwell children). As for her own family, she rarely mentions them
and seems to have had little correspondence with them. Friends,
mutual acquaintances, and polite soldiers stopping by get mention,
but the slaves never do. The letters usually contain some information about Susan's ill health, which typically ranged from a bad headache to all-day painful prostration, "similar as I have been when
taken with bilious colic."[17]

As the summer of 1861 wore on, Susan became more resigned
to the separation from her husband. This resignation produced
strength and increased her sympathy for the sadness of thousands
separated from their loved ones by the war. Susan kindly rejected
Lycurgus's proposals that the family join him in Richmond, emphasizing in her diplomatic way the burdensome costs of such a
move: "I think we must both content ourselves to live this way
till things are in a more settled condition, your salary is limited
and you will have use for every penny." As much as her heart
hurt, she knew she was also fortunate:

I am very anxious to see you, time seems very long since you
have left us . . . but I am not discontented or repine at my situation, for I am assured that you are more lonesome and suffer
more privations than I do. I have every thing around me to make
me happy. I am far better off than thousands who are compelled
to give up their husbands perhaps never to behold them in life
again—give them up to find a soldier's grave.[18]

Another wife and mother, Maria Louisa Wacker Fleet, was
equally fortunate to be able to see her husband, Dr. Benjamin Fleet,

remain out of military service. Dr. Fleet was one of the few physicians in King and Queen County, and with his health problems (not to mention pique over being offered a lesser rank than some younger physicians) and his manifold responsibilities as physician, plantation owner, "keeper of a ferry," and magistrate, it is not surprising that he declined a Second Assistant Surgeon's commission in the Confederate army.[19] The choices were different for Dr. Fleet's two oldest sons, Alexander Frederick (age seventeen) and Benjamin Robert (age fourteen). For Alexander ("Fred"), the choice was essentially to go along with his friends at the University of Virginia or to stay out and please his mother. For Benjamin ("Benny"), the choice he wanted to make—to join—was denied him because of his age. For his five younger brothers and sisters, there was no choice but to stay at home.

The war came slowly but steadily into Fred's life during his first year at the University of Virginia, 1860–61. When Fred went off to college in September 1860, he leaned toward the defunct party of his father, the Whigs. Having no party to promote in 1860, he gravitated toward John Bell's Constitutional Union Party. But his roommate, Pat, fell in with the majority of students at the university, favoring John Breckinridge, and even tacked up a picture of Breckinridge on the mantelpiece in their dormitory room. Fred seemed happier to report that in the election held at the university, Virginia students gave Bell the edge by five votes: "There was a tremendous hurrah for Bell, & then cheers for Virginia." Fred did not appear to be as ardent a supporter of Bell as his younger brother Benny was; Fred wrote to him in November 1860 that he tentatively agreed with the affirmative side of a debate he had heard on a Sunday night at the university, "Should the South secede now that Lincoln is elected?" Fred said, "Upon due deliberation, I reckon, although I am not certain, that the South had better secede now, while she can & not to wait until she cannot." Although Benny was too young to vote, he made his preference clear in his diary entry of November 5, 1860: "Tomorrow is the Election Day and I only hope and pray to God that Bell and [Edward] Everett may be elected." Their father took a more sanguine view of the election, writing to Fred that "even though Lincoln's election is a fixed fact, the Union need not of necessity be dissolved. My confidence is that over-ruling Providence will save us from the horrors of dissolution."[20]

It is not surprising that Fred's father, Dr. Benjamin Fleet, had no wish to see war come to Virginia; he had too much to lose. The last of four sons born to Captain William Fleet and Sarah Browne Tomlin Fleet, he decided to take money rather than land for his inheritance. He used his inheritance to pay for medical training at the University of Pennsylvania, then returned to King and Queen County where in rapid succession he married Maria Louisa Wacker, bought a fine house just east of the Mattaponi River, Pickle Hill, which he and Maria renamed Green Mount, and began his dual career as a county physician and plantation owner. Just four years apart in age, the young doctor and his wife had seven children between 1842 and 1856, all of whom survived the war except the journal writer, Benny. Although Dr. Fleet's father, Captain William Fleet, was clearly a member of the "ruling class" of Revolutionary-era Virginia (he was a member of the Virginia Constitutional Convention of 1788), he was by no means among the so-called old elite (100 families identified by historian Lorraine Eva Holland in her pioneering study, "Rise and Fall of the Antebellum Virginia Aristocracy"). Captain Fleet's youngest son, Benjamin, on the other hand, comes much closer to fitting Holland's "new elite" of the nineteenth century (real and personal property worth over $30,000). With fifty slaves and over 3,000 acres under his control, Dr. Fleet was in the upper 10 percent of Virginia's planters in terms of acreage and number of slaves owned. Yet if someone had told Dr. Fleet that he was a member of the "ruling aristocracy" in the 1850s, he would have laughed. Like many, he probably looked at old families such as the Carters and Cockes and "new" families such as the Riveses of Albemarle County as truly wealthy; he may have regarded himself as a hardworking country doctor with a good plantation to run. He did not have the benefit of statistics that would have shown that he had followed the path of many well-to-do males in Virginia: going into the "professions" to augment income generated by agricultural production.

Being a rural doctor was not a cushy job in the nineteenth century; a doctor was responsible for the good health of hundreds of people within a county. In Dr. Fleet's case, he also acted as magistrate; supervised crop production on four large parcels of land within the county besides the land around Green Mount; and operated several granaries, two ferries, a toll bridge, and a barge, or lighter. Given this wide range of responsibilities, it is understandable that Dr. Fleet preferred peace and order to war and chaos. In fact, the supervisory load may have been too great for him at times; family members' letters and journal entries are dotted with references to "Pa's" drinking problem.[21]

As for Fred, he was given an extensive private education. His mother taught him to read, and his father taught him the Greek alphabet before he was five years old. Then it was off to Goshen, where Mary Chapin of Washington, DC, taught Fred, Benny, and some of their cousins. When he became a teenager, Fred attended Fleetwood Academy, then Rumford Academy, and finally Aberdeen Academy, whose superintendent, James Calvin Councill, would be the commanding officer of Fred's company in the 26th Virginia Infantry in 1861 (Fred was moved from school to school as his parents sought a better education for him and his brother Benny.) Then, as mentioned earlier, it was off to the University of Virginia in the fall of 1860.[22]

It was at the university where Fred's Whiggish, pro-Union views began to erode under the assault of opposing opinions and the march toward secession. Even within his family, though, he was not alone in his shift from staunch Unionist to cautious Secessionist. In a letter written to his father in February 1861, he discussed some pragmatic reasons for secession:

> Your views expressed in your last letter exactly express mine and from what I have seen in all the papers, it will be the worst thing that could be done for the University if Virginia doesn't secede & go along with the South for a good many of the Southern students say that they will hold a meeting and all go home, & they, you know constitute about half or nearly half of the whole number. Then the Southern University that is being built would immediately rise while this would go down.

If pragmatism were not a strong-enough reason to change views, there was the peer pressure and the allure (to a young boy) of the very active military units on the campus. Fred wrote to his father, "The military companies make quite a display out on the lawn every evening, when on parade. They have red flannel jackets, black pants & glazed caps for their uniforms & have purchased muskets themselves."[23]

The firing on Fort Sumter would soon bring even the most dedicated Unionists around to the secession view. As Benny wrote in his journal on April 26, 1861, "We joined the Southern Confederacy yesterday, an overwhelming majority in the Convention. I have been for the Union all along until the first Gun was fired at Fort Sumter." Others within the family were not as enthusiastic as Benny. Fred's mother wrote to him on April 29, "With what anxiety the whole country looks to the future just now! Why does God allow so much misery to befall this once happy land." More directly, she told Fred, "Neither Pa nor I is willing for you to go to the War until there is greater necessity for it than there is at present." Her protective order took place within the context of considerable commotion. Her husband was helping the local militia to muster in, while rumors circulated that "vessels were coming up the river with the intention of burning and pillaging." That fear quickly vanished when no vessels appeared, but the building of four volunteer companies from the county went on apace, until 300 men had mustered in by May 8. Fred remained at college, however, which deeply pleased his father. Dr. Fleet wrote, "I am glad you have determined to remain at the University. You ought in justice alike to yourself & to me to do so, at least untill yr. services were actually required (which they are not at the present) by your Country."[24]

The rush of events forced the Fleets to continually reevaluate their positions. In late May there was the rumor of a slave uprising in King and Queen County. Dr. Fleet went out with "most of the gentlemen of the neighborhood" to patrol, while Mrs. Fleet stayed at home with her children and "three guns, a pistol and two clubs at hand." It was much ado about nothing, as Mrs. Fleet wrote to her son Fred: "(They) scoured the whole surrounding country, without finding anything amiss. Everything was unusually quiet—whether the calm before the storm or not, I cannot say." Then there was the continuing question of Fred's enlistment. Even Mrs. Fleet was beginning to waver on this subject, as she wrote to Fred on May 20: "I have been anticipating so much pleasure when you come home in July and now I don't know what you will have to do, for of course you can not sit idly by when our country expects every one of her sons to be up and doing." Her mind turned to the advantageous side of enlistment: "Will your acquaintance with General Lee's son help you in any way to a more desirable situation than the militia under Captain Wilson?" Even the ever-enthusiastic Benny was overwhelmed by the sudden and dramatic changes. On May 31 his school superintendent, James Councill, "broke up" the school to begin his next position, captain of a rifle company. Benny wrote in his journal, "I have left maybe never to go to school again. I feel very disconsolowtory & meloncolly."[25]

Fred Fleet finally resolved the dilemma he faced in the same manner as thousands of his contemporaries, by enlisting in a newly formed military company. He joined the Jackson Grays on June 14, the same day he returned home from college. He was elected first sergeant, serving under his former teacher, Captain James Councill. He had very little time for training; on June 23 the sixty-plus men who formed the nucleus of Company I, 26th Virginia Infantry, sailed off for Gloucester Point. There they went into camp, struggling against dysentery and homesickness rather than against Union forces. While Fred suffered the effects of a bout of dysentery, he was soon comforted by potions sent by his father ("Blue Mass & opium pills . . . also some Epsom Salts and Jamaica ginger"); the services of a free black man, Meredith, whom his parents paid to "look after" him; and plenty of food ("two quarters of lamb already cooked, some chickens . . . loaf bread, eggs, etc."). Fred was undoubtedly cheered by a visit from his father and his brother Benny, who in the last week of July brought news of the Battle of Manassas, good wishes from family and friends, and food. As Fred wrote to his mother in early August, "if I can keep my health as well as I have done heretofore (for I have been as well as I ever was in my life), I will be pleased with a soldier's life, but I have nothing like as hard a time as I expected."[26]

NOTES

1. *RDD*, June 20 and 28, 1861; Elizabeth R. Varon, *We Mean to Be Counted: The Roles of White Women in Politics in Antebellum Virginia* (Charlottesville, 1998), 1–2 .

2. See Chapters 1–2 in Faust, *Mothers of Invention*, for much more on this subject.

3. Edmonds, *Journals*, xxiii, vii, viii, ix.

4. Ibid., August 14, 1857, 3; August 24, 1857, 4; August 27, 1857, 5; unidentified obituary and editor's note, 248; November 3, 1857, 7; April 22, 1858, 13; auction of Belle Grove, July 12, 1859, 29; April 22, 1858, 13; June 13, 1859, 28; December 25, 1857, 9–10; August 28, 1857, 5.

5. Ibid. Weddings are noted on December 14, 1859, 37, April 17, 1860, 39, July 15, 1860, 41, and December 15 and 17, 1860, 43; meets George Leech, January 5, 1858, 11, September 14, 1858, 17, December 10, 1858, 21, February 10, 1859, 24; meets Wirt Lemert, January 3, 1859, 22, March 11, 1859, 25, April 9, 1859, 26, March 14, 1861, 46.

6. Ibid., December 13, 1860, 43; July 26, 1860, 41; February 28, 1859, 25.

7. Ibid., December 2, 1859, 34; November 11, 1859, 32; November 13, 1859, 33; April 17, 1861, 47; May 23, 1861, 48–49. The great nephew was Second Lieutenant John H. Washington.

8. Rable, *Civil Wars*, 46. In *We Mean to Be Counted*, Varon quotes a 13-year-old girl to make a small point that youth favored secession (action) over inaction (152–53). Neither Varon, Faust, nor Rable dig deeply into the question of how age might have affected a woman's response to secession and war; they tend to lump all white women together. This subject deserves further investigation.

9. Caldwell, *Letters*, Susan Caldwell to Lycurgus Caldwell, June 28, 1861, 21.

10. Ibid., editor's notes, 14–16 and 12.

11. Ibid., Susan Caldwell to Lycurgus Caldwell, July 20, 1861, 34.

12. Ibid., editor's notes, 15, 16, 62 (n. 55), and 14–15.

13. Ibid., Susan Caldwell to Lycurgus Caldwell, July 17, 1861, 32; Rable, *Civil Wars*, 46.

14. Caldwell, *Letters*, Susan Caldwell to Lycurgus Caldwell, July 17, 1861, 32–33.

15. Ibid., Susan Caldwell to Lycurgus Caldwell, July 20, 1861, 33–34. An initial foray into the expanding debate about definitions and roles of the concept of "manhood" before, during, and after the Civil War should begin with Gerald Linderman's *Embattled Courage*; then move on to Reid Mitchell's *Civil War Soldiers* (New York, 1988) and *The Vacant Chair*, E. Anthony Rotundo, *American Manhood* (New York, 1993), and some essays found in Catherine Clinton and Nina Silber, eds., *Divided Houses: Gender and the Civil War* (New York, 1992).

16. Discussions of marriage relations among white middle- or upper-class Southerners can be found in Sally G. McMillen, *Southern Women: Black and White in the Old South* (Arlington Heights, IL, 1992), 35–47, and Joan Cashin, " 'Since the War Broke Out': The Marriage of Kate and William McClure," in Clinton and Silber, eds., *Divided Houses: Gender and the Civil War*, 200–212. The effects of the Civil War on marriage and roles of women in white families are covered extensively in Faust and Rable. Faust also has a brief but illuminating discussion of "separate spheres" in footnote 7 on page 263 in *Mothers of Invention*. For

an extended discussion of the history of "separate spheres" as an ana-
lytical construct, see Linda Kerber, "Separate Spheres, Female Worlds,
Woman's Place: The Rhetoric of Women's History," *Journal of American
History* 75, no. 1 (June 1988): 9–40.

17. Caldwell, *Letters*, Susan Caldwell to Lycurgus Caldwell, June
23, 1861, 19; Susan Caldwell to Lycurgus Caldwell, June 28, 1861, 22;
Susan Caldwell to Lycurgus Caldwell, July 10, 1861, 25; Susan Caldwell
to Lycurgus Caldwell, August 22, 1861, 45.

18. Ibid., Susan Caldwell to Lycurgus Caldwell, August 13, 1861,
43.

19. Fleet, *Green Mount*, Maria Louisa Wacker Fleet to Fred Fleet
("Ma" to Fred), December 25, 1861, 93; Benny's journal entry, December
20–25, 1861. Benjamin ("Benny") Fleet began his journal in 1860 when
he was fourteen and continued writing until his death in 1864. The letters and journal use familiar addresses of Ma and Pa, and I have retained them for ease of use.

20. Ibid., Benny Fleet's journal, September 26, 1860, 30; Fred Fleet
to Benny Fleet, October 3, 1860, 32–33; Fred Fleet to Benny Fleet, October 29, 1860, 38; Fred Fleet to Benny Fleet, November 10, 1860, 40; Benny
Fleet's journal, November 5, 1860, 39; Ma and Pa to Fred Fleet, November 24, 1860, 42.

21. Ibid., xxiii and xxiv; Lorraine Eva Holland, "Rise and Fall of the
Antebellum Virginia Aristocracy: A Generational Analysis" (Ph.D. dissertation, University of California, Irvine, 1980), 310–11, 318–31, 366–
71, and 338.

There are many references to Dr. Fleet's drinking "problem." He
went on a five-day drinking binge in mid-December 1861, quit when he
got an order from Colonel Gresham to report for duty, then started drinking again the day before he was scheduled to leave home. He was unable to attend the militia muster on December 18 or to leave with the
unit for Gloucester Point on the nineteenth. As Benny tersely wrote in
his journal entry for December 18, 1861, "Colonel Gresham just sent Pa
word to come down when he got well." See Benny Fleet to Fred Fleet,
December 17, 1861, in *Green Mount*, 90–91, and Benny's journal entry of
December 18. Pa's drinking brought even more shame upon his head.
He asked the pastor of St. Stephen's Church if he could quietly "withdraw" his membership in January 1862; the pastor acceded to his wishes.
Dr. Fleet to Reverend Joseph Garlick, January 17, 1862, and Reverend
Joseph Garlick to Dr. Fleet, January 20, 1862, 98–99.

As for the refusal to accept the commission, it is hard to tell whether
Pa refused because he was passed over for First Surgeon, because of the
lingering effects of an illness suffered in 1859, or because he hated to
leave behind the comforts and security of home. He and some members
of his family discussed all three possibilities in a series of letters, with
no single cause emerging as primary. See Pa to Fred, December 28, 1861,
93–94; Pa to Fred, December 29, 1861, 94–95; Pa to Fred, January 1, 1862,
95–96; Benny's journal entry, December 25, 1861, 91; and Ma to Fred,
December 25, 1861, 92.

22. Fleet, ed., *Green Mount after the War*, 5–6.

23. Fleet, *Green Mount*, Fred Fleet to Pa, February 18, 1861, 48. The Southern University that Fred refers to is the present-day University of the South in Sewanee, Tennessee. Peter Carmichael discusses the pressure to support secession at the University of Virginia and other Southern colleges in "The Last Generation," 146–64.

24. Fleet, *Green Mount*, Benny Fleet's journal, April 26, 1861, 52; Ma and Pa to Fred Fleet, April 29, 1861, 52–54; Benny Fleet's journal, May 8, 1861, 54.

25. Ibid., Ma to Fred Fleet, May 20, 1861, 55–56; Benny Fleet's journal, May 31, 1861, 59. The Lee son referred to was Robert Edward Lee Jr., who, like Fred, was in his first year at the University of Virginia. Unlike Fred, young Lee returned to college in the fall, but left to join the infantry before the first term ended. See Paul C. Nagel, *The Lees of Virginia* (New York 1990), 276.

Mrs. Fleet was far more worried about the "awful war" than about a slave uprising. She wrote to Fred, "I should not be telling the truth to say I feel entirely composed as if I had not heard of it, but it is a thing I have never dreaded. They know how well armed the whites are at this time—I cannot believe them so deluded as to suppose they could ever have a successful insurrection."

Mrs. Fleet also had some strong opinions about local notables, which she did not feel free to mention to her husband. In the same long letter to Fred she remarked, "If we could send off our worst men to fight the Yankees as they do in New York, I would not mind the war so much. Peter Samuel, Dr. S. G. Fauntleroy and Col. Davis were the most violent advocates for war I ever saw, and not one has done more than talk. Of course, I would not write in this free way if Pa were not asleep and no chance of his reading the last part of this letter." See Ma to Fred Fleet, May 20, 1861, 56.

26. Fleet, *Green Mount*, Benny Fleet's journal, June 14, 1861, 61; Benny Fleet's journal, June 18, 1861, 61; Benny Fleet's journal, June 23, 1861, 61–62; Pa to Fred Fleet, July 2, 1861, 62; Ma to Fred Fleet, July 2, 1861, 63; Pa to Fred Fleet, July 16, 1861, 64; Benny Fleet's journal, July 24–26, 1861, 67–68; Fred Fleet to Ma, August 6, 1861, 70.

James W. Jackson was the proprietor of the Marshall House, a hotel in Alexandria. On the day Alexandria was occupied by Union forces, May 24, 1861, Jackson shot the man, Elmer Ellsworth, who tore down the Confederate flag that flew above the hotel. Jackson, in turn, was shot and killed by one of the men with Ellsworth. Benny referred to Jackson as "Martyr Jackson." Others felt the same; hence the name for the unit, the Jackson Grays. See Benny Fleet's journal, June 18, 1861, 61 and footnote 2 on page 61 in *Green Mount*.

CHAPTER THREE

FIRST BLOOD
Manassas, July 1861

LIEUTENANT WILLIAM THOMAS POAGUE'S first exposure to large-scale combat came, as it did for thousands of other young men, on a hot July day in 1861. The day began with his battery, led by the former rector of Lexington's Grace Episcopal Church and now Colonel and Chief of the Artillery of the Army of the Shenandoah, William Nelson Pendleton (West Point class of 1830), waiting for orders as they huddled near the railroad crossing at Bull Run. Late in the morning the batteries were ordered to join Brigadier General Thomas J. Jackson's 1st Virginia Brigade as it established a line on the back side of Henry Hill. The small, slender 25-year-old lieutenant with the intense gaze and serious mien found himself on a rollicking race to the battlefield.[1]

Because this was the first real battle for Poague, the impressions became indelibly stamped into his memory. He recalled a swirl of images: "a terrific roar of cannon and musketry is heard in front; wounded and stragglers come creeping along to the rear, dodging into the fence corners to avoid our battery in its headlong rush." As smoke rose above the treetops, Poague felt a "wild and joyous exhilaration." He added, "Nothing ever equalled it afterwards." Poague's actual role in his first battle was quite limited; he had to look after the caissons. He did show the presence of mind to report to his superior officer that one of the Rockbridge Battery's pieces was not being used, and the officer instructed him to find a good spot for it. Poague positioned it at the right of the battery and left it under the command of Sergeant J. C. Davis. After about two hours of firing, the batteries were ordered to withdraw to the Lewis House ridge, while the Stonewall Brigade began its famous charge on the Union lines. Poague recalled that the drill master of Alburtis's battery, Lieutenant John Pelham, displayed his own initiative when he stopped the movement of the battery at the top of a ridge and ordered its men into formation and to commence firing on one section of the Union line, saying, "I'll be dogged if I'm going any further back."[2]

Poague gave a remarkably clear description of the coolness under fire, or what Bell Wiley described as the "complete indifference to the pandemonium raging about them," that he and so many other soldiers have experienced in combat. He wrote, "I was at no time frightened, nor was I excited after we had reached the battle line. . . . The thought repeatedly came to me that I was in the hands of a kind heavenly Father, and that His merciful care and protection were over me." He also described what we now call an adrenaline rush: "With all this was a most novel sensation, hard to describe, a sort of warm, pleasing glow enveloping the chest and head with an effect something like entrancing music in a dream." Yet in the midst of this "glow," his "observing, thinking and reasoning faculties were normal."[3]

In his memoirs, Poague does not mention feeling the "deep depression" that Wiley says most Confederate soldiers underwent after their first battle. Yet he writes poignantly of returning to the field the day after the engagement, and finding "many a friend and acquaintance, stiff in death, with whom as boys I had gone to school and college." He specifically remembered coming across the body of Jim McCorkle, "lying on his back, with a note addressed to his wife pinned to his shirt front." He struggled to give meaning to this tragic sight, resorting to the simplest of summaries: "One could hardly imagine a greater contrast in every respect between that day and the day before."[4]

It had been a swift journey from fledgling lawyer to green artillery officer for William Thomas Poague. In May 1861 the young lawyer had left his practice to join the recently formed Rockbridge Artillery, which was almost immediately sent north to join other Shenandoah Valley units at Harpers Ferry. His record from May 1861 to April 1865 is fairly well detailed in his memoir and official reports; it is his life before military service that is hazier. The bare biographical facts do not reveal much about the man's upbringing. He was the eldest of the four sons of John Barclay and Elizabeth Stuart Paxton Poague. Born on December 20, 1835, he was raised on a midsize farm near Falling Spring Presbyterian Church in Rockbridge County. His early education must have been thorough, because he matriculated at Washington College, graduating in 1857. Following the custom of the day, he pursued the study of law by attending a private school run by Judge Brockenbrough in Lexington, then passed a law examination conducted by three judges. For unstated reasons, he decided to start a law practice in St. Joseph, Missouri, and moved there in the spring of 1860.

Poague found neither success nor happiness in St. Joseph. Although he found the place to be a "stirring border town of about twelve thousand people," he thought that the competition for legal business was too fierce and underhanded. "Only a few men of preeminent abilities could afford to ignore the tricks, shortcuts, and unprofessional methods of the majority," he wrote. Not wanting to employ such methods, he left for more "favorable conditions," which just happened to be in his hometown, Lexington. He felt that he was part of a large "return" movement of young men to the east at this time, where they would "be ready for the impending struggle."

Poague discovered a crucial difference between the citizens of Lexington and those of St. Joseph in 1860. The people of Lexington were not as "stirred up as they were in St. Joe." Moreover, "the great majority believed that the two sections would not come to blows, that an adjustment would be reached and the danger averted." In St. Joseph, on the other hand, he found the electorate to be at a "white heat" when Abraham Lincoln was elected (most of the town's residents opposed him).[5]

Back in Lexington, Poague was offered a partnership with James W. Massie, a "prominent lawyer." The offer came despite the fact that the two men had distinct political differences. Massie was a Breckinridge Democrat, and Poague, like the majority of voters in Rockbridge County, had supported John Bell of the Constitutional Union Party. These differences soon disappeared in the wake of Lincoln's call for volunteers from Virginia to suppress the insurrection in the South. In response, Poague believed that Virginia "took her stand in front of her Southern sisters to resist the invader of her soil." Rockbridge County was no exception; its two volunteer companies organized after John Brown's raid, the Rockbridge Rifles and Rockbridge Dragoons, joined

other Shenandoah Valley militia companies heading north to occupy Harpers Ferry. One of the men in the Dragoons was James
Poague (William's younger brother), who left his medical studies at the University of Virginia to serve with his company.[6]

Initially, however, William had to stay behind. His senior
partner, James Massie, "felt it to be his duty to go into military
service at once," leaving William to tend to the business. Like so
many others, Massie believed that "at the last moment a satisfac-
tory adjustment would be found." He would quickly learn how
wrong he was.

For the middle-aged Poague, reflecting on his youthful
choices, the reasons to join and to fight were eminently clear: "It
was the act of Mr. Lincoln and his party that precipitated the conflict which many think was inevitable. . . . The North was the
aggressor. The South resisted her invaders." He also remained
hopeful that the current (turn-of-the-century) Northern interpretations of the South's motivation would change. "History will
vindicate her course,"[7] he wrote.

William Poague would soon have his chance to serve in the
military. In just three days, seventy men formed the Rockbridge
Artillery, led by the previously mentioned Reverend William
Nelson Pendleton ("Old Penn"). The men elected William Poague
to the post of junior second lieutenant, after he refused to allow
his name to be offered for first lieutenant or senior second lieutenant. Poague's reluctance to lead came not from fear but from
a sober assessment of his skills; as he wrote, "I did not want an
office in the company simply because I was not qualified for it.
Afterwards I keenly felt my deficiencies." As usual, Poague was
being quite modest; as his service record will show, he consistently demonstrated courage, wisdom, and resolve in his commands. That he might have preferred to be in the ranks is not
surprising in light of the fact that over half of his company were
either college students or professionals, surely one of the highest
percentages in the entire Confederate Army.[8]

After a few weeks of training, the Rockbridge Artillery was
sent north to join other Valley companies occupying Harpers
Ferry. Here, Poague came under the command of a former VMI
instructor, Colonel T. J. Jackson, whose tireless efforts to shape
the volunteers into soldiers included reorganizing the militia units

into regiments, supervising the construction of camps and fortifications, and drilling the men to the point of exhaustion. He was
not yet "Old Jack" to these raw recruits; he was more the "Tom
Fool" of VMI ridicule to his men. That would soon change, as
did most expectations, on the rolling fields of the Widow Henry's
farm in Manassas.[9]

Poague would experience fire even before that fateful day in
late July; he was involved in a skirmish with Union troops near
Hainesville on July 2. The Rockbridge Artillery was accompany-
ing the 5th Virginia Infantry Regiment as it marched north from
Winchester toward Williamsport to determine the size and
strength of a Federal force moving south. Somewhat to the surprise of Colonel Jackson, he soon faced a much larger Federal
force under General Robert Patterson. The Federals attempted
two charges, both of which were repulsed by the 5th Regiment.
In the second charge, the Rockbridge Artillery, using one of its
four 6-pounder guns, played a crucial role by firing into a group
of cavalry attempting to turn to the unit's left and then exchanging fire with the Union battery posted on a crest near the main
road. Poague well remembered this "affair at Hainesville," recalling that "the impression made was wonderful, exciting various emotions and creating an intense desire to see and take part
in the fight." But was this fighting real, or was it a dream? Poague
soon knew: "Then came another boom from our gun! And another! Presently a limping man supported by a comrade comes:
blood dripping from his sleeve! Yes, the war is on!" With the benefit of hindsight, Poague could calmly rank this first experience
in battle as a mere glimpse of what was to come. The 1st Virginia
Brigade was ordered back to Winchester, where the men would
wait impatiently for new orders. The orders came quickly enough;
on July 18 the brigade was instructed to abandon Winchester and
to march east to reinforce Confederate units at Manassas.[10]

At Manassas the 1st Virginia Brigade and Colonel Wade
Hampton's South Carolina Legion, aided by General Bernard E.
Bee's 4th Alabama Infantry Regiment, withstood the Union assaults for most of the afternoon, earning for Jackson the immor-
tal sobriquet, "Stonewall," and for Bee, a hero's death. The tide
of battle suddenly turned when the long-awaited secondary Confederate reinforcements arrived—first, General Edmund Kirby

Smith's 5th Brigade, then Colonel Jubal Early's 6th Brigade. Their timely arrival and charges, coming on the heels of disappointing Union attacks all afternoon, broke not only the Union offensive but also their will. The retreat quickly turned into a rout, as fleeing soldiers competed with supply wagons, artillery caissons, and even some local civilians in carriages for precious space on the dusty dirt roads leading back to Washington. With Confederate artillery bombarding them and some Confederate companies chasing them, it was almost impossible for Union commander General Irvin McDowell and his subordinates to restore order. Somehow he and his staff managed to find enough organized units to erect a defensive line outside Centreville, while the majority of Union troops fled pell-mell back to the safety of Washington.[11]

The joy in Confederate cities like Richmond was tempered by the lengthy casualty lists and the trains packed with dead and wounded that wended their way back to the capital all the next week. The first news of the battle had been scattered and contradictory. President Jefferson Davis had sent a personal telegram to his wife upon his arrival on the battlefield late in the afternoon of the twenty-first, assuring her of his safety (he arrived too late to fight, but in sufficient time to follow the chase of some Union troops) and of Confederate victory. While the capital buzzed with rumors, Attorney General Judah P. Benjamin sought out Mrs. Davis and asked if she had heard from her husband. He passed on her news to the other cabinet members, and the joy of the War Department was soon echoed in the streets when Davis's official telegram announcing the Confederate success came in just before midnight: "Our forces have won a glorious victory." Davis's telegram made it into the morning's newspaper, along with many dispatches from Manassas, some of them inaccurate (Davis commanded the center of the army and General Joseph E. Johnston the left, for example). So many reports arrived on Monday that the *Richmond Daily Dispatch* printed an "Extra" on Tuesday, beginning the lead column on the first page with the headline, "We Have Met the Enemy and They Are Ours." Inaccurate information continued to be printed, as it would be for some time before the commanding officers had time to regroup their troops and write complete battle reports. (For instance, Confederate casualties were estimated to be 1,500 to 2,500, compared to 12,000 to 15,000 on the Union side, bringing the aura of truth to the prewar boast that any Reb could beat ten Yankees.) Tuesday also saw the return of President Davis, who gave a stirring speech to the huge crowd gathered outside his residence at the Spotswood Hotel. On the same day, though, Richmonders saw the other side of war. The bodies of Colonel Francis Bartow, General Bee, and Lieutenant Colonel Benjamin Johnson were brought to the city and carried by three separate hearses to the Capitol, where they were attended by an Honor Guard that evening.[12]

As the week wore on, the details of the battle began to take clearer shape, and the excitement over victory began to subside as more wounded and dead came into the city of Richmond. Cooler heads realized that one battle would not decide a war. Although the wounded men suffered "like heroes—scarcely a groan escapes them" as they were moved from the trains to homes or hospitals—the same dignified manner was not exhibited by some of the male observers who milled around at the train station: "The ill-timed levity of boys and thoughtless men should be discouraged by every sober-minded person present." As for the battle, people were still undecided about its name, with earlier correspondents referring to it as "the Battle at Stone Bridge." Reputations were being enhanced, such as those of Beauregard, Johnston, and Jackson, and mistaken impressions corrected (Davis was *not* in command of the center of the line, for instance). Lingering questions remained about the performance of some units, transportation, and the quartermaster corps. The biggest question of all was, Why did the Confederates let the Union army slip back into Washington? The answer was common knowledge, but no one wanted to discuss it, because the truth was so obvious and painful. After the battle, the Confederate army was in almost as much disarray as the Union forces, and it could not have pursued the entire Union army if it had wanted to.[13]

For the time being, though, celebrations and accounting were the order of the day. There would be plenty of time to reevaluate performances in the battle and, even more important, plenty of time to equip and train these boisterous civilians to become soldiers prepared to endure a war, not just a single action. The soldiers would go into their first winter quarters awaiting the appearance of spring and the resumption of battle. The next clash would take place much closer to home for many of these young men, in the woods and fields and farms to the east of Richmond—on the Peninsula.

NOTES

1. Poague, *Gunner with Stonewall*, 7 and front photograph, no page; James I. Robertson Jr., *Stonewall Jackson: The Man, the Soldier, and the Legend* (New York, 1997), 261–62.

2. Poague, *Gunner with Stonewall*, 8–9.

3. Ibid., 11; Wiley, *The Life of Johnny Reb*, 29.

4. Poague, *Gunner with Stonewall*, 10–11. Poague's matter-of-fact views of the death and destruction he observed on the battlefield seem to be in the middle of a spectrum of responses, ranging from the depression noted by Wiley to the macabre enjoyment of battle and its aftermath by some, such as Lieutenant William W. Blackford. See William W. Blackford, *War Years with JEB Stuart* (1945; reprint, Baton Rouge, 1993), 44–46, for his description of the field "the day after."

5. Poague, *Gunner with Stonewall*, xiv and 1; Rockbridge County, Virginia, Census, 1860, roll #1378, page 090; Poague, *Gunner with Stonewall*, 1–2.

6. Poague, *Gunner with Stonewall*, 2–3; James I. Robertson Jr., *The Stonewall Brigade* (Baton Rouge, 1963), 5. Robertson opens his superb account of this storied brigade with a riveting description of the nighttime capture of Harpers Ferry by Virginia militia companies on April 18, 1861—the day *after* the secession convention passed the secession ordinance. Governor Letcher had asked Valley militia companies to form and quickly occupy Harpers Ferry; they followed his order with alacrity.

7. Poague, *Gunner with Stonewall*, 3–4.

8. Ibid., 4; Douglas Southall Freeman, *Lee's Lieutenants: A Study in Command*, 3 vols. (New York, 1942), 1:614; Robertson, *The Stonewall Brigade*, 17. According to Robertson, Colonel T. J. Jackson "found it necessary to restrict its membership, lest its numbers swell out of proportion to the other units." The first roll of the company included "28 college students, 25 theological students, and 7 men who held master's degrees from the University of Virginia" (17).

Wiley mentions the Rockbridge Artillery and other famous units with high proportions of "elites" in their ranks. He notes just how exceptional these units were, especially in regard to education and social background. For understandable reasons, more memoirs have come from members of these units than from others. Wiley, *The Life of Johnny Reb*, 335–36.

9. Poague, *Gunner with Stonewall*, 4–6; Robertson, *The Stonewall Brigade*, 8–9 and 23–28; William C. Davis, *Battle at Bull Run: A History of the First Major Campaign of the Civil War* (New York, 1977), 204–5.

10. Robertson, *The Stonewall Brigade*, 28–35; Poague, *Gunner with Stonewall*, 6–7. The three other 6-pounders of the Rockbridge Artillery had been placed "at a strategic location along the road" behind the marchers. Robertson, *The Stonewall Brigade*, 31.

11. Davis, *Battle at Bull Run*, 194–95, 201, 213–19, 225, 231–36.

12. Jefferson Davis to Varina Davis, July 21, 1861, U.S. War Department, *The War of the Rebellion: A Compilation of the Official Records of the Union and Confederate Armies*, 128 vols. (Washington, DC: Government Printing Office, 1888–1901), vol. 2, 986 (hereafter cited as *OR*; all *OR* references are to series 1 unless otherwise noted); Davis, *Battle at Bull Run*, 243, 250, 244 (President Davis's telegram on p. 244); *RDD*, July 22, July 23 (Extra edition), July 24, 1861.

13. *RDD*, July 25, 1861; Davis, *Battle at Bull Run*, 248–49 and 244–45. The Confederates had just over 2,000 casualties, while the Union suffered over 3,000 casualties. Ibid., 245 and 253.

CHAPTER FOUR

THE WINTER OF DISCONTENT, 1861–62

THE LONG FUNERAL procession moved slowly through the muddy streets of Richmond, the mournful notes of martial music broken only by the clopping of horses' hooves, the muffled tramp of soldiers' boots, and the sobs of women in the large crowd. A detachment of the Richmond Blues, some men from Wise's Legion, members of Richmond's Company F, Freemasons, Mayor Mayo, Governor John Letcher, and members of the family all marched toward St. James Episcopal Church in the largest funeral procession since the burial of President John Tyler in January and the ceremony honoring the fallen leaders at the Battle of Manassas the previous July. The hearse, pulled by four gray horses, carried the coffin with the body of Captain Obadiah Jennings Wise of the 46th Virginia Infantry Regiment. The coffin was covered with a Confederate flag and wreaths of evergreens. The eldest son of former governor Henry A. Wise had suffered mortal wounds in the disastrous rout of Confederate troops at Roanoke Island. He had been shot twice while directing his company's fire, and shot yet a third time while aboard a small boat headed for his father's headquarters at Nag's Head, North Carolina. While the island battle raged, General Wise lay on his sickbed, confined by the painful coughs and searing fevers of pleurisy. He did not see the body of his favorite son until it was brought back to Virginia a few days later. There he cried out, "My noble boy, you have died for me! You have died for me! You have died for your father!"[1]

Roanoke Island was another setback in a string of disappointments and losses that only got worse as winter eased into spring. People had accepted the fact that Confederate forces had been unable to capture the entire Union Army in the wake of the Battle of Manassas, basking as they were in the glow of that signal

victory. Then troubles at the top emerged into public view, with
the hero of Manassas, General P. G. T. Beauregard, being deprived
of his command and sent west, owing to excessive feuding with
President Davis. His immediate superior and the actual architect
of the Manassas victory, General Joseph E. Johnston, also had numerous difficulties with Davis and his cabinet, problems that
would handicap Johnston's entire career in the Confederate Army.

Worse than the feuding between civilian and military leadership were the military defeats. They began in the rain and rug-
ged terrain of western Virginia in September 1861, when one of
the Old Dominion's favorite sons, General Robert E. Lee, had to
regroup his forces after a disappointing offensive around Cheat
Mountain. In November, Union ships under the command of Flag
Officer Samuel F. Du Pont destroyed Confederate defenses at
Hilton Head and Port Royal, securing that vital stretch of South
Carolina coast for the Union for the remainder of the war. In January the Confederates were defeated at the Battle of Mill Springs
(Kentucky), followed by losses at Roanoke Island, Fort Donelson,
and Nashville in February. March saw the Confederate forces
beaten in battle at Pea Ridge (Arkansas) and Glorieta Pass (New
Mexico). With General McClellan's huge Army of the Potomac
embarking for Fort Monroe and an expected push up along the
Peninsula toward Richmond, the future for the chastened and
now truncated Confederate States of America looked very dim
as the fledgling government began its second year of existence.[2]

Disappointment over the rifts among leaders and losses on
the battlefield was magnified by the disease, boredom, and homesickness that plagued the Confederate Army of the Potomac that
long winter. Diseases ranged from the debilitating—malaria,
measles, dysentery, and diarrhea—to the deadly—pneumonia and
typhoid. More than 35,000 of the 50,000 soldiers in this army suffered from one or another of these diseases in the first nine months
of the war, with typhoid being the most feared and deadly. William Poague was an early contractor of typhoid, coming down
with it two days after the Battle of Manassas. His friend, Dr. John
Leyburn, sent Poague back to Lexington on a train, "sick . . . (and)
delirious part of the time." He stayed at home for nearly three
months, nursed by his parents and a black slave. Even when he
returned, he did not feel completely well, complaining of "im-

paired memory." He wrote, "I recognized my friends and acquaintances in the battery but could not recall the names of many of them." Gradually his memory improved, though he would write many years later, "I am inclined to think it has never been as good as before that terrible attack of fever."[3]

Robin Berkeley had a much more severe case of typhoid. Stricken on October 5, 1861, he was soon carried to Richmond by his company commander. Unable to eat, wracked by fever and occasional delirium, he was taken home by a family friend and a physician, where he was confined to bed for "nearly six weeks." He stayed at home until his reenlistment in the Hanover Artillery in March.

Berkeley may have returned to this unit too soon, because he had several spells of chills and high fever that rendered him unable to fight in some of the Peninsula battles in May and June. As late as July he wrote, "I was, during all this time, very poorly and unwell, suffering with chills and fevers which our surgeon, Dr. Lawson, seemed unable to stop." Fortunately for Robin, the symptoms did finally pass.[4]

Since the Battle of Manassas the houses of several Warrenton residents had been opened to wounded soldiers, including the home of Susan Caldwell. Seventy ailing soldiers were brought into town on July 31 alone; some had battle wounds, others measles, and a few typhoid. On July 24 the Caldwells welcomed a Mr. Robinson from Huntsville, Alabama, who "was slightly wounded in his shoulder." He recovered in a few weeks, but that was not the case for some of the other soldiers convalescing in Warrenton.

In one instance, Captain Brown from Georgia died from typhoid on a Saturday night, two days before his wife arrived. When she got to Warrenton and learned the horrible news, she "went into spasms. . . . Yesterday she went to the Graveyard and stretched herself on her husband's grave." Captain Brown was the first of several to die from disease. As Susan wrote to her husband in late September, "Our town is filled with sick soldiers. Some die each day."

A good number of these soldiers were from Susan's home state of South Carolina, and she took particular interest in one, 18-year-old Paul Miller. He arrived in Warrenton in early December with a case of the mumps. Soon the doctors diagnosed typhoid, too. Although "he was cheerful and never complained," on "Monday he was taken worse and died on Thursday." When his father did not come, Susan "sent a `green` wreath to put on his coffin and went out to the Graveyard to see him buried." With a husband away in Richmond, parents barely escaping a fire that swept through Charleston, two sons with the mumps, a 2-month-old baby to nurse, and scarlet fever coursing through the children of Warrenton, Susan must have felt particularly saddened and frightened by the sudden death of this "beautiful boy" with a "very intellectual countenance."[5]

The many soldiers stationed in Virginia in the winter of 1861–62 who escaped or survived their greatest enemy, disease, still had daily to face their second greatest enemy—boredom. For Fred Fleet, stationed at Gloucester Point with the 26th Virginia Infantry Regiment, his one moment of excitement came in early December, when a "blockading steamer came within 5 or 6 miles of this place, nearer than it ever has been before." His regiment was put on alert, and militia units from three counties were ordered to Gloucester. Their readiness was all for naught, however, because the "blockading steamer steamed off Friday, and has not been in sight since." Fred's bigger concerns were personal during this period: what to do about his father's "drinking binge," how to advise his father on joining the service (Dr. Fleet decided against it), how to avoid contracting measles, and, in February, whether to help Joseph Pollard muster a new company.[6]

Fred was torn between loyalty and opportunity. If he helped Joseph Pollard form a new company, he would be assured of a promotion to first lieutenant from his rank of first sergeant. On the other hand, if he reenlisted with his current commander and former teacher, Captain James Councill, he might "get up a little." He was smart enough not to share his dilemma with Captain Councill. As he waited to see how many men in the company would take Councill's offer of "$50 bounty & 30 days furlough," Fred wrote passionately to his father about the problems of reenlistment and electioneering. "If the men had only been paid up promptly and been allowed furloughs in as large numbers as could be spared, I think there would have been little difficulty in causing them to re-enlist, but as it is they are disgusted with the service."[7] Fred took the advice of his parents and stayed with his company, a decision that paid off in the May elections of new officers. He was elected Second Lieutenant of Company I (the former Jackson Grays), while Pollard was elected First Sergeant of the same company and Councill was elected Lieutenant Colonel of the reorganized 26th Virginia Infantry Regiment.[8]

William Poague made use of the reenlistment furlough too, "as only a soldier can," which turned into a recruitment drive as well. He was gone over a month, returning to the 1st Rockbridge Artillery Battery with nearly sixty new men just in time for the Battle of Kernstown (March 23, 1862). The next month he was elected captain of the battery, a position Poague regarded with mixed feelings: "I never felt myself qualified for the command of such a splendid body of men, but as I seemed to be so considered by them, I accepted the responsible position."[9]

Poague had earned the respect of the men through his leadership in the December skirmishes in northwest Virginia and the bitterly cold Romney Campaign of January 1862. While most of the soldiers stationed in Virginia in the winter of 1861–62 had been idle, General Jackson marched his troops out of winter quarters near Winchester and on toward Dam No. 5 on the Chesapeake and Ohio Railroad Canal. His goal was to destroy the dam, rendering the major route for coal shipping to the North unusable. Despite several efforts to sever the dam's supporting wooden cribs and numerous artillery exchanges over a period of days, the entire effort came to naught. Poague remembered one time when his battery came under heavy artillery fire, and he and other officers were "dodging first to one side and then to the other." The exceptions were General Jackson, who "occasionally bowed to those infernal shells," and the incredibly brave cavalry officer, Colonel Turner Ashby, who walked "back and forth near the deserted guns in the open field . . . totally indifferent to the hellish fire raining all about him."[10]

It was the Romney Campaign, however, that put the leadership of the officers and the fortitude of the men to the test. Setting out on January 1, 1862, on a freakishly warm winter morning, the Stonewall Brigade and the newly arrived Army of the Northwest under the command of General W. W. Loring marched out of Winchester in high spirits. That mood would be broken by nightfall. A cold snap blew out of the northwest, bringing snow and sleet in its wake. Over the next two weeks, there would be snow or sleet almost every day, turning muddy roads into rutted ice slicks and ensuring that the supply wagons were always a day or more behind the cold and hungry troops. The Confederates captured Bath on January 4 and Romney on January 14, but these were hollow victories, for Union troops under General Benjamin Kelley evacuated each tiny town before the Confederates arrived. Even the normally reserved and generous Poague had harsh words for this campaign, deeming it a "failure" that was "simply terrible—terrible in the sufferings of man and beast, in demoralization of a great part of the army and in the number of deaths that followed, and all without any substantial fruits." Poague was in Romney with his company, escaping some of the worst of the weather by sleeping in "the high pulpit" of a Methodist church. Few were more pleased than Poague when the Stonewall Brigade was ordered back to Winchester, and he summed up the campaign in unequivocal language: "In all the war I never had a similar experience—never endured such physical and mental suffering as on this trip."[11]

While most participants and historians would share Poague's views of the Romney Campaign, Sergeant John Worsham of F Company, 21st Virginia, provided an alternate vision. While acknowledging the cold "terrible weather" that necessitated men replacing horses as wagon and caisson pullers, he highlighted the lessons learned (leave snow on the ground as the first layer between your oilcloth and the ground) and the ingenuity of his mess, as they found a woman who sold them her broken-down stove (which served them well throughout the war), another woman to cook their rations in Romney, and a hotel in the small town that made "buckwheat cakes in splendid style," which they cleaned out in three days. Only at the end of his description of this campaign did he tally the cost of this expedition, calling it the "most terrible experience during the war."[12]

Perhaps Worsham was not as critical of Jackson as others were because he and the 21st Virginia had just finished a frustrating 5-month stint in the mountains of western Virginia. The regiment had left Richmond in July, traveling by train as far as Staunton. From there the regiment marched through Buffalo Gap, McDowell,

Monterey, Napp's Creek Valley, and Huntersville, before setting up camp at Valley Mountain. The regiment's biggest foe was disease; at one point as many as one-third of the men were sick with measles or typhoid. Not long after General Lee's arrival, the 21st went into action at Conrad's Mill on September 11, engaging in some light skirmishing with Union troops. When Union forces withdrew, the 21st did likewise, returning to Valley Mountain. Worsham blamed the lack of success on the mud. He wrote, "In all my experience of war I never saw as much mud. . . . I saw dead mules lying in the road, with nothing but their ears showing above the mud." When General Lee joined General John B. Floyd's forces at Sewell's Mountain, the 21st Virginia was left behind to guard Valley Mountain. In late September the 21st Virginia headed back east, burning five wagons full of baggage the men had brought from home. The regiment camped near Greenbrier for most of October, then headed east again, returning to Staunton in early December. The 21st left Staunton on December 10, joining the Stonewall Brigade in Winchester on the twenty-fifth. All told, the 21st had marched over 600 miles, rarely engaging the enemy and suffering no casualties except those hospitalized for illness.[13] It had not been a glorious war so far for these eastern Virginia boys—but Stonewall Jackson would soon take care of that.

The chance for action came at Kernstown, a tiny village four miles south of Winchester. In early March, General Jackson put his army of just over 4,000 men on the march, daring General Nathaniel Banks to do battle with his army of 25,000 recently arrived from Frederick, Maryland. Banks did not take up the challenge, and Jackson's army withdrew southward to Mount Jackson. It was followed by General James Shields's division of 9,000 men, which temporarily camped at Strasburg. When Colonel Turner Ashby reported that Shields's division was leaving Strasburg on March 21, Jackson decided to catch him. Jackson's orders were to detain as much of Banks's army as possible, so as to keep his 25,000 men in western Virginia, allowing General Johnston to move the bulk of the Army of the Potomac south to defend Richmond.

On Saturday, March 22, Jackson's Stonewall Brigade marched twenty-six miles, camping at Cedar Creek. The next morning the tired men set out again, marching ten miles before bumping into the tail end of Shields's division. Colonel Ashby reported that only four regiments were in Jackson's way, so Jackson decided to give battle. Poague's battery was rushed up to open fire in support of the 21st Virginia, which was ordered to occupy and hold the hills on the Confederate left. For over two hours the exhausted men of the 21st fired at attacking companies of Union troops, as Shields rushed six regiments from his left to his right. Worsham recalled, "Some of F Company were kneeling down, firing from behind the fence, some were standing straight up, soon all were standing, and taking deadly aim as they fired. As the excitement increased, they mounted the fence, and many sat on it, loading and firing until every cartridge was shot away." With their ammunition spent, the 21st retreated. The retreat thoroughly angered Jackson, who shouted at one soldier who said he had run out of ammunition, "Then go back and give them the bayonet!" As the 21st fell back, so did the rest of Jackson's small army, a decision largely made by the commander of the Stonewall Brigade, General Richard B. Garnett. That decision would cost Garnett; after the battle Jackson relieved him of command and ordered him arrested.[14]

As for the 21st, it had performed well in its first battle and learned a valuable lesson as well—take whatever cover you can. As Worsham noted, "The men along the fence left its protection and fought as I never saw any fighting during the war. After this, they were glad to take advantage of anything." F Company counted six wounded, which was a remarkably light number considering that its men were in the thick of the battle (the 21st reported sixty casualties, about 20 percent of its total strength). Jackson's army suffered 700 casualties that day, exceeding the 590 reported by Shields. Equally important, Jackson's army lost its belief in its invincibility. As Worsham wrote, "We were whipped after desperate fighting." Others blamed Jackson for engaging an exhausted army prematurely, without adequate information on the enemy's size. Yet in the larger scheme, the small battle had accomplished Johnston's objective: to frighten the top authorities in Washington into keeping Banks's army of 25,000 Union troops in the Valley, thus denying General George McClellan some of the troops he demanded and allowing General Johnston to safely evacuate the Army of the Potomac from northern Virginia.[15] The evacuation, which began on March 7, would have enormous consequences for the residents of northern Virginia. For the first time, they would be left unprotected by Confederate forces. It did not take long for Union troops to exploit this opportunity.

Occupation began in sudden, unpredictable ways. Susan Caldwell and her family were at the Baptist Church in Warrenton on Sunday, April 6, attending the first service there since the retreat of Johnston's army in March, when a black man burst into the church and told the minister to dismiss the congregation because the "Federal Army was approaching the town." The parishioners flocked to the street, where "you could see them as far as the eye could take in." Soon "every lady was at her door, no one seemed daunted in the least, the women seemed anxious to see what the *yankee* soldiers were made of." For Tee Edmonds, the first glimpse of Union troops came on April 10, as they set up camp in the hills around Paris. It was the next night, however, when war came to Tee's door. She wrote, "Last night scarcely had I gone snugly to bed and in a doze, before a tremendous barking of the dogs aroused me and then the noise of horses' feet. I jumped out of bed, raised the curtain and there were six or seven Cavalry men riding away." They had come for whiskey, not fighting, finding such at Ben Triplett's distillery later that night. And when lead elements of General Shields's troops came marching into Front Royal on April 27, Lucy Rebecca Buck and her family were on their way to church. They watched the troops go by, "a file of infantry with their bayonets glistening and arms flashing in the morning sun." Then the family went on to church, the women wearing "thick brown veils," so as not to "let a Yankee see our faces."[16]

The appearance of Union soldiers was a bitter pill to swallow for a young, proud daughter of one of Front Royal's leading families. Lucy Rebecca Buck was nineteen years old when the war broke out, the eldest daughter of William Mason and Elizabeth Ann Ashby Buck. Mr. Buck owned the fine estate of Bel Air, which still stands a quarter of a mile east of downtown Front Royal. He also owned a store in town and co-owned the well-known Capon Resort Hotel. He was the father of eleven children; the oldest two—Alvin and Irving—had joined the Confederate forces and the youngest, Frank ("Dixie"), was born on November 27, 1861. Lucy began her diary on December 25, 1861 (for unstated reasons). As the oldest child at home, her major concerns were her brothers and cousins in the army; her immediate family, especially the sister closest to her, 17-year-old Nellie; and the education of her younger brothers and sisters. An incurable romantic, Lucy filled her diary with long passages of high-flown rhetoric such as this one:

> My thoughts reverted to our own little bands of patriots, and my heart thrilled gratefully as I remembered how gallantly they had hitherto repelled the advances of the insolent foe, and I felt an exulting confidence that ere another winter's frost should have browned the woodlands with the blessing of heaven we should have been welcomed into the family of nations, an honored and respected member of the vast fraternity.

Lucy's diary is full of keen observations of human conduct and behavior as well as details about her own desires and disappointments. She had a budding affection for her neighbor serving in the army, Scott Roy, though she wrote in her diary, "I like him, but can't exactly understand his varied and variable moods."[17]

Of more pressing concern to Lucy in the spring of 1862 was the Union occupation of Front Royal. The behavior of the soldiers ran the gamut from larcenous to generous, with the major determinant appearing to be the principles and leadership of the Union officer in charge. William Buck offered hospitality to some of the soldiers, which was repaid in protection provided first by Lieutenant Daniel Hildt and later by Corporal Charles McGetigen. None of this mattered, however, when General Nathan Kimball's 1st Brigade (Shields's Division, Department of the Rappahannock) set up camp in Front Royal on Wednesday, May 14. Appropriating Bel Air as his headquarters, Kimball's staff pitched three tents in the Bucks' backyard "ten feet from the door," while across the great rolling lawn that ran down to Happy Creek soldiers busied themselves stealing fencing for their huts and fires. General Kimball soon ordered his men to leave "outside enclosures" alone, but not before the rails and planks of the railroad and wheat field fences were almost completely gone. Ironically, even as the fences were being dismantled and some livestock stolen, there occurred one of those quaint moments of gentility that distinguish this war from more modern conflicts. Out of nowhere, the indefatigable Corporal McGetigen appeared, racing up the hill to see if he could help the Bucks. He ran by the staff's tents, answering General Kimball's question, "Why are you here?" with a curt reply, "I have business with Mr. Buck." He asked if he could appoint a safety detail for the family, but Mr. Buck told him one had already been assigned. He then tried to stay on, but was encouraged to leave. The family was left alone with Kimball's staff, and Lucy was despondent over her father's helpless rage: "He could only walk the pavement with folded arms and drooping head looking helplessly on the scene of desolation . . . (this) day was doing the work of years bowing his form and furrowing his brow. This distressed us more than anything else."[18]

The distress would grow even greater, as the brigade stayed for two days. The family ate meals with the general and his staff and slept at night with sentinels posted outside their bedroom doors. Lucy and her sister Nellie delighted in devising nicknames for some of the soldiers, but Lucy took no pleasure in conversations or chance meetings with the chaplain of the 8th Ohio Regiment, a man named Freeman. Quick to anger, Lucy more than once almost lost her temper around Freeman, especially when he told her "three consecutive falsehoods without any apparent violence to his feelings." And one night the chaplain drove Lucy up to her room with a "severe headache" by asking a regimental band to play "Yankee Doodle."[19]

With the exception of Freeman, though, Lucy noted that the "officers have conducted themselves with as much courtesy and delicate consideration as I ever saw in my life." General Kimball had several earnest conversations with Mr. Buck about abolitionism; a staff officer criticized the chaplain for being too politically involved; the fine band played some of the favorite songs of the period ("Mocking Bird," "Annie Laurie," "The Dearest Spot on Earth"); the younger Buck children were given fruits and candies by the general's aide; and 5-year-old Willie was given a silver half-dollar by General Kimball (a souvenir he kept all his life). Yet despite all this kind and polite behavior, Lucy still did not trust these "Yankees," writing about one staff officer who had befriended the children, "I am reluctantly half inclined to think he's a good-hearted fellow. But no doubt he is an accomplished hypocrite and his suavity assumed to subserve some selfish purpose." After the brigade had marched out on May 16, Lucy summed up this singular experience: "Oh me!—what an intense relief this is!—to be without a houseful of Yankees once more."[20]

The presence of the Union soldiers equally irked Lucy's contemporary, Amanda "Tee" Edmonds of Belle Grove. At first the family was visited by small bands of soldiers; then on April 14 an entire company appeared, demanding the use of the barn for lodging. Tee hated the officers and men alike. As she heard their "German and Dutch brogue," or Pennsylvania Dutch, it created "feelings inexpressible." Well, not exactly inexpressible—after she heard a soldier singing in "broken Dutch," "I vish I vas in Dixie, avay, avay," she wrote, "I trust you may find a resting place in Dixie—and soon!" The officers were no better in her eyes. She wrote, "We were *dishonored* with two at the supper table— Shumaker and Memenger, whom I hope will be registered with the fallen." The only relief was that they left as abruptly as they came, leaving Tee feeling "twice as free tonight, more like a bird out of a cage."[21]

The burden of occupation did not trouble Susan Caldwell as much, perhaps because her house was barely disturbed or because the welfare of her children and husband were of greater concern than the presence of Union troops. Maybe it was the humbling meeting she had when the Union troops first arrived that set the tone for the early days of occupation. On the Sunday the Union troops came into town, word reached Susan that a "gentleman" wished to see her. She had no desire to see this mystery man, but he and a friend appeared at the door anyway, at 9:00 P.M. It was First Lieutenant William J. Mackey and a fellow officer from Company P, 28th Regiment, Pennsylvania Volunteers. Mackey and his wife had boarded in the Jeffordses' house in Charleston for two years, and apparently Susan and his wife had grown close enough for Mackey to ask Susan to write a letter to her that he would send. Susan wrote of their initial conversation, "Why Mr. Mackey how do I see you—do I meet with you among the enemies of the South—my heart was deeply pained and I saw too he felt it also—he said don't let us talk on that subject." But the subject could not be avoided. Mackey insisted that he "loved the South," "abhorred abolition," and, before he would allow Susan to "be harmed he would suffer himself." The officers shared a glass of wine with Mr. Finks that evening and so impressed him that he invited them over for breakfast the next morning, where they took a "cup of Rye." Then they were off as quickly as they came, blaming the "low Dutch" in their units for any depredations that occurred.[22]

The Union army returned in force in late May. General James Shields's division of the Department of the Rappahannock marched into Warrenton on May 17, established headquarters in the home of Mrs. James V. Brooke, then left the next day. There were reports of theft—especially of livestock—but General Shields either made or promised restitution in most cases, earning from Susan a generous compliment: "Genl. Shields and most of the army behaved very well."

Although Susan and Lycurgus worried about each other's safety and yearned to be together, they wisely accepted the counsel of Confederate officers and local friends who thought it better for Susan and the children to stay at home than to leave. As Susan wrote to Lycurgus before the Union troops came, "Several officers of Virginia Reg. told us yesterday it was far better for us to remain . . . if we left everything would be destroyed as a matter of course." She added in a subsequent letter: "I feel that we are much better off at home—children are comfortable and get healthy food."[23]

One sizable group of Virginians did not choose staying in their communities over leaving: the thousands of slaves who sought and found liberation in the camps of the advancing Union army. As Union troops moved into northern Virginia, slaves in towns and the countryside fled from their masters. Susan Caldwell wrote to her husband about this movement in June 1862, "You would be astounded to hear of the numbers of servants left town for Alex [Alexandria] and Washington." Tee Edmonds noted the same trend in her diary in April: "It is thought the *remaining ebonys* will take to themselves the wings of liberty as some have declared as much." She added, "Let them go, yes, the last one, provided we never be harassed with the same unfaithful ones again." Yet she would soon learn what Susan Caldwell learned the hard way: the escape of one slave reduced the trust held in the slaves who remained, while simultaneously increasing the value of those who stayed. In early June the Caldwell family discovered one night that "light Cinda was missing—and we are pained to believe she has gone to the Yankee Camp." Not only had she taken some of her owner's clothes with her, but she also raised the family's suspicions of all their slaves because Cinda had "ever said she disliked the Yankees." Susan wrote to Lycurgus, "Since Cinda has left we begin to distrust Aunt Lucy."[24]

Susan did not get it. Cinda wanted something as dear to her as it was to Tee Edmonds, Lucy Buck, and herself—freedom.

NOTES

1. *RDD*, February 17, 1862; Alfred Hoyt Bill, *The Beleaguered City: Richmond, 1861–1865* (New York, 1946), 99–100; Craig Simpson, *A Good Southerner: The Life of Henry A. Wise of Virginia* (Chapel Hill, 1985), 265–68; Putnam, *Richmond during the War*, 97–98. Most likely the band played George Frederick Handel's "Dead March," but the sources do not state this for certain. See C. Vann Woodward, ed., *Mary Chesnut's Civil War* (New Haven, 1981), 107 (July 22, 1861) and note 8 on the same page, for a discussion of the use of this musical piece.

2. For a lively overview of troubles at the top of the Confederacy, see Freeman's *Lee's Lieutenants*, vol. 1, 98–143. For a more sympathetic treatment of Davis during this period, see William C. Davis, *Jefferson Davis: The Man and His Hour* (New York, 1991; HarperPerennial edition, 1992), 354–413. For an overview of the battles, see Emory M. Thomas, *The Confederate Nation, 1861–1865* (New York, 1979), 120–28; and Long, *The Civil War Day by Day*, 117, 135–36, 162, 170–72, and 175.

3. Wiley, *The Life of Johnny Reb*, 251–53 (Wiley notes that typhoid was estimated to have caused "one-fourth of all the deaths from disease in the Southern armies," 253); Poague, *Gunner with Stonewall*, 11–12. Wiley found the same proportion of deaths from typhoid among Union soldiers, "one fourth." Bell Irvin Wiley, *The Life of Billy Yank: The Common Soldier of the Union* (Baton Rouge, 1952; paperback reprint, 1992), 134.

4. Berkeley, *Diary*, October 5, 1861, 8; October 14, 1861, 8–9; February 23, 1862, 11; May 5, 1862, 16; May 7, 1862, 17; May 23, 1862, 17; June 4, 1862, 18; June 25, 1862, 18; June 26, 1862, 18; July 8, 1862, 23.

5. Caldwell, *Letters*, Susan Caldwell to Lycurgus Caldwell, July 24, 1861, 37–38; July 31, 1861, 39–40; August 8, 1861, 41; September 5, 1861, 51–52; November 13, 1861, 59–61; December 21, 1861, 62–63. The Caldwells' fourth child, Lucy Lee, was born on October 1, 1861, in Warrenton.

There was another side to the conversion of Warrenton into a giant hospital; it meant more business for merchants like John W. Finks. In mid-August he asked Lycurgus Caldwell to send him quinine, opium, morphine, "six quires of note paper, with Flag," and "*3000 Envelopes @ 10ct. pack—6 rms paper @ 2.50.*" John W. Finks to Lycurgus Caldwell, August 16, 1861, 44–45, in ibid.

6. Fleet, *Green Mount*, Fred Fleet to Benny Fleet, December 15, 1861, 90; Benny Fleet to Fred Fleet, December 17, 1861, 90–91; Pa to Fred Fleet, December 28, 1861, 93; Pa to Fred Fleet, December 29, 1861, 94–95; and Fred Fleet to Pa, February 1, 1862, 100–101.

7. Ibid., Fred Fleet to Pa, February 1 and 3, 1862, 100–102. Councill's offer was a bit less than that proposed by the Furlough and Bounty Act passed by the Confederate Congress in December 1861. It had offered $50 and sixty days of furlough to all those who agreed to reenlist for three years. It also allowed soldiers to change companies and elect officers. See *RDD*, December 12, 1861, for the act.

8. Fleet, *Green Mount*, Fred Fleet to Pa, May 14, 1862, 125–26, on the election results; Ma to Fred Fleet, February 7, 1862, 102–3, and Pa to Fred Fleet, February 8, 1862, 103–4. (Ma wrote, "You are better off than a private, and there are many better men than—privates in the army.") For a summary of Fred Fleet's military service record, see Alex L. Wiatt, *26th Virginia Infantry* (Lynchburg, 1984), 55.

9. Poague, *Gunner with Stonewall*, 18, 19, 21.

10. Ibid., 18, 21, and 14.

11. Robertson, *Stonewall Brigade*, 55–57; Poague, *Gunner with Stonewall*, 12–14 and 17–18.

12. Worsham, *One of Jackson's Foot Cavalry*, 43–48.

13. Ibid., 25–36; Riggs, *21st Virginia Infantry*, 3–6.

14. Robertson, *Stonewall Brigade*, 68–78; Poague, *Gunner with Stonewall*, 18–19; Worsham, *One of Jackson's Foot Cavalry*, 54.

15. Worsham, *One of Jackson's Foot Cavalry*, 54; Riggs, *21st Virginia Infantry*, 11; Robertson, *Stonewall Brigade*, 77–78. As is often the case, Poague's succinct account, "our battery of six guns did good work," leaves out many dramatic details. For example, Poague's guns directly stopped several Union infantry charges by firing canister at distances of as little as 150 yards! See Robert Driver Jr., *The 1st and 2nd Rockbridge Artillery* (Lynchburg, 1987), 16–17.

16. Long, *The Civil War Day by Day*, 180; Caldwell, *Letters*, Susan Caldwell to Lycurgus Caldwell, April 10, 1862, 93–94; Edmonds, *Journals*, April 11 and 12, 1862, 73–74; Buck, *Diary*, April 27, 1862, 54.

17. Buck, *Diary*, introduction, 7; December 29, 1861, 14–15; February 1, 1862, 62.

18. Ibid., April 29, 1862, 56; May 4, 1862, 60–61; May 13, 1862, 64; May 14, 1862, 65–66.

19. Ibid., May 14, 1862, 67–68. The nicknames were: Breakfast, Rawhead and bloody bones, Wasp, Freckles, Redhead, Mouth, Nose, and Mutton.

20. Ibid., May 15, 1862, 68–72, and May 16, 1862, 72–73.

21. Edmonds, *Journals*, April 12, 1862, 74–76; April 13, 1862, 76–77; April 14, 1862, 77–78; and April 15, 1862, 78–80.

22. Caldwell, *Letters*, Susan Caldwell to Lycurgus Caldwell, April 10, 1862, 93–98.

23. Ibid., Susan Caldwell to Lycurgus Caldwell, May 21, 1862, 120–22; Susan Caldwell to Lycurgus Caldwell, March 14, 1862, 86; Susan Caldwell to Lycurgus Caldwell, March 20, 1862, 88.

24. Jordan, *Black Confederates and Afro-Yankees*, 69–85; Caldwell, *Letters*, Susan Caldwell to Lycurgus Caldwell, June 1, 1862, 124; Edmonds, *Journals*, April 19, 1862, 82; Caldwell, *Letters*, Susan Caldwell to Lycurgus Caldwell, June 9, 1862, 131.

Chapter Five

Confederate Resurgence, Spring and Summer 1862

THE WAR IN THE EAST began in earnest in the spring of 1862. While General McClellan moved the bulk of the Army of the Potomac to the Peninsula, three separate Union armies tried to defeat General Stonewall Jackson's small army of 15,000 in the Shenandoah Valley. The roles played by the soldiers in this study in those crucial few months were as varied as the battles themselves. While some saw much fighting, others were barely engaged. Taken together, their experiences encompass the full range of military activity from boring inaction to horrific combat.

Captain William T. Poague and Sergeant John Worsham endured enough fighting that spring to last the entire war. As part of Jackson's army of self-styled "foot cavalry," they marched over 500 miles in one month, fighting in five separate battles. This small army neutralized over 50,000 Union soldiers, kept the Shenandoah Valley in Confederate hands, and made Washington authorities reluctant to send General McClellan every last soldier. Their collective efforts would be named the Valley Campaign, and their achievements in that one month are studied to this day.[1]

In the roll call of Confederate victories at McDowell, Front Royal, Winchester, Cross Keys, and Port Republic, the grandest and most dangerous moment for John Worsham came at the Battle of Winchester. Worsham's 21st Virginia Infantry was part of Jackson's command that chased the fast-retreating army of General Nathaniel Banks down the Valley Pike after the quick victory at Front Royal on May 23. After marching his men eighteen miles by mid-afternoon on the twenty-fourth, Jackson allowed them only a brief rest before ordering a night march to Winchester. Wading through swamps and tripping over bushes, the weary soldiers slogged on, falling where they stopped near dawn when they were given an hour's rest.[2]

When Union troops were spotted on a hill, the men were roused, and the Stonewall Brigade was ordered to take the hill. The brigade got as far as the crest but was stopped there by fierce artillery fire. The Rockbridge Artillery under Captain William T. Poague was called up to drive the Union cannons back. Supported by the 21st Infantry, Poague's battery endured enfilading fire as its men fired their own shells at the Union battery. Finally, Poague was ordered to destroy a stone wall protecting a Union regiment, which he promptly did. This action paved the way for Colonel Richard Taylor's Louisiana Brigade, which turned the Union troops to the right in what Worsham called the "grandest (charge) I ever saw during the war." He wrote, "They marched up the hill in perfect order, not firing a shot!" Near the top of the hill they were ordered to charge, and "over the stone wall they went." This disciplined move broke the Union line, which quickly retreated. The 21st Virginia gave chase, slowing only to receive the grateful cheers of the citizens of Winchester, some of whom even hugged the soldiers as Union bullets flew through the streets! To Worsham, "the reception at Winchester was worth a lifetime of service."[3]

After this signal moment of glory and jubilation, the 21st Virginia was assigned the more mundane task of guarding Union prisoners. The regiment missed the battles of Cross Keys and Port Republic. It finally rejoined the 2d Brigade in Charlottesville in mid-June, marching on toward Richmond to join up with General Lee's forces.[4]

For Captain Poague, the Battle of Winchester was a stern test of his men and his leadership. Fortunately for Poague, he passed the test with flying colors. The commander of the Stonewall Brigade, General Charles S. Winder, commended all the artillery batteries in his report, writing, "Of Captains Poague, Carpenter, Cutshaw and their officers and men I cannot speak too highly. The skill, judgment, and bravery displayed by them at all times, under a heavy fire of artillery and infantry, reflect the greatest credit upon themselves." The victory, however, came with a heavy price. Poague reported that his battery had suffered two killed

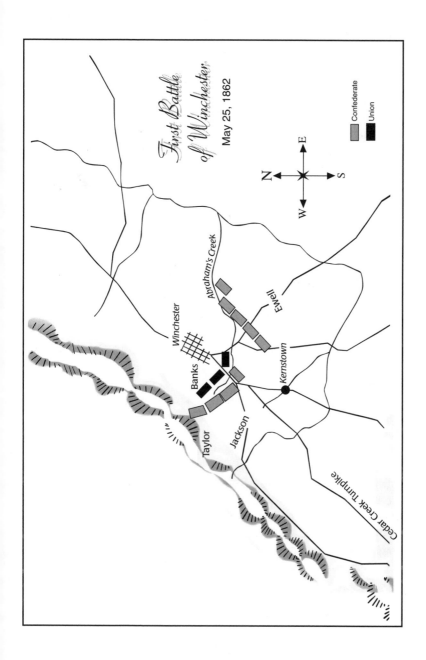

First Battle of Winchester
May 25, 1862

Confederate
Union

and fifteen wounded, a casualty rate of nearly 20 percent in his 89-man unit. He also hinted that not every one of his soldiers had acted bravely, writing that he could "testify to the good conduct of all the officers, non-commissioned officers, and privates, with a few exceptions among the latter." He probably referred to Jonathan Agnor, who, according to Poague's memoirs, refused to go to the front line as ordered. Poague personally rode up to him and ordered him to move; and while Agnor was reluctantly in motion, he was killed. Poague would learn a bitter lesson about command from this incident: that officers must shoulder the responsibility for all the deaths under their command, regardless of their particular role in each death. Poague wrote in his memoir, "After the war his old father complained bitterly of my having caused his son's death."[5]

Poague had no time to reflect on the battle because soon he was ordered to take his battery up to Charlestown. Hardly had the men had time to bivouac when they were directed to head south and rejoin the bulk of Jackson's forces at Strasburg. Once reunited, the whole army kept moving south until it reached Harrisonburg. Then the army turned east, toward Port Republic.[6] Here, Poague would have two more brushes with fame. The first nearly destroyed his budding reputation, while the second helped restore it.

The first incident occurred when General Jackson rode up to Poague's position on a hill above the village of Port Republic. On that hot June morning, Jackson found Poague's battery firing on Union troops as they marched from the east toward the main bridge into the village. When Jackson saw a group of blue-clad soldiers heading for the bridge with a 6-pound gun, he ordered the battery to fire on them. At this moment occurred one of the classic confusing incidents of the war, and the only instance when William T. Poague deliberately defied his commanding officer. Poague told Jackson that those men were Confederates wearing Union uniforms. Jackson then ordered the guns to be moved before firing, and Poague's cannoneers refused to budge. For the last time, Jackson gave an order: "Bring that gun up here, I say." Fortuitously, the blue-clad soldiers then pointed their gun at the hill, proving Jackson right. Poague's men commenced firing at the small band of men, and they soon retreated. Fortunately for

Poague, this incident did not preoccupy Jackson, and Poague had a second chance to prove his worth the next day.[7]

Well before dawn on June 9, Poague and the rest of the Stonewall Brigade were up and moving toward Union General James Shields's recently reinforced division. On this morning, Shields's men held the high ground, partly protected by the brush and trees on the ridge they occupied. Across a long, open wheat field the Stonewall Brigade advanced that morning, never making it to the ridge. While the 2d and 5th Regiments attempted to flank the Union line, Captain Poague's battery tried to protect the huddled troops of his brigade from the deadly fire of the Union battery positioned in the charcoal clearing (or "coaling") on the east side of the ridge. For two hours the opposing batteries barked at each other while the Stonewall Brigade endured a punishing enfilading fire from Union infantry brought up on the left. Slowly, even the tough veterans began to drift back across the wheat field, and when Poague ran out of ammunition, he ordered his cannons back. In vain, General Jackson tried to rally the men. Just when the battle seemed lost, the Union battery in the coaling stopped firing—Colonel Taylor's Louisiana Brigade had once again saved the day with a daring assault. Now the Union army began retreating pell-mell, and the weary Confederates gave chase to no avail. The Confederate losses were the heaviest of the entire Valley Campaign (800 casualties), but the battle had been won and the Valley saved. It was with relief that the veterans of the historic Valley Campaign went into camp for five days of well-earned rest.[8]

The well-deserved rest soon came to an end. On June 17 the men were ordered to move east, to help protect Richmond. With some soldiers marching and some riding trains, the entire body of Jackson's army did not reach Hundley's Corner (four miles from Mechanicsville) until the later afternoon of June 26, too late to help out at the Battle of Mechanicsville.

Jackson's army was able to participate in the bloodiest battle of the Seven Days Campaign, the Battle of Gaines's Mill. Not all the brigades shared equally in the pain and glory of this engagement. To begin with, each brigade got confused in moving across dense thickets and swamps. Nonetheless, each one arrived in time to participate in the late afternoon assaults on the well-fortified

Union lines. The Stonewall Brigade helped take one part of the ridge, while the 21st Virginia of the 2d Brigade helped carry what Worsham called the "strongest point I saw occupied by either army during the war."[9]

In one of the many ironies of this long war, and in particular of this fierce battle involving over 96,000 men from both sides, the 1st Rockbridge Artillery missed the entire struggle. Instead, it was camped to the rear of the Confederate lines that hot June day, exchanging a "twelve-pound howitzer . . . for a captured Napoleon [a type of artillery gun]."[10] At Malvern Hill, however, the roles of the 1st Rockbridge Artillery and the 21st Virginia Infantry were reversed. On that blistering July day (the first), Poague's and Carpenter's batteries fired for six hours on the massed Union batteries on the hill. Their efforts came to naught. The Union batteries stayed in place, ready to wreak their horrifying toll on the thousands who charged up the hill that evening.[11]

The worst for Poague and his battery came late in the day. The battery was ordered to the rear of General D. H. Hill's line and, while waiting for further orders, they had "to endure the most trying of ordeals, staying idle under terrific fire." It was with immense relief that Poague and his fellow officer, Carpenter, finally received an unexpected order: "Rejoin your command." One casualty of this intense barrage was John Brown, a private assigned to guard the ambulances positioned 400 yards to the rear of the battery. Proving that there is no place of safety on a battlefield, Brown was decapitated by a shell from a Union gunboat on the James River. The complete injustice and randomness of war were further confirmed by another event of that day. According to Poague, a "blustering bully" from Lexington serving under his command "couldn't stand the racket and broke for the rear." This 28-year-old "bully," John Craig, would survive the war, while 35-year-old John Brown, a farmer from Fancy Hill, would leave a widow to carry on without him.[12]

As for the 21st Virginia Infantry, it was ordered to the edge of the battlefield, where it too endured a horrific shelling until darkness began to fall. The men then marched to another spot on the field, where the regiment was ordered to stay for the night. Consequently, the 21st never got dragged into the maelstrom of death and destruction on Malvern Hill, although Worsham had his own private, chilling experience. He gave food and water to a wounded comrade, then let him sleep the night under his blanket, which Worsham shared as the night grew colder. When Worsham tried to rouse his friend the next morning, it was to no avail—he was dead.[13] After Malvern Hill, both the 1st Rockbridge Artillery and the 21st Virginia Infantry went into camp, enjoying a well-deserved rest before setting off for central Virginia in mid-July.[14]

Robin Berkeley had a completely different experience from Poague or Worsham in the Seven Days Campaign. Berkeley spent more time in bed than in combat, and when his unit was engaged, it was usually in movement, not in battle. Ordered to the Battle of Seven Pines (May 31), the battery got as far as the intersection of Williamsburg and Charles City roads, where "deep mud" prevented the battery from hauling its "big and heavy" guns any farther. Most of June was spent in a temporary camp set up in an oak grove near the farm of John Poe. It was a miserable time for Robin, because he shook and sweated from "chills and fever" that afflicted him every day. He had such a bad case of the chills that he missed his battery's participation in the Battle of Mechanicsville. Rallying a bit on June 27, he was detailed to bring some sick men to the hospital in Richmond. While there he saw a makeshift infirmary in action at the Central Depot, with surgeons "dressing wounds and amputating limbs" as the "ladies of Richmond . . . moved like ministering angels among these sufferers." The only saving note was that he found no member of his company at the infirmary. As he made his way back to his company, he crossed the battlefields of Mechanicsville and Gaines's Mill. There he glimpsed "one of the most awful sights of war"—the "swollen" and blackened corpses of dead Confederates. Thankfully, none of his unit was among the dead. Instead, they were camped near Gaines's Mill, resting after two days of fighting.

On June 30, Robin finally got into a fight; his battery engaged in an artillery duel with opposing Union batteries at White Oak Swamp. Remarkably, no man was injured in three hours of firing; the battery lost four horses, however (and supporting Confederate batteries had eight casualties). The Hanover Artillery withdrew in the late afternoon, watching fresh batteries take its place and General Jackson's troops pass them in "battle order." The next day the company moved to Fair Oaks, where it encamped on the stormy night of July 1, the men listening to the "noise" of the awful Battle of Malvern Hill. The rest of July was spent in camps near Richmond, where Robin continued to suffer from "chills and fevers" and his mess spent its "leisure time in abusing Wash [Captain G. W. Nelson] and his lieutenants for their laziness and want of energy."[15] For Robin, the time to "see the elephant" (experience combat for the first time) had yet to occur.

Another soldier who saw virtually no action was Fred Fleet. After the excitement of regimental elections in early May (when Fleet was elected lieutenant), the 26th Virginia Infantry Regiment was sent to Richmond to join General Robert E. Rodes's brigade. The 26th hardly had time to adjust to its new commander before it was reassigned, this time to the remnants of General Henry A. Wise's "Legion" (now more properly called Wise's Brigade, as it numbered under 1,000 men as late as June 30, even with the addition of the 400 men of the 26th).[16] For a young man still seeking the glory and honor that came with battle, this latest reassignment could not have been worse.

By this time, Wise's reputation as a poor military officer had been set. He had lost western Virginia, Roanoke Island, much of eastern North Carolina, and Norfolk. Still, he retained the support of President Davis and General Robert E. Lee, probably more out of convenience (he was better in the army than out of it as a critic) than respect. He did not have the backing of General Joseph E. Johnston, however, who had already been overheard stating that he no longer wanted Wise's troops. General Lee was not willing to alienate Wise completely (although he may have shared Johnston's view of Wise's commanding abilities), and Wise's Brigade was ordered to protect the heavy batteries at Chaffin's Bluff on the James River, a necessary defense but also a posting that kept the brigade far from the intended center of action.[17]

As the great and horrible battles of Fair Oaks and the Seven Days raged near Richmond, Fred Fleet had the chance to reevaluate his views of combat. He wrote to his mother on June 5, "I have always thought heretofore that I wd: like very much to be in battle & run the risk of being shot, but since I have heard of the severe wounds & death of some, I think I will be satisfied to keep out." Still, he had not turned into a shirker. He continued, "If we were ordered, however, I wd: cheerfully go to do my duty."[18]

Despite the strenuous efforts of General Wise, Fred never had the opportunity to challenge his fears or fully test his resolve during the Seven Days battles. Defying "strict orders" to remain at Chaffin's Bluff, Wise took his brigade to reinforce Major General Theophilus H. Holmes on June 30. The brigade was sent to the extreme right of Holmes's forces, just 600 yards from Malvern Hill. The 26th Virginia came under heavy artillery fire but did not buckle. As Fred later wrote to his father, "I felt very calm, altho' shells were bursting all around us." That was about as close to the action as the 26th would get. The next day they were marched closer to Malvern Hill but never called up to fight. On July 2, as the dead and wounded were being carried off Malvern Hill, Wise's Brigade was ordered to return to its original post at Chaffin's Bluff.[19] Martial glory had again eluded Henry A. Wise and Fred Fleet.

The Battle of Malvern Hill proved decisive for both commanding generals. Reluctant to attack, McClellan ordered his entire army to retreat to the safety of Harrison's Landing, the huge dock on the James River that had served the historic Berkeley and Westover plantations. There, under the protection of Union gunboats, the 90,000 men of the Army of the Potomac and all their horses, mules, and supplies squeezed into a narrow strip of riverland, four miles long and one mile wide, awaiting new orders from their general, who wrote to President Lincoln that he had moved the army there "to take a different base of operations."

Chastened by the enormous number of Confederate casualties (5,640) incurred by the futile attacks on Malvern Hill, General Lee ordered reconnaissance of the land near Harrison's Landing until the strength of McClellan's position was fully appraised. On July 4, 1862, General Lee made the decision to leave McClellan alone; he would not repeat Malvern Hill. Lee was exhibiting his ability to grow in command, as his better coordination of divisions would show in future battles. McClellan had already demonstrated his aversion to combat, both personally and for his men. He would cement this reputation when he evacuated his entire army in August (as ordered by General Henry W. Halleck, the president's military adviser, and endorsed by Lincoln).[20]

As for the four soldiers in this study, only two, William Poague and John Worsham, had directly experienced combat. Little could they know, however, that they had already achieved their pinnacle of fame, back in the dust and mud and blood of the Valley Campaign. Robin Berkeley and Fred Fleet had been close to battles but never deeply involved. Circumstances had placed them in regiments that would see little action for at least another year, demonstrating clearly that in war, circumstance and chance are the only constants.

NOTES

1. Modern studies of Jackson's Valley Campaign include Robertson, *Stonewall Jackson*, 359–457; Robert Gaither Tanner, *Stonewall in the Valley* (Garden City, NY, 1976); Robert K. Krick, *Conquering the Valley: Stonewall Jackson at Port Republic* (New York, 1996); Richard L. Armstrong, *The Battle of McDowell, March 11–May 18, 1862* (Lynchburg, 1990); Brandon H. Beck and Charles S. Grunder, *The First Battle of Winchester* (Lynchburg, 1992); Robertson, *Stonewall Brigade*, 79–113.

2. Robertson, *Stonewall Brigade*, 92–94.

3. Ibid., 94–97; *OR*, vol. 12, pt. 1, 734–37 (report of General Charles S. Winder); *OR*, vol. 12, pt. 1, 761–62 (report of Captain William T. Poague); T. Michael Parrish, *Richard Taylor: Soldier Prince of Dixie* (Chapel Hill, 1992), 185–87; Worsham, *One of Jackson's Foot Cavalry*, 73–74.

4. Riggs, *21st Virginia Infantry*, 14–15.

5. *OR*, vol. 12, pt. 1, 737; *OR*, vol. 12, pt. 1, 762; Poague, *Gunner with Stonewall*, 24.

6. Robertson, *Stonewall Brigade*, 99–105.

7. This dramatic story was first recounted by two men at the scene, E. A. Moore and William Allan. See Moore, *The Story of a Cannoneer under Stonewall Jackson* (New York, 1907), 68–69; and Allan, *History of the Campaign of General T. J. (Stonewall) Jackson in the Shenandoah Valley of Virginia, from November 4, 1861 . . . to June 17, 1862* (Philadelphia, 1880), 270–71. The story is retold in Freeman's *Lee's Lieutenants*, 1:442–43; Robertson, *Stonewall Brigade*, 106–7; and Robertson, *Stonewall Jackson*, 433–34. Poague simply referred readers to Allan's work. Poague, *Gunner with Stonewall*, 26.

8. Robertson, *Stonewall Brigade*, 108–13; Robertson, *Stonewall Jackson*, 442–45; Parrish, *Richard Taylor*, 205–15; Krick, *Conquering the Valley*, 350–435; Poague, *Gunner with Stonewall*, 26–27.

9. Robertson, *Stonewall Brigade*, 116–20; Worsham, *One of Jackson's Foot Cavalry*, 84–85.

10. Stephen W. Sears, *To the Gates of Richmond: The Peninsula Campaign* (New York, 1992), 335; Driver, *1st and 2nd Rockbridge Artillery*, 25.

11. According to Sears, the Confederates did not use their artillery wisely on July 1 and a few batteries, including Poague's, paid the heaviest price for the poor overall management of all the artillery resources. See Sears, *To the Gates of Richmond*, 318–21. Also see Robertson, *Stonewall Brigade*, 120–21.

12. Poague, *Gunner with Stonewall*, 29–30. The shell that killed John Brown first passed through the trunk of an oak tree 30 inches in diameter, ibid.; Driver, *1st and 2nd Rockbridge Artillery*, 63 and 61.

13. Worsham, *One of Jackson's Foot Cavalry*, 87–88.

14. Driver, *1st and 2nd Rockbridge Artillery*, 26; Poague, *Gunner with Stonewall*, 31–32; Worsham, *One of Jackson's Foot Cavalry*, 89. While resting near Richmond, Poague was visited by his father, who brought him a much-needed present, his "first handsome Confederate uniform." Poague, *Gunner with Stonewall*, 32.

15. Berkeley, *Diary*, May 23, 1862, 17–18; June 2 and 4, 1862, 18; June 25, 1862, 18; June 27, 1862, 19; June 29, 1862, 19–20; June 30, 1862, 21; July 1, 1862, 21; July 2, 3, 8 and August 15, 1862, 22–23; July 8, 1862, 23.

16. Alex L. Wiatt, *26th Virginia Infantry* (Lynchburg, 1984), 5–6; Simpson, *A Good Southerner*, 265–69.

17. Simpson, *A Good Southerner*, 267–68. According to Simpson, Wise was acutely aware of the criticism about him, both real and imagined. Although he would accept no blame for his failures, he also could not exert enough political influence to get his troops placed in the "hot" spots.

18. Fleet, *Green Mount*, Fred Fleet to Ma, June 5, 1862, 132.

19. Wiatt, *26th Virginia Infantry*, 5–7; Simpson, *A Good Southerner*, 269–70; Fleet, *Green Mount*, Fred Fleet to Pa, July 3, 1862, 145. Wise's decision to leave his post and join Holmes is shrouded in controversy. See Wiatt and Simpson, the same pages as above, for this story.

20. Sears, *To the Gates of Richmond*, 316–17, 324, 326, 392, 335, 327, 332, 335–41, and 350–56. McClellan had demanded more troops, a demand Halleck and Lincoln were unwilling to meet.

CHAPTER SIX

CONFEDERATE OFFENSIVE, SUMMER AND FALL 1862

As GENERAL ROBERT E. LEE waited all through July to see what General McClellan would do, he kept track of new threats in the northern tier of Virginia. Major General John Pope had come from the western theater with orders to unify the three separate forces that had fought Jackson into one command, the newly designated Army of Virginia. Combined, the corps of Generals McDowell, Banks, and Sigel would total nearly 50,000 men. By July 12, McDowell's corps occupied Culpeper Court House, the county seat of Culpeper County. Just twenty-seven miles away lay Gordonsville and the absolutely vital Virginia Central Railroad, Richmond's rail connection to the Shenandoah Valley. Gordonsville had to be protected, so General Lee and President Davis sent General Jackson with 11,000 men to do the job. Facing them were bitter veterans of the embarrassing spring campaign in the Shenandoah Valley, and the most boastful general in the Union Army. To inspire his new command, General Pope told his men that he had "come to you from the West, where we always see the backs of our enemies." To challenge this taunt and with some harsh occupation orders, Jackson led his weary troops to Gordonsville by rail and on foot.[1]

General Jackson's small army soon had its chance to test Pope's strength. On the blistering afternoon of August 9, the two enemies met in the woods and fields just north of Cedar Mountain. Naturally, if Jackson was there, so were Poague and Worsham. As chance would have it, Worsham's beloved 21st Virginia found itself in the epicenter of the battle, fighting for its very survival as a unit.

The combat began in the afternoon with cavalry skirmishing, followed by artillery duels. Around 5:45 P.M., the battle shifted to a more intense phase. General Nathaniel Banks ordered General Christopher C. Augur's three brigades to march across a cornfield to attack the Confederate regiments under the command of Generals William B. Taliaferro, Edward L. Thomas, and Jubal A. Early. Augur obeyed and thousands of Union troops marched on toward the Confederate lines, enduring withering artillery fire from Confederate batteries placed strategically on Cedar Mountain. While fighting raged on the fields east of Crittenden Lane, an annoyed General Banks sent General Samuel C. Crawford's "three and six-tenths regiments" to attack the Confederate left huddled along the woods north of Crittenden Lane. Showing tremendous courage, 1,500 Union soldiers charged across a wheat field, pushing into the Confederate lines despite a heavy volley from the defenders. They rolled on relentlessly, sending the 1st Virginia Battalion fleeing and breaking the 42d Virginia into fragments by the force of the surprise attack in the rear of the 42d. The scattering of the 42d left the rear of the 21st Virginia unguarded, thus setting the stage for one of the fiercest short struggles of the war.[2]

Despite losing hundreds of men to bullets or just plain confusion, approximately 900 men from the 28th New York, the 5th Connecticut, and a portion of the 46th Pennsylvania Regiments kept moving through the woods, falling upon the rear of the 21st Virginia and half of the 48th Virginia Regiments. The lead Union troops opened fire at thirty paces, catching the Confederates by surprise. The Union troops kept coming, and the tough veterans of the 21st Virginia soon found themselves in hand-to-hand combat. Lieutenant Colonel Richard Cunningham tried to organize a retreat, but his voice of "loud compass" had been reduced to a whisper by illness, so he asked John Worsham to convey his order. Worsham managed to reach the men close to him, and as they started to retreat down the lane, they encountered more Union troops, which meant that the 21st was surrounded. Then ensued "such a fight as was not witnessed during the war; guns, bayonets, swords, pistols, fence rails, rocks, etc. were used all along the line." Historian Robert Krick maintains that this fight had "an intensity never exceeded on this continent." Worsham's F Company alone lost two-thirds of its numbers (six killed and six wounded), which essentially meant the dissolution of the

"Old F." Bearing the regimental colors was a particularly deadly job; each of the four men who picked up the flag was killed. With some firing at will and some fighting hand-to-hand, the 21st maintained its discipline until its valiant commander, Cunningham, was shot as he mounted his horse. According to a Union observer, the 21st then "stampeded" down the lane. Worsham uses the softer term "overwhelmed" to describe the moment.[3]

As the remnants of the 21st fell back, they soon found themselves part of a vast, chaotic retreat of Confederate regiments, including the four regiments under Colonel Alexander Taliaferro and the four regiments under General Jubal Early, as the combined force of Crawford's attack on the Confederate left flank and John Geary's frontal attack forced them to fall back. To the credit of some of the men and officers, the retreat did not turn into a rout, as some units, supported by Captain William Pegram's four guns, fought a disciplined movement backward. Then, just as the entire Confederate left had collapsed, three events happened almost simultaneously: General Jackson rode into the ranks of retreating soldiers, waving his sword *and* a flag to rally the men; fresh troops under General Lawrence O. Branch and Colonel James J. Archer burst forth from the woods into the flank and rear of Crawford's regiments; and Crawford's amazing advance simply ran out of steam. Quickly the tables turned as the scattered elements of Crawford's regiments scurried back across the wheat field. Once again, Jackson had watched (and this time immeasurably helped) a potential disaster turn into a springboard for success. He also had added another chapter to the book of legends growing around him.[4]

John Worsham had survived this "hell spot" and went on to participate in the Confederate counterattack that swept across the fields, driving the Union troops back. But the cost for his company, his regiment, and his brigade was enormous; two-thirds of his company, nearly half of his regiment, and over one-third of his brigade were counted as casualties. Robert Krick notes that the 2d and 3d Brigades of Jackson's Division "bore nearly one-half of the August 9 burden of blood [for the Confederates]. On none other of Virginia's major battlefields did the butcher's bill fall so unevenly among the Confederate units charged with paying the price."[5] After describing the deaths of Cunningham and

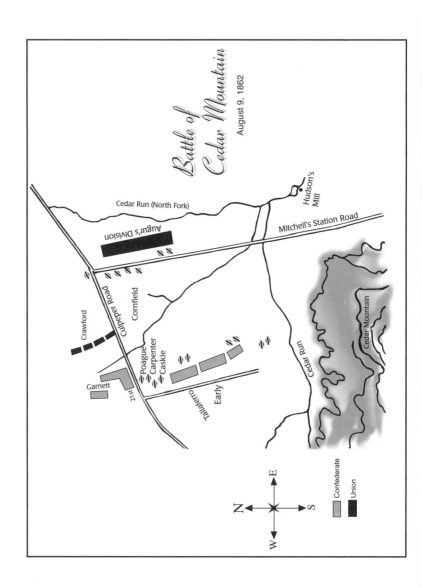

Battle of
Cedar Mountain
August 9, 1862

the commander of the Stonewall Brigade, General Charles S. Winder, Worsham brings home the awful reality of this war by listing the dead and wounded, some of whom were his friends, all of whom were his comrades: "Henry Anderson, Joe Nunnally, William Pollard, and Roswell Lindsay were killed, Bob Gilliam was shot through the leg, Clarence Redd through both wrists, Ned Tompkins through one arm and in the body, Porter Wren in the arm, Harrison Watkins through the body, and Clarence Taylor through the hip." Miraculously, Worsham survived without so much as a flesh wound.[6]

Another tough veteran of Jackson's campaigns, William Poague, also came through the battle uninjured. As usual, Poague minimized his role, not even mentioning in his memoirs the accurate firing of his battery in the late afternoon before the Union attack began. He does describe the effect of the Confederate retreat on his battery: "My guns were rendered useless, being surrounded by our infantry and all we could do was try to rally the infantry and restore order, for it was on the verge of panic." He also passes out more credit to others besides Jackson for reining in the frightened soldiers: "In the melee the most conspicuous persons, as I remember it, were General Jackson, General W. B. Taliaferro, and David Barton, a private in our battery." In his memoir he explains why his official report of the battle is a "meager affair," because the "battery did not require the reports of its commanders to help make and maintain its reputation."[7]

Even as the armies buried their dead and nursed their wounded on the bloody fields below Cedar Mountain, more divisions were on the move from the north and the south, gathering force for their inevitable collision. Cavalry and infantry skirmished along the Rappahannock River, as Pope and Lee attempted to outmaneuver each other. Lee, however, knew that he had a limited amount of time for such feints. By mid-August it became common knowledge that McClellan's large army was being moved corps by corps to Alexandria, and before long the two Union armies would be united. Consequently, Lee decided he would move north, toward Maryland, drawing Pope and McClellan away from the vital crops and stores of central Virginia. He would not seek a major engagement, but he would not pass on a battle either, if an opportunity presented itself. To accomplish this movement, though, Lee made a tremendously risky decision. He would split his army of 55,000 men, sending Jackson ahead with 24,000 men to seize the Orange and Alexandria Railroad. Once that was secured, the rest of Lee's army would join Jackson and move on toward Maryland. Jackson's men began marching before dawn on August 25.

To a large degree, Lee's bold plan worked as intended. Jackson's quick march and seizure of the stores at Manassas Junction forced Pope to chase him. He finally caught him on August 29 near Sudley Springs, just north of Groveton. A day's worth of attacks failed to dislodge Jackson's army. Undeterred, Pope attacked again the following day. On the second day, though, James Longstreet's corps was there to help Jackson, and once again Pope's attacks were stopped. By September 1, Pope had had enough, and his army was ordered to return to Washington. Within two weeks he found himself transferred to the West, to fight a different enemy, Native Americans. He would never be given command in the Civil War again. Lee had achieved his objective of dislodging Pope and keeping McClellan at bay, and he now stood poised to bring the war to the North.[8]

In the thick of things, as ever, were Poague and Worsham. The tiny 21st Virginia had no time to recuperate after the hard fighting at Cedar Mountain. It marched with the 2d Brigade under the command of General Taliaferro, the replacement for General Winder. On August 29 the 2d Brigade joined in a flank attack on Colonel James Nagle's 1st Brigade of the 2d Division of the 9th Corps. There were two stages to the attack. As Worsham described the first stage, the men of the 21st "emptied our guns into the enemy, and [then] charged them with empty guns." Holding on to a railroad line cut, the 21st reloaded and reformed, awaiting a counterattack. It came quickly, as three lines in succession marched toward the 21st and the other regiments in Colonel Bradley T. Johnson's 2d Brigade. At 100 yards the Confederates opened fire and subsequently broke each Union advance. The 2d Brigade then charged the disintegrating Union regiments, pushing them through a patch of woods. At this moment, the 2d was ordered to return to the railroad cut. As the men retreated, a Union artillery battery raked the Confederate lines. Worsham witnessed another gruesome spectacle of this war: four men killed by a single cannon ball, with one man still standing, his head blown off, "with a stream of blood spurting a foot or more from his neck." The 21st nevertheless continued its retreat and soon settled into uneasy bivouac for the night.[9]

The next day brought more unrelenting sun and heat and, by 3:00 P.M., a fresh Union attack on the now familiar site, the railroad cut. Colonel Bradley Johnson's 2d Brigade again defended the cut, with the 21st Virginia and the 1st Virginia Battalion held in reserve in a woods 200 yards back. Soon ten Union regiments surged across an open field and up an embankment, where they took cover and engaged in what historian John Hennessy calls "one of the war's most intense musketry battles." Colonel Johnson needed his reserves, and he called up the 21st Virginia and the 1st Virginia Battalion. After surviving murderous fire as they crossed an open field, the 300 men took their positions and soon exacted their revenge for an earlier battle. Worsham wrote, "Every man in the Second Brigade at this moment remembered Cedar Run, each one loaded his gun with care, raised it deliberately to his shoulder, took deadly aim, and pulled the trigger!" The fierce firefight lasted over thirty minutes before the Confederates began running low on ammunition. Then a soldier suggested they use rocks, and thus was born another legend of this war, when the 2d Brigade heaved and hurled rocks at their Union counterparts. Finally, "a short struggle on top of the bank, and in front of the cut, and the battle was ours!" After a brief pursuit of the retreating Union soldiers, the 2d Brigade returned to the railroad cut.[10]

Another soldier in the thick of the 2-day battle was William Poague. He and his Rockbridge Battery ably assisted the Stonewall Brigade as it stoutly battled the storied Iron Brigade for over two hours near Groveton on August 28. As the chief historian of the Stonewall Brigade, James Robertson, writes, "Few battles in the Civil War equaled the one these two brigades waged in the waning afternoon. It was mostly a stand-up fight, with the two lines at times less than seventy yards apart." When darkness stilled the fire, the Confederates retained control of their orchard, but at a staggering cost: nearly one-third of the Stonewall Brigade became casualties.[11]

The next day Poague and his battery were engaged again. Posted near a railroad cut, the battery sprang into action when Captain James Cooper's Battery B, 1st Pennsylvania Light Artillery opened fire on the Confederate right. Poague quickly ordered his guns "out into the fields and somewhat on the flank of the enemy's battery." After some "lively" firing (from as close as 600 yards), the Union battery withdrew, leaving a disabled gun on the field. When General Jackson saw Poague's handiwork, he offered rare praise to the young officer: "Good morning, Captain, that was handsomely done."[12]

On the third and climactic day of the battle, August 30, Poague's battery joined Colonel Stephen D. Lee's 18-gun battalion on a ridge overlooking Mrs. Dogan's pasture. From here the guns of Poague and Lee helped repel three Union advances on Jackson's thin line in the afternoon. During that long, hot afternoon, the courage of Poague's men was severely tested and not found wanting. At one point a shell came tumbling toward one of Poague's guns, smoking as it drew nearer. Poague wrote, "On it came and exploded under the trail of the gun. Not a man budged from his position. . . . What an honor to command such men!"[13]

After the timely arrival of Longstreet's army and the subsequent rout of the Union forces, Poague rode over to see the former position of the Union army, finding the "enemy's dead so thickly strewn that I could not ride among the silent ranks." A lone Union soldier almost stood up, then fell to the ground. Poague felt "an almost uncontrollable impulse to end his apparent agony with my pistol." Poague allowed himself a rare moment of introspection: "Here, as on other fields, I experienced most divers and conflicting emotions—sincere sympathy for individual suffering and wishing I could give relief, and an inner rejoicing and intense satisfaction at the sight of hundreds of my country's foes deliberately put to death."[14]

Poague had little time to reflect on mortality, however. On September 1 he and his battery were marching again, this time heading north through Chantilly and Leesburg toward Frederick, Maryland. Camped near Frederick from September 5 to 10, the officers of the Stonewall Brigade took their meals at a "Dutch" farmhouse, and Poague fondly recalled: "I never enjoyed good things to eat, as much in my whole army experience." It was fortunate that Poague and his men had their break from the war, because they would soon be embroiled in what Poague called "the awful fight at Sharpsburg—in my opinion the most terrific and most trying to his troops of all of Lee's battles."[15]

As Poague and Worsham (camped near Frederick as well) got some well-deserved rest after the month of fierce fighting, General Lee outlined plans to President Davis and others to occupy western Maryland and, if necessary, march into Pennsylvania—perhaps even farther north. As long as he stayed in western Maryland, he kept the war away from Virginia and the pressure on McClellan to either protect or attack.[16] At first everything worked in Lee's favor. Confederate forces occupied Hagerstown, Maryland, on September 11, captured Harpers Ferry (and 12,000 soldiers) on September 15, and survived a tough battle against superior numbers at South Mountain on September 14. Yet in the midst of success, trouble came. A copy of General Lee's orders for the Maryland campaign had been lost by Confederate couriers and then found (wrapped around cigars!) by Union soldiers on September 13. Even though General J. E. B. Stuart told Lee of the intelligence loss the same day, the damage had been done. Now even General McClellan had few reasons not to press an attack on Lee's divided army.

General McClellan managed to find reasons, though, even in the best of circumstances. He failed to strike on September 16, when Lee's scattered corps had not yet assembled along Antietam Creek. Instead, he waited until September 17 to attack, giving the Confederates time to arrive and deploy. When the battle did take place, it would be one of the longest single days of fighting in the entire war and definitely the bloodiest.

For John Worsham, Sharpsburg would be another tough battle in a season of difficult fights. After a hard day's march from Harpers Ferry on September 16, the 2d Brigade got a few hours of much-needed rest before fighting began at first light. Commanded by General William E. Starke (who replaced General John R. Jones after Jones had been temporarily disabled by an air burst of a cannon shell), the 2d Brigade fought in the fierce, seesaw battle for control of the fields around the Dunker church just north of town on the Hagerstown Turnpike. Worsham's action came in the morning, beginning around 7:00 A.M. In just three hours of fighting, "over 8,000 men" were "killed or wounded . . . Northerners and Southerners in nearly equal measure," according to historian Stephen Sears. He also notes that because the lines were so close, at times no more than thirty yards apart, veterans "would remember this as quite simply the worst fighting they had ever experienced."[17]

Worsham's main memories included the shooting of General Starke, who was mortally wounded as he led a charge. Worsham also noted that after the Second Battle of Manassas, F Company had been reduced to three men. At Sharpsburg one of the men was sick; another, Reuben Jordan, performed admirably as a skirmisher; and the third (Worsham), served with Captain A. C. Page of Company D, and once again survived a major battle without a wound. Worsham reported of Captain Page, however, that "this gallant and good man had to pay the penalty of commanding F Company, losing a leg in the battle." Captain Penn, acting commander of Jones's Brigade after Jones and Starke were wounded, also lost a leg. The 21st Regiment officially listed nineteen casualties at Sharpsburg, which was primarily an indication of its tiny size that day, not its location on the battlefield. As for F Company, the old Richmond militia unit that "formed the nucleus" of the 21st Infantry Regiment, it had experienced an enormous and sad decline in its ranks, from ninety-five men in April 1861 to three men in September 1862. But as long as one man remained, the proud company had a chance to replenish its rolls as it went into camp in Jefferson County for almost two months after the Battle of Sharpsburg.[18]

Captain William Poague was on the bloody field near the Dunker church that morning as well, commanding his battery as it exchanged fire with both the short-range guns to its front and long-range guns at its flank. Soon he had to retreat, as did Jones's entire division. Poague found a gap in the Confederate line of 200 to 300 yards, so "two guns were immediately put in position and fire opened directly to the front on the enemy's line of battle." That too ended abruptly when the infantry on Poague's right retreated, forcing him to do the same. Poague was then ordered to report to General J. E. B. Stuart on the "extreme left, and with other guns kept up an advancing fire on the retreating enemy until he found shelter under a number of reserve batteries." The reserve batteries must have returned devastating fire, because in his official report Poague noted that "several of my men were wounded, and a large proportion of the horses of two of the pieces killed or wounded, rendering the pieces unserviceable. They were at once sent to the rear."[19]

Reduced to just one artillery piece, Poague's men were ordered to retreat. While moving back, the group passed General Robert E. Lee. Seeking new orders, Poague rode up to Lee. Then occurred one of the poignant moments for which the Civil War is remembered. One of the soldiers who accompanied Poague was Private Robert E. Lee Jr., who wrote in his memoirs that "the general, listening patiently, looked at us—his eyes passing over me without any sign of recognition." General Lee ordered Poague to return to Stuart with his one active piece. Private Robert Lee then approached his father and spoke with him for a few seconds. Young Lee recollected their parting words: "General, are you going to send us in again?" General Lee replied, "Yes, my son. You must do what you can to help drive these people back." So back the tired band of cannoneers went to General Stuart, who sent them on to Major John Pelham. Unbeknown to Poague and some other artillerists, Pelham had been ordered to fire on the large Union battery of thirty-four pieces, testing whether General McClellan's right flank could be turned. With no more than ten guns hidden in a small patch of trees, Pelham ordered his ad hoc command to fire on the Union batteries. Laughing, he told his protesting subordinates: "Oh, we must stir them up a little and slip away." Stir them up they did, as Poague tersely noted in his official report: "[We were] . . . silenced in fifteen or twenty minutes by a most terrific fire from a number of the enemy's batteries." Within an hour, General Stuart ordered a retreat of Pelham's small artillery group, learning in a matter of minutes that there would be no turning of McClellan's right at that time.[20]

After this battle, Poague and the Rockbridge Battery had a well-deserved rest at several camps in the lower Shenandoah Valley. It was the first extended rest the battery had had during the year and the men enjoyed it, except for one aspect of the reorganization of artillery that took place that fall. Artillery batteries were detached from infantry brigades and brought together, which made great logical sense. It caused emotional hardship, however, because many batteries were severed from brigades they had fought with for over a year. Such was the case with the Rockbridge Artillery; the men had to say farewell to their friends in the famed Stonewall Brigade.[21]

Poague had an additional disappointment, one that offered insight into the difficulties and subtleties of promotion in the Army of Northern Virginia. In his memoirs, Poague wrote that he heard "it was contemplated to give me promotion," but owing to claims for the same by other captains of batteries, his promotion was put on hold. Poague added, "I had been without a friend at court after Captain Alf. Jackson, a college mate and 'frat' chum gave up his place as assistant adjutant general to 'Old Jack.' " Captain Jackson had been replaced by General Jackson's favorite aide, the engaging Alexander "Sandie" Pendleton, Poague's "day room mate at college," but Poague said he had learned on "good authority" that he "could not count him as a friend, but rather against me with any influence he might have." Why? "I could not exactly understand his attitude to me, unless it was because some of his friends in the battery had been disciplined." No promotion came that fall for Poague.[22]

Another soldier profoundly affected by the artillery reorganization was Robin Berkeley. In his case, the change proved beneficial. Robin and his mess had long rued the day that the battery had elected G. Washington Nelson as captain. Robin wrote in his diary in July 1862, "The company is going to the dogs, and unless something is done, and done very soon, it will all go to pieces." Nelson was a brave man, but not a "hard-working, industrious man of good executive ability." Robin complained that horses had died from poor care, and proof came in early September, when the Hanover Battery had to stay in Leesburg with "broken-down horses" while most batteries moved on to Sharpsburg.[23]

Not being under General Jackson, Berkeley's battery missed the battle at Cedar Mountain (August 9). As part of Major General D. H. Hill's division, the Hanover Battery had remained in Richmond until McClellan's exodus from Harrison's Landing became assured. On August 15 the Hanover Battery began its slow march north. The leisurely pace offered Robin and his cousins the opportunity to visit home. They had a "royal dinner" with their families on August 23, replete with "ice water and ice cream." Robin called this day one of the "most pleasant and happy" he ever spent in camp, adding that the "home people made heroes of us, yet we had only done our duty."[24] The battery never made it to the Second Battle of Manassas, nor did it make it to Sharpsburg, hampered in its movement by poor horses and later by the weight of additional guns. Robin's entries during this period describe slow movement between camps, "pretty girls" in Leesburg, and numerous stories about procuring and preparing food, including the time John Hill put such bitter-tasting beets in a hash that the mess had to eat "dry bread."[25]

When the great reorganization of the artillery occurred in October 1862, the Hanover Battery was disbanded. Twenty men went to Captain Kirkpatrick's Amherst Battery, and forty men went to Captain Woolfolk's Hanover Battery. The men apparently voted on which battery to join; Robin said his mess "decided to join Captain Kirkpatrick's company" under the advice of their old captain, now major, William Nelson. The mess felt a bit vindicated when the despised Captain G. W. Nelson lost his command, and would have been heartened to read General William Pendleton's comment on Nelson: "he is not, in some respects, adapted to take care of a battery."[26] On the other hand, too much should not be read into this statement. After the Battle of Fredericksburg, G. W. Nelson got a new job on Pendleton's staff; he became an "inspector of batteries." Perhaps someone in the high command had a deep sense of irony.

Robin's mess also helped drive out one of Nelson's hated subalterns, Lieutenant Martin Stringfellow. Robin personally handed Stringfellow a "communication signed by every man present, asking him to resign." The men accused Stringfellow of cowardice during the Seven Days battles. Either this communication or some other prompted Stringfellow to leave the Army of Northern Virginia. The records last show him fighting with General John Magruder in Texas, where Magruder commended him for fighting with "remarkable gallantry" at the Battle of Galveston.[27]

The remnants of the Hanover Battery met Captain Kirkpatrick on October 8 and seemed favorably impressed. The men stayed at their camp in Warren County, nicknamed Camp Nineveh for a church of the same name nearby. Perhaps because of the reorganization, artillery units proved susceptible to the tug of religion when the first great revival swept through the Army of Northern Virginia that October. The Reverend William Jones noted that one of the "most powerful revivals" occurred in Kirkpatrick's Battery, with as many as fifty of the 115 men experiencing conversion. Robin did not say how the revival affected him; he only noted that it happened. In November and December the battery was on the move again, finally seeing action at the Battle of Fredericksburg.[28]

Such involvement after a long period of inactivity did not occur for Fred Fleet's 26th Virginia. He spent the summer, fall, and winter at Chaffin's Farm, commenting on the fortunes of war and his own boredom. On August 13 he wrote to his mother that he hoped the talk of the 26th Virginia "going to Jackson" was true—but it was not. In October he witnessed an exchange of prisoners in Richmond. He found the process fascinating, except when Confederate officers would "go on board [a ship] and drink with them [Union officers] and talk as friendly as brothers almost." Fred thought the exchange should be businesslike, though he did manage to talk with some Union officers himself. He discovered that they were "as much in earnest as we are." Based on these conversations, Fred thought there was "no probability to the end of the war."[29] After the excitement of the exchange, camp life settled into its monotonous routine. Fred wrote to his father, "Everything is unusually dull with us, just as there is a complete lull in the armies of the Potomac." The quiet continued for Fred into winter, broken only by news from Fredericksburg and a visit at Christmastime from his brother Benny.[30]

There would be no quiet for the bulk of the Army of Northern Virginia in early December. Lincoln had removed McClellan—again—and replaced him with Major General Ambrose E. Burnside. After considerable movement of both armies, the Confederates entrenched themselves along the foot of Marye's Heights in Fredericksburg. There, on a cold December day (the thirteenth), Burnside demonstrated his aggressiveness by hurling Major General Edwin Sumner's "Right Grand Division" (Burnside temporarily reorganized the Army of the Potomac) into desperate, futile assaults against the well-defended Confederate line at the foot of Marye's Heights. He called off the offensive at nightfall, then withdrew his weakened army the following evening. Burnside had demonstrated his willingness to go on the offensive, but at a terrible cost in the lives of his men: 12,600 Union casualties versus 5,300 Confederate casualties.[31]

Three of the soldiers in this study fought at Fredericksburg. John Worsham's 2d Brigade was there with Jackson's corps, but never suffered a fierce attack nor charged. Robin Berkeley saw action for the first time since the Battle at White Oak Swamp. He witnessed the entire action from his vantage point on Lee's Hill. Although shelled all day by Union artillery, no one in Robin's mess was injured, protected as they were by breastworks. They did not "fire a single shot" either, because the Union troops never moved into their range. More important than the battle, apparently, was the "bright and beautiful" aurora seen in the sky the next night, which the "men took as an omen of victory." Robin stayed near Fredericksburg until late December, breaking the monotony by taking clothes from dead Union soldiers ("about a dozen pairs of drawers and an oilcloth"), watching Union soldiers bury their dead in a "deep pit," visiting a family friend in town, and enjoying a turkey that his father and Uncle Dick had brought from home.[32]

William Poague did not have a family reunion or a visit with a friend in Fredericksburg. Instead, he endured a forced march at night and the strangest, most troubling order he ever had from his beloved commander, Old Jack. The night march proved to be the easier of the two orders to carry out. Near sunset on December 12, Poague received an order to move his battery to Fredericksburg to help fight the Union forces. With the main road in bad shape, Poague found a local resident to guide him over back roads and farm lanes on a 16-mile forced march on a bitterly cold night. The battery reached Hamilton's Crossing by daybreak, where the men "made roaring fires and got a nap and breakfast." Poague's men arrived before the batteries (which had a shorter distance to travel) of the commanding officer, Colonel Brown, got to Hamilton's Crossing. For his rapid movement, Poague earned praise from Brown and General Jackson.[33]

In the afternoon, however, Jackson gave an order to Poague that still haunted him thirty years later. By early afternoon Poague's Rockbridge Battery was positioned at the top of Dead Horse Hill (Prospect Hill), sent there to relieve the "badly smashed" battalion of Colonel Lindsay Walker. As they placed their guns, Poague remembered that "never before have we seen as much infantry and artillery of the enemy at one time." General Jackson soon appeared, surveyed the field with binoculars, then ordered Poague to fire at a Union battery in front of the Rockbridge Battery. Jackson asked, "Can't you silence that battery?" Poague replied, "We can try, General." Jackson then added, "Well then open on it, and if they get too hard for you, turn your gun on their infantry and try and stampede that!"[34]

It was the second half of the order that mystified Poague. As he wrote in his memoirs, "the words burned themselves into my memory—never to be forgotten." Only Poague's battery had been ordered to fire on the Union artillery, and Poague knew that an old artillerist like Jackson knew what the result would be: "Such a tempest of shot and shell I never have witnessed anywhere during the war." The sole explanation Poague had was that Old Jack wanted to draw the Union fire so he could "locate" the positions with "as little damage as possible to his own" batteries to the left of the Rockbridge Battery. Even Jackson's biographer, James I. Robertson, calls the order "illogical, to say the least." Nevertheless, the good soldier Poague carried it out until Lieutenant Colonel Lewis Coleman rode up and told him to cease firing, saying, "I take the responsibility of ordering you to stop." Soon after, Coleman suffered a mortal wound, thus not living to see the consequences of his bold decision. Two of "the finest soldiers in the battery . . . Lieutenant Baxter McCorkle and Private Randolph Fairfax" were also killed, along with Private Arthur Robinson. Total casualties for the Rockbridge Battery (including two guns in action under Lieutenant Graham, which had been detached to Major Pelham's artillery battery) were six killed and sixteen wounded, the heaviest loss of life sustained by any one Confederate battery that day.[35]

Poague himself barely escaped death; as he was speaking to Colonel Brown a piece of shell cut through his hat brim, "producing a sensation of much heat about my eyes and forehead." Brown also nearly died when a "heavy shot struck within three feet of him." But Brown remained "perfectly cool and self possessed in all the fiery ordeal," proving to Poague that he and Coleman "were of the right stuff and 'would do.'" Yet the brief battle would bother Poague for years: "I could not understand Jackson's order and our own sacrifice seemed senseless." Harsh words from a loyal follower of Old Jack, but also from a wise and brave young officer who "never ceased to mourn the loss of those splendid officers and men."[36]

NOTES

1. Robertson, *Stonewall Jackson*, 510–11; *OR*, vol. 12, pt. 3, 473–74; Sutherland, *Seasons of War*, 117–30.

2. Robert K. Krick, *Stonewall Jackson at Cedar Mountain* (Chapel Hill and London, 1990), 47–49, 57, 60, 73, 53, 68, 116, 117, 122, 142–43, 150–51, 156, 161, and 177.

3. Ibid., 177–83; Worsham, *One of Jackson's Foot Cavalry*, 96–97; Harrison A. Tripp, "The Charge of Cedar Mountain," *Grand Army Scout and Soldiers Mail* 5, no. 38 (1886), quoted in Krick, *Stonewall Jackson at Cedar Mountain*, 183; Worsham, *One of Jackson's Foot Cavalry*, 97.

4. Krick, *Stonewall Jackson at Cedar Mountain*, 184–231. The maps on pages 188 and 218 are particularly helpful. Krick's superb analysis makes sense of this dramatic, chaotic battle.

5. Worsham, *One of Jackson's Foot Cavalry*, 97–99; Krick, *Stonewall Jackson at Cedar Mountain*, 370–72 (quotation on 372). There are discrepancies between Worsham's and Krick's figures, with Worsham's casualty numbers being higher. Consequently, I have described the casualties in general terms.

6. Worsham, *One of Jackson's Foot Cavalry*, 99–100.

7. Krick, *Stonewall Jackson at Cedar Mountain*, 98–99; *OR*, vol. 12, pt. 2, 213 (report of Captain William T. Poague); Poague, *Gunner with Stonewall*, 33–34; Sutherland, *Seasons of War*, 131–51.

8. John J. Hennessey, *Return to Bull Run: The Campaign and Battle of Second Manassas* (New York, 1993), 92–95 and 456–72.

9. Ibid., 259–63; Worsham, *One of Jackson's Foot Cavalry*, 111 (first quotation), 112 (second quotation), and 113; Hennessey, *Return to Bull Run*, 264–67.

10. Hennessey, *Return to Bull Run*, 340–48 (quotation on 347), 358–59; Worsham, *One of Jackson's Foot Cavalry*, 115. Losses were low for the 21st in this major battle: three men killed and nine wounded, according to Riggs, *21st Virginia Infantry*, 22; Worsham, *One of Jackson's Foot Cavalry*, 116 and 115.

11. Hennessey, *Return to Bull Run*, 186–93; Robertson, *Stonewall Brigade*, 146 (quotation) and 147.

12. Hennessey, *Return to Bull Run*, 200 and 207–8; Poague, *Gunner with Stonewall*, 37 (first quotation) and 40 (Jackson quotation).

13. Hennessey, *Return to Bull Run*, 315–16; Robertson, *Stonewall Brigade*, 150; Poague, *Gunner with Stonewall*, 39.

14. Poague, *Gunner with Stonewall*, 39.

15. Driver, *1st and 2nd Rockbridge Artillery*, 31; Poague, *Gunner with Stonewall*, 42 and 45.

16. Worsham, *One of Jackson's Foot Cavalry*, 120–21; Stephen W. Sears, *Landscape Turned Red: The Battle of Antietam* (New York, 1983), 64–69.

17. Sears, *Landscape Turned Red*, 96–97, 151–55, 114–50, 112–17, 163–69, 191 and 202 (quotation).

18. Worsham, *One of Jackson's Foot Cavalry*, 125, 126, 128 (quotation), 129–30; Riggs, *21st Infantry Regiment*, 51 and 1.

19. *OR*, vol. 19, pt. 1, 1010 (Poague's report).

20. Robert E. Lee Jr., *Recollections and Letters of General Robert E. Lee* (New York, 1904), 78; Poague, *Gunner with Stonewall*, 48 and 47; *OR*, vol. 19, pt. 1, 1010; Sears, *Landscape Turned Red*, 291.

21. Poague, *Gunner with Stonewall*, 50–51; Driver, *1st and 2nd Rockbridge Artillery*, 33–34.

22. Poague, *Gunner with Stonewall*, 51. A good discussion of the complexities of promotion within the Army of Northern Virginia is found in J. Boone Bartholomees Jr., *Buff Facings and Gilt Buttons: Staff and Headquarters Operations in the Army of Northern Virginia, 1861–1865* (Columbia, 1998), 23–26; Robertson, *Stonewall Jackson*, xiv and 301; Poague, *Gunner with Stonewall*, 51. Sandie Pendleton, a son of General W. N. Pendleton, was a graduate of Washington College and the University of Virginia (MA in 1861). See Freeman, *Lee's Lieutenants*, 2:436–37, for a longer description.

23. Berkeley, *Diary*, July 8, 1862, 23, and September 7, 1862, 27.

24. *OR*, vol. 19, pt. 1, 1019; Berkeley, *Diary*, August 15, 1862, 23, and August 23, 1862, 25.

25. Berkeley, *Diary*, August 28, September 1, 6, 7, 11, and 12, 1862, 26–28.

26. Ibid., October 5, 6, and 7, 1862, 30–31; *OR*, vol. 19, pt. 2, 646–54.

27. *OR*, vol. 19, 565, 567, and vol. 25, pt. 2, 613; Berkeley, *Diary*, October 6, 1862, 31; *OR*, vol. 15, 218, and vol. 26, pt. 2, 65–66.

28. Berkeley, *Diary*, October 7, 8, 9, and November 1, 1862, 31–33; J. William Jones, *Christ in the Camp, or Religion in Lee's Army* (Richmond, 1887), 283–311; Berkeley, *Diary*, November 1–30 and December 1–13, 1862, numerous entries on movement, 33–36.

29. Fleet, *Green Mount*, Fred to Ma, August 13, 1862, 160, and Fred to Ma, October 6, 1862, 170–71.

30. Ibid., Fred to Pa, October 21, 1862, 175; Fred to Pa, December 5, 1862, 187–88; Ma to Fred, December 10, 1862, 188–89; Benny's journal, December 23–26, 1862, 190.

31. Daniel T. Sutherland, *Fredericksburg and Chancellorsville: The Dare Mark Campaign* (Lincoln, 1998), 6–77. See also Edward J. Stackpole, *Drama on the Rappahannock: The Fredericksburg Campaign* (Harrisburg, 1957); and Gary W. Gallagher, ed,, *The Fredericksburg Campaign: Decision on the Rappahannock* (Chapel Hill, 1995).

32. Worsham, *One of Jackson's Foot Cavalry*, 133; Berkeley, *Diary*, December 13, 1862, 37; December 14, 1862, 37; December 18, 1862, 39; December 20, 1862, 39.

33. Poague, *Gunner with Stonewall*, 53 and 54 (quotation on the latter page). In his official report, General Jackson wrote of Poague, "the promptitude with which he responded to the order by a fatiguing night's march is worthy of notice." *OR*, vol. 21, 633. Colonel Brown's report follows General Jackson's in ibid., 639–40.

34. Poague, *Gunner with Stonewall*, 55 and 56 (quoted dialogue).

35. Ibid., 56–57; Robertson, *Stonewall Jackson*, 659; Poague, *Gunner with Stonewall*, 57–58; Driver, *1st and 2nd Rockbridge Artillery*, 36; Jennings Cropper Wise, *The Long Arm of Lee, or The History of the Artillery of the Army of Northern Virginia*, 2 vols. (Lynchburg, 1915; reprinted edition, 1991), 1:408.

36. Poague, *Gunner with Stonewall*, 58 and 60.

Chapter Seven

"Our Strength Was Equal to Our Day"

Civilian Life, May 1862–May 1863

THE SQUAD OF UNION cavalry suddenly appeared in Front Royal on a cold January morning, searching for contraband. First they broke into Weaver's Store, where they stole "cakes and candy . . . tobacco, blacking brushes, boxes of little fancy notions and finally the mail bags." They read letters, then tore them up. The destruction of the mail was the worst for Lucy Buck, then in town; she felt so "excited and vexed I could scarcely restrain myself." Still, she managed to hold her tongue, even as the soldiers seized horses and took lodging in a local hotel. She and her mother left for home at twilight.

The ordeal continued into the next day. Soldiers began searching private residences for contraband. The Bucks hid not only the "official" contraband ("letters, papers, money, etc."), but food as well: "The turkeys were put in the dark cellar next to Harriet's room and the bacon in a packing box under the boys' bed." Most important, the horses were sent off.

A squad of soldiers finally marched up to the house around 4 P.M. They searched the house thoroughly, even examining the "bandboxes and Ma's dress pockets." They found the meat, but did not take it. At one point in the search Lucy decided she wanted to be with her mother, which meant she had to walk through a file of soldiers who "stared and shuffled as rudely as possible." The soldiers left with two haversacks, a shotgun, and a musket, and Lucy felt that she could "shoot the man who carried it off." That night the neighbors gathered to swap horror stories, and the Bucks found out they were more fortunate than others because they were not "robbed of meat, etc." Lucy joined some children and young adults who ended the exciting day by playing "Blind Man's Bluff," "Tap the Rabbit," and cards. The next morning, the Union troops left as suddenly as they had appeared two days earlier.[1]

The second year of the war brought hardship, occupation, and adventure for the three women in this study. Each woman's family endured sudden searches and plunders by Union troops, the absence of family members, and the deterioration of the institution they depended upon—slavery. George Rable argues that, by the end of 1862, "Southern independence seemed farther away than ever; increasingly obsessed with their own suffering, families teetered on the verge of despair, if not disaffection."[2]

When the focus is narrowed from the general to the particular, however, a more complex story emerges. The three women, for instance, continued to support the Confederacy on the same terms they had when the war began. Susan Caldwell dwelled on problems, Lucy Buck attempted to find meaning in the chaos and misery of war, and Tee Edmonds had a good time. Some of their responses were shaped by circumstance, but the primary determinant of response was character.

Tee Edmonds's life during the second year of the war clearly illustrates the influence of character. Situated in the very heart of the Mosby Confederacy, Tee's beloved Belle Grove often had visits from Confederate and Union soldiers. Whether entertaining young Confederates or defying Union soldiers, Tee found excitement in these new challenges.

By isolating one typical month in the early years of the war, November 1862, we can see the variety of visitors and experiences that the conflict brought to Belle Grove. On November 1 the family woke to find that only four of their five Confederate soldier guests from the night before were still there. One had run away rather than go back to his unit and stand trial for desertion. The next day the family "entertained seven soldiers from Mecklenburg." That same day, the Confederates set up defensive lines near Paris, expecting a battle. The residents of Paris were ordered to evacuate, so the Edmondses packed up and moved to Uncle Abner Settle's house, Mount Bleak. When no battle occurred, the family returned to Belle Grove, where they found "Mr. and Mrs. Newlon, Mr. De Barr and family from Upperville, Aunt

Margaret's girls and Sallie. I had brought three Rogers girls, so we pile them up tonight—plus a dozen soldiers." Everyone left the next morning, and later in the day Tee watched a brief artillery duel between rear guards of the two armies. Then, while having tea with several soldiers, the Edmondses' longtime slave, "poor old Aunt Polly," suddenly felt ill and died within minutes of "hemorrhage of the lungs." Tee turned to a passage from the Anglican liturgy to convey her feelings: "Truly 'in the midst of life, we are in death.' "[3]

The next day, Tee's brother Bud left to rejoin his unit. It was lucky that he did, because that evening "two gentlemen Yanks" asked to stay the night. One was an artist from England, drawing for the *Illustrated London News*, while the other was a reporter for the *New York Times*. The artist left Tee a sketch of a "young lady" (perhaps it was Tee; she does not say).[4]

After the gentlemen left on November 5, the Edmondses were visited by General Winfield Scott Hancock and his staff. Tee described the energetic Hancock as "the finest looking man I have ever seen in either army, and very handsomely dressed." Hancock said he would make Belle Grove his headquarters, then changed his mind. He left a Union guard at the house, which was needed that evening as stragglers came by, some "cursing the 'd——Secesh' [Secessionists] off the face of the earth." The Union division moved on, and within a week the Edmondses were visited by their son Bud (November 8 and 10), Tee's cousin "Cap" Settle (November 10), and Tee's brother Syd (November 16 and 18). Syd and Bud stayed through the following week, finally leaving for camp at Harrisonburg on November 25. The next morning another of Tee's cousins, Robert Humphrey, stopped by on his way home from the hospital, where he had been recovering from a leg wound.[5]

The month closed out with another reported injury, this time to a friend of Tee's, Kate Brown. Kate and Cornelia Triplett had decided it would be fun to watch a skirmish, so they rode an "old nag" out to Upperville in search of a show. They were not disappointed. On their way back home, they got caught in a cross fire between Union and Confederate cavalry. Their horse was shot and it "fell on Kate, breaking her leg." Under a white flag of truce a group of Union soldiers rescued Kate and carried her to a friend's house. Such kindness meant nothing to Tee. She wrote in her diary, "The hateful wretches pretended to be sorry."[6]

Other months were similarly busy at the Edmondses' home. What gave the war its dashing, theatrical tone in their county was the location of Belle Grove and the very nature of cavalry activity. Paris was on the Ashby's Gap Turnpike, the main east–west road in northern Virginia (Route 50 today), and just a few miles north of the railroad stop at Piedmont (Manassas Gap Railroad). Armies threatening or protecting Washington or moving into or out of the Shenandoah Valley would have to pass through Ashby's Gap or one of the several other gaps in the Blue Ridge Mountains. The region perfectly fits historian Stephen Ash's definition of "Confederate frontier" as an area "within the reach" of Union soldiers but not regularly occupied. Communities in these frontier regions usually kept operating throughout the war, but they also suffered from the fear that was "part of everyday existence." When armies were not on the move in this section of Virginia, cavalry from both sides would be out scouting or foraging in Loudoun, Fauquier, Warren, and Fairfax counties. The area was excellent terrain for small bands, the countryside lush with woods and fields and farms. It was here, for instance, in the Salem-Rectortown-Paris area, that John S. Mosby established his mobile "center of operations" from 1863 to 1865.[7]

Yet even before Mosby began his exploits, the residents had become accustomed to the constant movements of horsemen. In the Edmonds family, Tee's brothers, Syd and Bud, had joined Captain Richard Henry Dulaney's Company A of the 6th Virginia Cavalry. Throughout 1861 and 1862 they served near their home, which partially accounts for their frequent visits to Belle Grove. The other reason is the apparently liberal view of "duty" taken by Captain Dulaney and other commanding officers. As long as Bud and Syd were not on maneuvers, they could easily spend the night at home and return to the unit in the morning. It was a great advantage to have the mobility and freedom that a horse offered and to serve in a regiment stationed so close to home. Of course, this mobility was shared by the Union cavalry. On several occasions Confederate soldiers visiting Belle Grove had to flee before the arrival of swift-moving Union horsemen.[8]

Fortunately for the Edmondses, they had to endure only two Union occupations in the first year and a half of the war, and the appearance of General Hancock and his staff in November 1862 was more of a visit than an occupation. The tides of war could shift swiftly and unexpectedly, however. On February 10, 1863, a cold winter's day, Tee was visiting her sister Mary in Paris when a small group of Union cavalry suddenly appeared in town. They began searching houses for "arms and powder," and when they found none in Mary's house, they headed for Tee's horse, Nelly, tethered in the yard. Tee held tightly onto the bridle, declaring, "You shall not have her." The soldiers wrested the bridle away from her, pulled the saddle off, and led Nelly away. All Tee managed to save was the bridle. Her anger had not subsided by the time she described the scene in her diary. Of these soldiers, she wrote, "such a set of angry wolves were never seen before, among all the Yankees." This same party of soldiers also grabbed Bud's cavalry horse and other horses in town, for an estimated loss of $7,000.[9]

After the shock of the confiscation had passed, life returned to its usual busy pace. Syd was home for much of February, resting his arm, which had been broken while wrestling with friends. He somehow found time to go sleigh riding, so he could not have been suffering very much. Syd's convalescence was eased by frequent visits from friends in Company A, including the commissary sergeant, John Gibson, who stopped by while on a foraging expedition in late March of 1863.[10]

As for Tee, she continued to both hate and love the war. In July 1862 she had written, "O! Please come to an end, senseless war." Yet in the same month she composed a 32-line poem about its effects on her for her cousin, Margaret Humphrey. She wrote, in part:

But this plagued, horrid, awful war
Has proved to me romance too long.
But yet 'tis grand, sublimely so,
In all its varied scenes and ways.
Who can but own its brilliant feats
Will live to never ending days.

In a similar vein, Tee wrote on September 6, "All scenes and late changes suit my wild restless spirit. It is thus I should like to pass my life—no dull monotony but all change and variety, full of novelty and romance." These feelings were reversed in the cold holiday season, when she referred to the Christmas of 1862 as offering only "sad and gloomy pleasures." When the new year opened, she stated, "I have never said or felt before that I was glad at the departure of the old year, but I am now. . . . The past year has been one of pleasant memories, yet with them all was intermingled sadness and gloom for our Country's fate." As for the coming year, she did hold some hope that "war's alarm is much nearer being calmed."[11]

Lucy Buck also hoped that 1863 would be a better year. She felt that Southerners had passed through a "fiery ordeal" and that their "strength was equal to our day." Now, though, she wished for "their barques . . . (to be) floating in calmer seas." Unlike Tee Edmonds, Lucy did not express much excitement over the war. Rather, she strove to write grandly on its meaning. Her writing was suffused with Christian themes: "Then the thoughts of the many, many noble and precious lives that had been offered up on the altar of their country in propitiation for a nation's sins— of the torrents of blood that had been poured out, a priceless oblation to liberty." Yet through their hardships they had learned:

How sublime a thing it is
To suffer and grow strong.

Lucy went on to describe the new year, "melodious with the minstrelsy of thy rippling waters; glad in the joyous harmony of nature!"[12]

Lucy does appear to have fancied herself a writer, as shown by her frequent attempts to employ sweeping phrases or find larger meanings in daily events. In January 1863, for instance, Lucy went ice skating with her brothers and sisters, finding that the "bracing air invigorated body and spirit." Afterward she "climbed up on the high cliffs towering over the river and sat there under the pines and looking down on the river murmuring and flashing between its ice-bound shores I wished oh!—so earnestly, that my life were such a sunlit softly flowing stream." In April, she found more inspiration in nature; on a walk she rested

in "the tall dry grass with the warm balmy sunshine falling gold-
enly like a shower of loving smiles around me." In the same month
a friend of the family died. They buried Mrs. Turner in the garden she had so loved.

> Now that she was no more, everything would go on as usual,
> the flowers spring and bloom as brightly as if the hands that
> had planted and nurtured them were not mouldering into na-
> tive dust again, the sunshine visited every nook and corner of
> the place just as freely and goldenly as if the shadow of death
> had not been there . . . Oh!—'tis a humiliating thought that when
> our visible persons fade from the earth the traces, the influ-
> ences we leave behind are so soon erased, so soon forgotten.[13]

On the surface, Lucy shared similarities with Tee (they were
distant cousins, in fact).[14] They were both young (Lucy turned
nineteen in 1861, Tee turned twenty-two), unmarried, older children in large families, upper class for their area, well educated,
inquisitive, and intelligent. But their differences are pronounced.
Tee lacked a father, whereas Lucy's father was a powerful presence in the family's life. Tee's brothers served in a cavalry unit
active in northern Virginia; Lucy's favorite brother, Irving, served
on General Pat Cleburne's staff in the West. Most important, Tee
appears to have been more lighthearted, impetuous, adventurous, and flirtatious than Lucy. Tee constantly admired young men
or fell in love (George Leech before the war, Matthew Magner
during the war). In turn, Tee fended off numerous advances: Wirt
Lemert before the war, Douglas Gibson in September 1862 (he
asked for her "ambrotype," or photograph), and a "ladies man"
from Georgia, Lieutenant Gwynell of the 8th Georgia Regiment,
who wanted to walk her home one evening.[15]

It is difficult to say why Tee drew so much more male attention than Lucy. It was not for lack of male visitors, nor was conversation with men forbidden or limited in any way by parents.
Appearance may have played a role, but it is hard to tell from
photographs who would have been considered more beautiful.
Again from faded photographs, they both appear to have been of
average height for women of their time. Tee appears slimmer than
Lucy, though she actually outweighed her (Tee weighed 116 pounds
in 1857 [age eighteen], while Lucy weighed 111 pounds in 1862
[age twenty]). Given the Victorian-era "imperative to thinness"

for women, Tee may have come closer to the "short and slight" ideal of the times described by historian Lois Banner.[16] But appearance can only take this speculation a short distance; without comments from men known to both women, there is no solid comparison of male impressions. Therefore, personality must be the key. Tee was more fun and adventurous than Lucy as well as more open to flirting. Men found these aspects of Tee's character appealing and sought her attention. Lucy did not refrain from flirting, but she did not discuss it or the qualities of the young men she met nearly as often as Tee did. What mattered most to Lucy was her home, Bel Air, and her family. She kept up a steady correspondence with her brothers Irving and Alvin, whom she rarely saw.

After the high drama of the Union soldiers' search of the house in January 1863, life returned to its busy normalcy for Lucy and her family. There were even times of gaiety: Lucy and her brothers went ice skating; she made and received valentines; and she went on a fishing trip on a clear April day with "warm balmy sunshine." A friend brought over a "microscopic collection of our generals' and statesmen's photographs—Davis, Lee, Beauregard, Jackson, Hill, Morgan, Price, Bragg, and Semmes—all composed in the space of a large sized pinhead." One example of the omnipresence of the war, however, was noted in mid-April: while "sitting at the supper table it seemed so pleasant to have no one but our own immediate family together—such a thing had not occurred before in a year."[17]

Another unusual aspect of this war was the casual socializing of generals and civilians. In November 1862, General James Longstreet and his staff spent a night at Bel Air. Of Longstreet, Lucy remarked: "What a very quiet, dignified old gentleman he is—very fine looking though and with a countenance full of benevolences." (The general was forty-one at the time.) She had greater admiration for two men on Longstreet's staff, Majors Sorrell and Waldon, who "exactly realize my ideal of the chivalrous knights of yore, so courteous and delicate in their manner."[18]

The tides of war washed over Warrenton, too, but for Susan Caldwell the changes and hardships they brought did not inspire comparisons to Arthurian legends. Rather, ever greater burdens were heaped on a woman already consumed by the responsibilities of raising four young children and running a household. Responsibilities are the second greatest determinant of the attitudes toward the war of the women in this study. Susan had to manage a fairly large household; Tee and Lucy did not. Susan was married; Tee and Lucy were unmarried and childless.

In Susan's letters she worried about the health of the children, Lycurgus, and herself. She worried about her baby daughter's slow progress in learning to walk. She worried about high prices and shortages, although she had to admit in February 1863 that "we certainly have not as yet felt the effects of war." She worried about the continuing war; at one point she wrote to Lycurgus, "Oh! How I long for this unholy war to be at an end." She worried whenever Union troops came to town, as they did five times in the first half of 1863. In the late April raid, "Union troops detained some civilians, took provisions from farmers, established a 7 P.M. curfew and 9 P.M. 'No lights on' policy," and even attended Episcopal church services on Sunday. The troops left as suddenly as they came, not reappearing until May 31, when a group of Union soldiers "arrested every citizen on the street, took them out of town and questioned them to know if they had ever been in the rebel army, after a short time they were all released."[19]

Of all the things Susan worried about, none was as frightening as Lycurgus's persistent desire to join the army. In 1861 she had persuaded him to stay out, emphasizing his service to the Confederacy in his government position and the pain his loss would cause the family. She maintained her influence through 1862, writing forcefully in one letter, "Please don't think of joining Mr B's company. I will never consent."

Eventually, though, the dreaded news arrived: Lycurgus had volunteered. Never mind that it was only in the Home Guard, part of a "Local Defense" force organized in Richmond in the summer of 1863, comprised of clerks and laborers. It was still unacceptable to Susan. Initially, she used the toughest, most critical language she had ever employed in her letters to reprove him: "Pardon me for saying that I think you have acted very unwisely." Lycurgus's argument that the clerks who refused to join were "discreditable" did not wash with Susan. She replied, "No, I say they acted with true wisdom and are as brave at heart." She attempted to soften her tone near the end of the letter: "I do not censure you but I feel grieved to think you have done what was not compulsory."[20] Still, her message came through loud and clear: Lycurgus had made a mistake.

Susan's next letter conveyed more fear than criticism. She asked, "Now tell me *candidly*, are *you compelled* [to serve]? . . . Please tell me if you could not have avoided this trial to me?" If every man had to serve, that was different; she must "bow in submission to my fate." Still, fate could not claim her yet: "Oh, how I have been deceived in believing that you would ever be exempt from military duty." Noting that she had "strived hard for the past two years to be cheerful under all the trying circumstances that has passed over our country," she could not "rally" her spirits now to a vision of Lycurgus in uniform, fighting an "enemy outnumbering you." Most galling was the fact that Lycurgus had volunteered. "Now I want you to write me exactly what duties are expected of you, and if it is so that clerks are kept in the office to do government work, why *you preferred* to do *military* duty." Yet despite her many entreaties, Lycurgus remained in the Local Defense force and continued to toy with the idea of joining the regular army.[21]

One of the few fears the three women shared equally was the flight of slaves. Without slaves, the white women would have to carry the burden of household labor. This was a fact that none wanted to face. As Drew Faust argues, "In their reactions to slaves' departures, women revealed—to themselves as well as to posterity—the extent of their dependence on their servants." On a psychological level, she continues, "the elite Southerner's fundamental sense of identity depended on having others to perform life's menial tasks."[22]

Susan Caldwell's concerns reflected these realities. After Cinda left in June 1863, Susan warily watched the behavior of the slaves remaining in Warrenton. In her correspondence to Lycurgus in the fall and winter of 1862–63, she mentioned several times that there was a scarcity of slave servants. For instance, on December 28, 1862, she wrote that "I do not suppose there will be any hiring on New Years day—for there are but few servants in town, and even now they are talking about this new law after 1st of Jan meaning Emancipation bill—The darkies know everything." Susan predicted (or feared) as early as October the results of President Lincoln's Preliminary Emancipation Proclamation. She wrote to Lycurgus, "I feel much troubled in regard to Lincoln's proclamation in regard to the servants—I don't expect we will have one left anywhere in Va."[23]

Despite Susan's protestations and fears, a large number of slaves actually stayed on in Warrenton—at least until Union Major General William W. Averell's 2d Cavalry Division came to town in force in April 1863. Just before they departed, "about 150 servants left town on the cars." Moreover, "many more were to leave last night and regularly sold out." Susan did not know whom to blame, the Union soldiers or the slaves: "It looks as if the yankee soldiers were here for the very purpose of getting all off that would go—telling them Jeff Davis intended arresting all free and slave and making them either go into the army or work in the cotton fields." Were the slaves themselves to blame? Susan described the parting scene: "The negroes were as bold as they could be—those who were house keeping had auctions and sold out all their goods." Either way, between 100 and 200 slaves left town, and Susan stated the plain truth: "I dont think there will be many servants left."[24]

The fear and distrust now exposed between master and slave tainted their relations. The Caldwells most important slave, Lucy, had stayed on after her son George went to the Union army in March 1862, after Cinda left in June 1862, and even after the mass exodus of slaves in April 1863. Did this loyalty impress Susan? Not in the least. She wrote to Lycurgus, "Aunty Lucy seems faithful—but I dont feel like trusting any servant." Further signs of great loyalty had been shown by the slave John, who on two occasions in February 1863 had hidden a black colt from marauding Union patrols.[25] But these good deeds did not allay Susan's fears. Like many slave owners, she found herself worrying about the flight of her slaves rather than focusing on the devotion shown by Lucy and John (especially compared to Cinda, a free black who had left with Susan's wedding dress).

For the Bucks, a sign of trouble came in June 1862. While enduring the second Union occupation of their house and town, their trusted black employee, Rob Roy (described by the editor of Lucy's diary as a "free Negro"), took the side of the occupiers in a discussion one morning. Lucy wrote in her diary, "Rob Roy in whom we had so much confidence [is] even espousing the cause of the Yankee. I never was half so mad in my life."[26] The next year the entire household of slaves would flee for the Union lines.

The June 1863 day began with mystery. Lucy awoke at 5 A.M., finding no fires going and hearing no movement downstairs. She heard her father say to her mother, " 'All gone, horses and all.' " Every black servant, slave and free, had left, from the faithful cook Mahala and five of her six children to the inestimable Rob Roy. They had sneaked out of the house in the dead of night, loading all their baggage on three horses and setting out just before dawn. They did not travel alone; Mr. Kiger's servants fled too. What bothered the Bucks was not only the flight of their slaves but also the loss of the horses. Lucy wrote of her "wonder at their dexterity in baffling so successfully all suspicion of their movements and indignation at their ingratitude in taking the horses when they knew they were our main dependence of support." Supposedly, the horses were worth $16,000.

Lucy's father would not let the matter rest. He rode off to the Union camp at Winchester, where he met with General Robert Milroy and requested the return of his horses. In the odd legality that marked this war, Milroy partially acquiesced, giving Buck two of his horses but leaving the third with the former servants as their "lawful hire" since January. Buck also spoke with his servants, who said "they had no idea of leaving until noon that day before." Apparently, they heard Grandma Buck say all the slaves should be sent south, and when they saw a wagon going to the Kiger home, they assumed the worst and fled. Lucy did not believe the story, but she did not suspect them of plotting their escape for some time, either. Instead, she alternated between sympathy and condemnation, writing in her diary, "Poor miserable creatures! I do pity them rushing so blindly to a fate that they little foresee." She could afford to be charitable in her feelings because nearby family members and neighbors sent their slaves—Eliza, Evelyne, and Armanda—to help the Bucks with chores. Also, their sole remaining black employee, the "freeman" Gilbert, stayed on, declaring his "ignorance of the exodus."[27]

Tee Edmonds also recorded the flight of a slave in her diary, but had only a sarcastic comment as editorial. In May 1862 the slave named Charles ran away. Actually, he went to see his wife (destination unstated) and never returned. Tee wrote, "Charles broke the chains of bondage Saturday night. . . . Of Course he has gone to Heaven on Earth piloted by the Yankee Angels." Tee could afford to be smug, because the Edmondses still had slaves working for them.[28]

Despite occasional occupations by Union troops, military service for loved ones, the flight of slaves, and the constant influence of the war on their daily lives, the three women in this study remained loyal to the Southern cause in the second year of the war. Each had faced trials in her own style. As the war moved into its third and eventually its fourth years, the women would face even greater challenges to their strength and their support for the cause when they met the stiffest tests—death and destruction.

NOTES

1. Buck, *Diary*, January 12, 1863, 165–66; January 13, 1863, 167–68; January 14, 1863, 168–69.

2. Rable, *Civil Wars*, 209.

3. Edmonds, *Journals*, November 1, 1862, 123; November 2, 1862, 123–24; November 3, 1862, 124.

4. Ibid., November 4, 1862, 124–25; November 5, 1862, 125. The editor of the *Journals*, Nancy Chappelear Baird, notes that Frank Vizetelly worked for the *Illustrated London News* and was the "only special artist to accompany the Confederate forces." She does not give a name for the *New York Times* reporter. Edmonds, *Journals*, 256, endnote 23.

5. Edmonds, *Journals*, November 5, 1862, 125; November 8 and 10, 1862, 126; November 16 and 18, 126–27; November 25, 1862, 127. Contemporaries often remarked on Hancock's good looks. See David Jordan, *Winfield Scott Hancock: A Soldier's Life* (Bloomington, 1996) 11, 17, 54, and 57.

6. Edmonds, *Journals*, November 26, 1862, 127; November 29, 1862, 128.

7. Jeffrey D. Wert, *Mosby's Rangers* (New York, 1990), map on front flap, 37–39 (quotations on 39); Ash, *When the Yankees Came*, 92–93.

8. Michael P. Musick, *6th Virginia Cavalry* (Lynchburg, 1990), 112. Edward Gilbert "Bud" Edmonds, Tee's older brother by three years, joined Company A on September 20, 1861; Ben. J. Sydnor "Syd" Edmonds, Tee's younger brother by four years, joined Company A on July 24, 1861, at the age of eighteen; see Musick, *6th Virginia Cavalry*, 4–35, for movements of the 6th Virginia Cavalry from July 1861 to May 1863. Samples of Syd's visits home are in Edmonds, *Journals*, June 15, 1862, 99, September 5–7, 1862, 111–12, October 10, 1862, 121, and

December 25, 1862, 129; samples of Bud's visits are in Edmonds, *Journals*, August 9, 1862, 107, August 26, 1862, 109, September 6, 1862, 111, November 8, 1862, 126, and December 25, 1862, 129. For examples of Union troops almost catching Confederate soldiers at Belle Grove, see Edmonds, *Journals*, May 29, 1862, 94, August 25, 1862, 109, and May 6, 1863, 144.

9. Edmonds, *Journals*, February 10, 1863, 132–33. See Chapter 4 for a description of the first Union occupation of Belle Grove.

10. Ibid., January 26, 1863, 131; February 11, 1863, 133; February 23, 1863, 134; March 23, 1863, 135.

11. Ibid., July 22, 1862, 106; July 3, 1862, 103; September 6, 1862, 111–12; December 25, 1862, 129; and January 1, 1863, 130.

12. Buck, *Diary*, January 1, 1863, 160–61.

13. Ibid., January 19, 1863, 170; April 3, 1863, 177; and April 13, 1863, 180.

14. Edmonds, *Journals*, endnotes on 254 (note 30) and 256 (note 26).

15. In February 1862 a longtime acquaintance, Armistead Chappelear, made clear to his friends his interest in Tee. She did not return the interest. She wrote in her diary, "He would dearly love to have me blush for him. ha! ha! the idea!" Ibid., February 16, 1862, 67. Armistead never gave up, despite receiving little encouragement from Tee over the years. They married in 1870.

As for the other admirers, see Chapter 2 for the story of Wirt Lemert; and Edmonds, *Journals*, September 12, 1862, 114, on Douglas Gibson and September 8, 1862, 113, on Lieutenant Gwynell. According to historian Steve Woodworth, there was no Gwynell in the 8th Georgia. There was, however, a Melvin Dwinell, so Tee did not even get the name right. The source is a private note to the author.

Admiration ran both ways. When Tee met a soldier nicknamed "Little Peake," she thought highly of everything but his age. She wrote, "I believe I should have set my cap, if he were older. Oh, such flashing eyes and kind, sweet smile." Edmonds, *Journal*, September 29, 1862, 119.

16. Edmonds, *Journals*, September 15, 1857, 6; Buck, *Diary*, December 18, 1862, 155; Lois W. Banner, *American Beauty* (Chicago, 1983), 48 and 46 for quotations, 45–65 for a chapter on "The Ideal Woman."

17. Buck, *Diary*, January 19, 1863, 170; February 14, 1863, 173; March 17, 1863, 174; April 3, 1863, 177; and April 11, 1863, 179.

18. Ibid., November 1, 1862, 146, and October 31, 1862, 146.

19. Caldwell, *Letters*: On the children's health see Susan Caldwell to Lycurgus Caldwell, June 18, 1862, 133; Susan Caldwell to Lycurgus Caldwell, June 25, 1862, 137; Susan Caldwell to Lycurgus Caldwell, October 12, 1862, 150. On Lycurgus's health, see Susan Caldwell to Lycurgus Caldwell, November 29, 1862, 158. On Susan's health, see Susan Caldwell to Lycurgus Caldwell, February 5, 1863, 174, and Susan Caldwell to Lycurgus Caldwell, May 31, 1863, 190. Susan frequently had bad headaches.

On the baby's walking, see Susan Caldwell to Lycurgus Caldwell, December 18, 1862, 165. On high prices but the relative security of the family, see Susan Caldwell to Lycurgus Caldwell, June 29, 1862, 140, and Susan Caldwell to Lycurgus Caldwell, February 22, 1863, 177; Susan Caldwell to Lycurgus Caldwell, November 29, 1862, 155, for mention of the farm. On silence from Lycurgus, see Susan Caldwell to Lycurgus Caldwell, November 29, 1862, 158; Susan Caldwell to Lycurgus Caldwell, December 14, 1862, 162; and Susan Caldwell to Lycurgus Caldwell, July 13, 1863, 192. Susan scolded in the November 29 letter, "I have written you some four letters—would that I could get one line from you."

Her comment on the "unholy war" is found in a letter to Lycurgus dated June 29, 1862, 140. The Union army raids of April and May are described in Susan Caldwell to Lycurgus Caldwell, April 20, 1863, 186–87; Susan Caldwell to Lycurgus Caldwell, April 27, 1863, 187; Susan Caldwell to Lycurgus Caldwell, April 29, 1863, 188; Susan Caldwell to Lycurgus Caldwell, May 31, 1863, 189.

20. Ibid., Susan Caldwell to Lycurgus Caldwell, October 10, 1862, 157–58; Susan Caldwell to Lycurgus Caldwell, Wednesday Night, June 17, 1863, 191–92; Susan Caldwell to Lycurgus Caldwell, July 13, 1863, 192–93.

21. Ibid., Susan Caldwell to Lycurgus Caldwell, July 13, 1863, 192–93. For more on Lycurgus's military service, see Susan Caldwell to Lycurgus Caldwell, July 19, 1863, 195, Susan Caldwell to Lycurgus Caldwell, September 12, 1863, 197, and Susan Caldwell to Lycurgus Caldwell, September 22, 1863, 198–200.

22. Faust, *Mothers of Invention*, 77.

23. Caldwell, *Letters*: Susan Caldwell to Lycurgus Caldwell, June 9, 1862, 128; Susan Caldwell to Lycurgus Caldwell, November 29, 1862, 160; Susan Caldwell to Lycurgus Caldwell, April 29, 1863, 188; Susan Caldwell to Lycurgus Caldwell, December 28, 1862, 167; Susan Caldwell to Lycurgus Caldwell, October 6, 1862, 156.

24. Ibid., Susan Caldwell to Lycurgus Caldwell, April 29, 1863, 188.

25. Ibid., Susan Caldwell to Lycurgus Caldwell, June 9, 1862, 128 and 131; Susan Caldwell to Lycurgus Caldwell, April 29, 1862, 188; Susan Caldwell to Lycurgus Caldwell, February 5, 1863, 175; Susan Caldwell to Lycurgus Caldwell, February 22, 1863, 178.

26. Buck, *Diary*, June 18, 1862, 103; editor's afterword, 303.

27. Ibid., June 9 and 10, 1863, 191–92.

28. Edmonds, *Journals*, May 22, 1862, 92.

Chapter Eight

The High-Water Mark
of the Confederacy?
Winter Quarters, Chancellorsville, and Gettysburg

Across a wide field, John Worsham and the fifty-two men of F Company, 21st Virginia Infantry, watched dismounted Union cavalrymen pull apart fences and move toward some farm buildings. The Union troops had eight artillery guns wheeling into line. What should the small company of "substitutes and conscripts" do? They were outnumbered and outgunned. The veteran and new company commander, William A. Pegram, turned to the few remaining survivors of the Old F and said he had two choices: "attack or retreat." He chose the former, shouting, "Forward! double quick!" The men charged across the field toward the farm buildings.[1]

F Company poured over two fences still standing, then ran into the barnyard, all the while catching fire from the Union cavalry. The company quickly secured the farm buildings and set up a defensive line along more undisturbed fences. Inside the barnyard lay three dead Confederates, at the cost of fifteen Union soldiers killed, wounded, or captured. The Union cavalry kept increasing in size and the Union artillery began firing on the farm buildings, but F Company held a newly formed defensive line along a road. The firing continued on for hours, until nightfall. Then the Union troops withdrew.

As Worsham assessed the losses, which now included the new captain, William Pegram, he considered this brief battle "the best fight of F Company during the war." Why? They had stopped the lead elements of General John Buford's twelve regiments of cavalry from capturing the tiny river crossing at Williamsport on

July 6, 1863. They had protected General Lee's "entire wagon train" and done the fighting with little assistance except for some conscripted "armed wagoneers" and a regiment that had been guarding the Army of Northern Virginia's train. The "new men . . . behaved like veterans, and every one did his duty, and they covered themselves with glory."[2]

This dramatic yet relatively unknown firefight illustrates a theme of this chapter: Gettysburg was a *big* battle of the war for the Army of Northern Virginia, but not *the* battle. That interpretation came later, begun by some veterans but burnished over the years by countless retellings (the most recent popular treatment being the 4-hour movie, *Gettysburg*).[3] There were so many moments of terror and exultation, that to single out one battle as *the* battle for most of the soldiers is an egregious error. As the patient reader has seen, the veterans placed such adjectives as "best," "biggest," "hardest," or "hottest" on many different firefights, some large and well known, others small and unknown. Worsham's description of the importance of Williamsport to F Company is a prime example. Here is a soldier who had marched hundreds of miles with Jackson, fought hard in all the major conflicts of the Valley Campaign of 1862, and survived the inferno of Cedar Mountain (131 casualties out of 284 men). Still, he regarded the 3-hour battle at Williamsport as the "best fight of F Company during the war."

None of this denies the importance of Gettysburg. It was a huge and costly battle for the Confederates. It was Lee's last northern offensive. It temporarily disheartened some in the South and relieved some in the North, and it helped buy time for the North to grow stronger while the South grew weaker. But it was not the climactic battle of the war for the individuals in this study or for the majority of soldiers in the Army of Northern Virginia. It was just another big battle, as was Chancellorsville; and before Chancellorsville, the army had a chance to rest, reflect, and reenergize in the winter of 1863.

The soldier's soldier, William T. Poague, spent much of the winter at a "comfortable camp on the Gay Mont Estate owned by a Mr. Bernard" (near Port Royal), remembering later that "our larder was fairly well supplied." In March, Poague finally got his long-overdue promotion to major. This meant he had to leave his beloved Rockbridge Battery, and after a special prayer meeting came the farewells. Years later, he recalled that evening with great fondness, calling it "one of the happiest hours of my life."[4]

So it was with a heavy heart that Poague left his old battery, but he quickly found pleasure serving under Major David G. McIntosh in the reorganized Corps Reserve (Artillery) of the 3d Corps. Almost immediately he and Captain William P. Hurt's Alabama Hardaway battery were sent to watch for Union gunboats coming up the Rappahannock River. Finding none, Hurt and Poague found a good pasture for their horses, where they were trained and groomed daily. When the men rejoined the 3d Corps, Colonel Walker praised the officers for the quality of their teams of horses. In writing for his children, Poague saw an opportunity in this story to impress upon them the importance of doing one's task, no matter how lowly, with care and diligence. When Poague was given command of a new battalion of artillery after the Battle of Chancellorsville, he attributed it to his earlier effort to get the horses in shape: "My training on the [family] farm where I had learned about the care and handling of horses, stood me in good stead."[5]

The three other soldiers in this study returned home that winter. Second Sergeant John Worsham and the tiny remnants of his beloved F Company finally got rest and relief. In January 1863 they were ordered back to Richmond to recruit and train new soldiers for their company. They did this job well, growing from four men to fifty-two, although the new members of the company were "conscripts of boyhood and middle age and some old substitutes." Of the original company, only six men were fit to return to active duty. The men trained through mid-June, thus missing the Battle of Chancellorsville. On June 22, 1863, the remade F Company "bid family and friends good-bye" and rode the cars to Staunton en route to joining the Army of Northern Virginia.[6]

After setting up winter camp near Hewlett on the Virginia Central Railroad, Private Henry "Robin" Berkeley and his cousin John Lewis Berkeley got permission to go home. They left on December 27, 1862, and returned to camp on January 4, 1863. Robin could not have been more fortunate in the selection of his battery's winter camp; it was in the northern reaches of his native Hanover County, approximately 10 miles from his family home.

After returning to camp, the two young men continued their relaxed ways, staying in camp during the day and going out "nearly every night to visit homefolks, friends and neighbors." On January 14 the spell was broken. At 8:00 P.M. a courier arrived with a note from Bob Winston, a messmate. They had to report to camp as soon as possible—the battery had been ordered to Fredericksburg. Robin and John at first thought it was "a joke" of Winston's, but they concluded it was the truth. When they finally left, at 2:00 A.M., the young people had "sad and gloomy faces, and the old . . . thoughtful and prayerful looks."[7] Fortunately, the movement toward Massaponax Church in Spotsylvania County proved to be only activity, not battle. After a week there, the battery returned to the original winter camp near Hewlett, and the "boys" even enjoyed a postponed "candy stew" party on January 27.

The good times continued for the next three months. Robin mentioned a "big snowball" fight, a night of merriment (drinking), and a large, elaborate camp dinner party given for the "ladies . . . old folks and the children of Hanover County." The dinner took place in the commanding officers' double tent, with servants to attend to a guest list that included General William Nelson Pendleton, who had a "cannon fired to let the ladies see the effects of a shell." Robin also found time to be confirmed into the Episcopal Church. He never mentioned whether this was a long-delayed plan or belated response to the revivalism that had swept through his battery in the fall.

When the camp was finally broken up on April 30, Robin found himself marching back toward Massaponax Church. His battery moved three more times near Fredericksburg in the next week, one part of the feinting of Confederate Major General Jubal Early and Union General John Sedgwick's divisions while the bulk of each side's army slugged it out at Chancellorsville. Consequently, Robin's battery, like John Worsham's company, did not see action at Chancellorsville. [8]

Lieutenant Fred Fleet was close to home that winter too, but he had a virtually impossible task in actually getting there. Stuck in winter camp at Burton's Farm, he complained about his assignment and the furlough policy. Fred considered joining the cavalry, but rejected the idea because he felt "there was no discipline" in that branch. As usual, his "Ma" provided the best advice: "I would prefer you staying where the Hand of Providence has placed you, than see you exposed as I see some poor fellows."[9]

The furlough policy was another matter. Pa and Ma were furious when they saw Fred's commanding officer, Captain James Smith, in the neighborhood. Smith had decided to gather up those absent without leave and offer $50 bounties for enlisting. Pa was livid over the furlough policy, writing to Fred, "I am almost fretted enough at your not coming home to advise you to resign your commission, and join a cavalry company." Pa encouraged Fred to speak to General Wise directly, reminding him that Pa was "one of his earliest and fastest friends." Although Ma missed him, she advised him not to resign his commission.[10]

So Fred waited and watched as General Wise had a garden dug. Harrison Ball, a deserter, returned without penalty under the government's amnesty proclamation. Ball's return brought the company up to its full strength of 81, which had "not occurred since we have been in service." Fred finally got his furlough in late February; it was his first in almost a year. His eight days at home revived his spirits. He wrote a glowing characterization of the Southern army in March 1863: "What a difference in our army now & this time last year. . . . This year has witnessed no defeats to our armies, but victory has been granted us." He urged his father to plant "large crops of grain of all sorts this year," because he feared "we are in much more danger of scarcity of food than we are from the enemy."

Fred had a moment of excitement when the 26th marched to Williamsburg in late April. Finding the town deserted, however, the 26th returned to Burton's Farm and its lonely defense of Richmond. Thus Fred's unit once again missed the "big show," further north at Chancellorsville in May.[11]

None of the soldiers in this study participated significantly in General Lee's greatest offensive victory, the Battle of Chancellorsville. Worsham was recruiting in Richmond, Berkeley marched back and forth near Fredericksburg, and Fleet remained at Burton's Farm. Only Major Poague fought at Chancellorsville, but even he regarded his role there as "very little to do." His batteries were largely in the rear of General Jackson's fast-marching columns, only getting close to action on May 3, when they stood ready to assist in the firing on the Chancellor house (it had been the temporary headquarters of Union Major General Hooker). Poague's batteries suffered no casualties, unlike many others. A short time after the battle, Poague received uplifting news; he would get his own battalion. Tempering his joy, however, were the deaths of General Jackson, General Frank Paxton of the Stonewall Brigade, a relative of the family, John Henry Paxton, and Captain Greenlee Davidson of the Letcher Artillery. The last three men were from Rockbridge County, and Poague wrote to his children that "the blood of these three soldiers was of the same strain as that flowing in your veins." Poague also told a story, perhaps apocryphal, of a conversation he had had with General Paxton just before the battle. Paxton had said, "Ah, Poague, if the rest of us poor sinners had 'Old Jack's' religion and assurance of faith, with what little thought of personal safety we would go into battle." Paxton "had settled that great question by a confession of Christ."[12]

Poague had little time to reflect on such timeless questions in May. Soon he and his battalion joined the Army of Northern Virginia as it marched northwest toward Pennsylvania. With a much larger army defending Washington and an unrelenting siege of Vicksburg in the West, President Jefferson Davis and General Robert E. Lee had little choice but to take the war to the North again. If they could keep ahead of the Army of the Potomac, they could procure supplies in Pennsylvania and Maryland, keep the Union army away from Richmond, and weaken the resolve of the Northern people. General Lee got his three corps into Pennsylvania by mid-June, but with his key cavalry general, J. E. B. Stuart, swinging east and north around the entire Army of the Potomac, Lee did not know the exact location of the Union army. When solid intelligence told him that the Army of the Potomac had assembled on his flank, in Frederick, Maryland, he knew he must concentrate his three corps and either attack or be ready for attack. The most convenient place to concentrate his forces was in the Lutheran seminary town of Gettysburg.

For the next three days, July 1 to 3, Lee attacked portions of the Army of the Potomac, now under the command of the Mexican War veteran, General George Meade. The Army of Northern Virginia won on the first day, but the Union forces held firm on the next two. At the close of the day on July 3, with General George Pickett's division shattered after the failed assault on Cemetery Ridge, Lee ordered a retreat back to the safety of Virginia.[13]

Robin Berkeley watched much of the battle from the north side of town, assigned to General Richard S. Ewell's 2d Corps. Robin himself had a special role at Gettysburg; he served as a lookout for his battery from the cupola of Gettysburg Seminary. Again, though, his unit was not engaged. As he wrote in his diary, "A great battle has been fought and lost, and our battery has *not* fired a single shot."[14]

After encamping on Seminary Ridge on the night of July 1, Robin awoke to see part of the ill-fated Iverson's Brigade (Rodes's Division, 2d Corps), "seventy-nine North Carolinians laying dead in a straight line. It was perfectly dressed." The same day he also saw the "body of a Yankee . . . [whose] head, arms and about one-half of his ribs had been thrown against a fence . . . while some 10 feet off the lower part of the body had been thrown into a mud hole in the road." On July 4, Robin had to walk six miles from Gettysburg before he found fresh water. Along the way "every house, shed, barn and hut was filled with wounded, dying and dead men, both Yanks and Confederates." His battery left Gettysburg that night in a hard rain.[15]

For Major William T. Poague, Gettysburg was a much bigger affair, complete with "hot" battle scenes and a few key conversations with famous generals that have become standard sources for students. Poague spent most of July 1 with his battalion at Cashtown, awaiting orders from General J. J. Pettigrew. When they were finally called up, the battle around Cemetery Ridge had nearly ended, so his batteries saw no action that day. The next day proved to be more of the same. General William Nelson Pendleton ordered Poague's battalion "a little further to the right and further to the front," where it stayed, never firing its guns.

On this same day, however, Poague had two conversations with General Robert E. Lee. In the morning, Lee asked Poague if he had seen General James Longstreet or his men. Poague had not, and as Lee turned to leave, he said to a courier, "I wonder where General Longstreet can be." Poague used this conversation, Colonel Henderson's article, and the "belief well-nigh universal among Confederates" to blame Longstreet for the loss at

Gettysburg.[16] He would have plenty of company in his belief, particularly Virginia veterans who wrote about the war in later years, including prominent generals Jubal Early and Fitz Lee. But Longstreet had his defenders too, including another Confederate general and postwar apostate, William Mahone.[17]

Longstreet was not alone in suffering Lee's censure that day. In the afternoon, Poague's men spotted a mass of soldiers moving 3 to 4 miles away. Poague immediately sent the news to General Lee, who then called him in to give him a fuller report. Lee asked specific questions about numbers, designations, and direction. Poague could not answer a single one, and Lee's final question pointedly expressed his impatience: "Well, Major, what do you know?" Poague could merely reply, "Only what I reported." Lee then lectured him on the importance of obtaining all the details before making a report. Forty years later, Poague still felt the sting of Lee's words: "Although I felt conscious of no failure of duty under the circumstances . . . I was mortified."[18]

Despite Poague's embarrassment, Lee appeared to harbor no grudge the next day. He "often stopped" where Poague's battalion placed itself the morning of July 3, not chatting with the major but simply surveying the field before riding on. Poague had ten guns spread over two positions about 400 yards apart. Two batteries were at the "junction" of Longstreet's left wing and Hill's right wing, giving these batteries "the very best position to witness the attack."[19]

Poague's orders were simple: fire at the signal, stop until Pickett's brigade reached the crest of Cemetery Ridge, and then bring his guns up behind the troops. Poague witnessed the historic assault of Pickett's men from a distance. He saw a few troops reach the crest, but most fell back. As his batteries prepared to move up, he grew more alarmed by the increasing number of men falling back toward his guns.

As the men of Pickett's division streamed back, Poague had his memorable conversation—or virtual non-conversation—with General Pickett. Poague rode up to Pickett and asked him if he should still move his batteries up. Pickett made no reply; he "continued to gaze with an expression on his face of sadness and pain." Poague then saw a horseman carrying a Virginia flag ride back and forth along the stone wall. He asked Pickett if that flag was

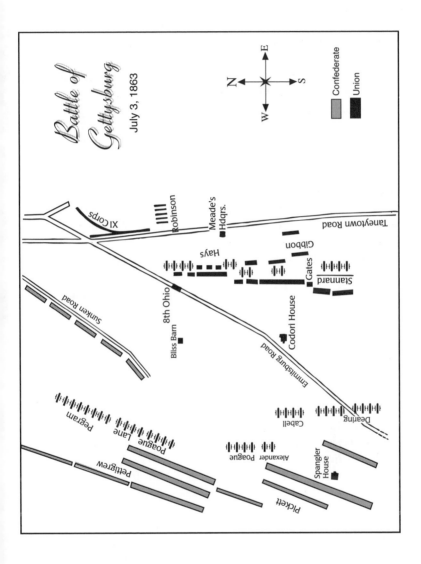

carried by friend or foe. Still no reply. He tried a third time, asking, "What do you think I ought to do under the circumstances?" At last the general answered him, "I think you had better save your guns." Then Pickett rode off.[20]

As it turned out, the flag belonged to aides of the victorious General Alexander Hays, who rode up and down the Union lines with the captured Virginia flags. Then, as hundreds of men streamed by Poague's position, General Lee and General Longstreet attempted to rally the broken and wounded men to form a line along Seminary Ridge. Although Lee and Longstreet kept their composure (as did Poague), Pickett had "tear-filled eyes," according to historian Lesley Gordon. He had failed that day and he knew it.[21]

Eventually, order was restored and lead elements of the army began the slow, hard retreat in the pouring rain back to Virginia. The accounts of Poague, Berkeley, and Worsham make no mention of Gettysburg as a turning point; rather, they offer detailed descriptions of troop movements after the battle. Worsham adds the drama of F Company's stand at Williamsport on July 6, but after that, the story is one of troop movements.[22]

Fred Fleet did not even mention the battle in correspondence with his family; his concerns were his dull posting and a rare firefight for his regiment. In August a Union ironclad and two wooden gunboats sailed past the "submarine batteries" on the James River. The 26th Virginia and some artillery pieces were ordered to fire on the ships. Apparently, the firing proved sufficient to convince their captains to reverse course. Even better, Fred's regiment "came out entirely unhurt." Shortly after this engagement, Fred received a long letter from his cousin, Charles B. Fleet, whose battery had fought at Gettysburg. Charles described the battle in detail, including Pickett's Charge. He concluded that "in a campaign of 19 days, I believe we endured as many hardships as any army ever did in the same length of time."[23]

Beaten but not vanquished, the Army of Northern Virginia limped back to Virginia. Perhaps Fred Fleet spoke for all four soldiers in this study in a letter he sent home in mid-July. Describing the Confederate losses of Vicksburg and Port Hudson as "tragedies," he offered a pessimistic prognosis: "I fear this will be a long war."[24]

NOTES

1. Worsham, *One of Jackson's Foot Cavalry*, 151.

2. Ibid., 152–53.

3. See Carol Reardon, *Pickett's Charge in History and Memory* (Chapel Hill, 1997), 38–61; Gallagher, *The Confederate War*, 33–41.

4. Poague, *Gunner with Stonewall*, 61, 62, and 63.

5. Ibid., 64–67; Wise, *The Long Arm of Lee*, 1:419–21.

6. Worsham, *One of Jackson's Foot Cavalry*, 140–42.

7. Berkeley, *Diary*, January 5–14, 1863, 41, and January 15, 1863, 42.

8. Ibid., January 16 and 27, 1863, 42; January 28, February 8 and 13, 1863, 43–44; April 30, May 1, 2, and 7, 1863, 45; and footnotes 1 and 2 on 45.

9. Fleet, *Green Mount*, Fred Fleet to Pa, November 19, 1862, 184; Fred Fleet to Pa, February 20, 1863, 206; Ma to Fred Fleet, February 17, 1863, 206.

10. Ibid., Pa to Fred Fleet, February 17, 1863, 204; Ma to Fred Fleet, February 17, 1863, 203–6.

11. Ibid., Fred Fleet to Pa, February 20, 1863, 206–7; Benny's journal, February 28, 1863, 207; Fred Fleet to Ma, March 19, 1863, 209–10; Fred Fleet to Pa, April 22, 1863, 218–20; Fred Fleet to Ma, April 25, 1863, 220–23.

12. Poague, *Gunner with Stonewall*, 64–67; Ernest B. Furgurson, *Chancellorsville, 1863: The Souls of the Brave* (New York, 1992), 246–50; see also Stephen W. Sears, *Chancellorsville* (New York, 1997).

13. McPherson, *Battle Cry of Freedom*, 647–65. The literature on the Battle of Gettysburg could fill a library. The longest modern monograph is Edwin B. Coddington, *The Gettysburg Campaign: A Study in Command* (1968; reprint, Dayton, 1979). Dozens of provocative essays on this major battle are brought together in three outstanding books edited by Gary W. Gallagher: *The First Day at Gettysburg: Essays on Confederate and Union Leadership* (Kent, OH, 1992), *The Second Day at Gettysburg: Essays on Confederate and Union Leadership* (Kent, OH, 1993), and *The Third Day at Gettysburg and Beyond* (Chapel Hill, 1994).

14. Berkeley, *Diary*, July 1, 2, 3, and 4, 1863, 46–52 (quotation on 52).

15. Ibid., July 2, 3, and 4, 1863, 50–51.

16. Poague, *Gunner with Stonewall*, 70 (quotation) and 73.

17. Longstreet had more defenders in the last quarter of the twentieth century than he had in the 100 years after the war. Students should start with William Garrett Piston, *Lee's Tarnished Lieutenant: James Longstreet and His Place in Southern History* (Athens, GA, 1987) and Jeffrey Wert, *General James Longstreet: The Confederacy's Most Controversial Soldier, A Biography* (New York, 1993).

18. Poague, *Gunner with Stonewall*, 72–73.

19. Ibid., 73–75 (quotation on 75).

20. Ibid., 75. A riveting account from a soldier who charged the wall and survived is William N. Wood, *Reminiscences of Big I* (Wilmington, NC, 1992), 46–47 and 123–24.

21. George R. Stewart, *Pickett's Charge: A Microhistory of the Final Attack at Gettysburg, July 3, 1863* (1959; reprint, Dayton, 1980), 230, 287, 246, and 253–59. Two recent studies of Pickett add varied interpretations to the dramatic event. Lesley Gordon uses the Poague story in her account and stands squarely with Stewart, arguing, "Pickett stood transfixed in horror and disbelief as his Virginia division crumbled before his tear-filled eyes. In his self-absorbed despair, he failed to answer the needs of his battered troops." Gordon, *General George E. Pickett in Life and Legend* (Chapel Hill, 1998), 116. Carol Reardon presents a different picture of Pickett at that moment, quoting from his defenders and detractors to show the clash of competing memories. She also criticizes George Stewart for treating "all those disconnected threads as equally valid historical sources." Reardon, *Pickett's Charge*, 154–61 and 207. While Poague's recollection of the conversation is the only one available, the position of Pickett to the rear of his command and his temporary lack of composure after the failed charge are generally agreed upon.

22. Poague, *Gunner with Stonewall*, 75–77; Berkeley, *Diary*, July 5–20, 1863, 52–55; Worsham, *One of Jackson's Foot Cavalry*, 154–56.

23. Fleet, *Green Mount*, Fred Fleet to Ma, July 16, 1863, 251–52; Ma to Fred Fleet, July 26, 1863, 253; Fred Fleet to Pa, August 7, 1863, 255–56; C. B. Fleet to Fred Fleet, August 8, 1863, 257–59 (quotation on 259); C. B. Fleet to Fred Fleet, August 20, 1863, 260–62.

24. Ibid., Fred Fleet to Ma, July 16, 1863, 251.

CHAPTER NINE

A TIME TO REST AND REBUILD, AUGUST 1863–APRIL 1864

AFTER THE ARMY of Northern Virginia safely crossed the Potomac River, it went into "summer camp" at Orange Court House and Montpelier, the old estate of President James Madison. It was a time for resting, recuperating, refitting, and recruiting. Meade's Army of the Potomac was on the move too, but closer to Washington. No one knew when or where Meade might attempt to strike. In the meantime, the tired soldiers of the Army of Northern Virginia began to revive and, for John Worsham's 21st Virginia Infantry, it proved to be the "longest rest of the war."

To keep the men sharp (and to help restore fallen spirits), General Lee ordered a "Grand Review" of the 2d Corps in September. On the fourth, tens of thousands of Confederate soldiers marched past their proud leader, brass shining and flags flying.[1] For one glorious summer day, the battle-weary veterans could suppress their thoughts about Gettysburg and all their fallen comrades and believe once more that the old dream of Southern independence could yet be realized.

Many of these same men did not put all their faith in their leaders and their cause. They sought a greater security in the hands of God, as a massive religious revival showed. Thousands turned out to hear preachers give the word of God, and then veterans and recruits alike dedicated their lives to Christ. John Worsham described how the men built log seats for 2,000 and a wooden stage, then lit the evening revival services by burning firewood in iron hoops placed atop stakes 15 feet high. As a "red glare" shone out from the stage, the congregation would make "hill and dell ring" as they sang hymns.[2]

Not all the soldiers in this study could enjoy this needed respite as much as John Worsham. Major William T. Poague suffered from "chills and fever" in August and September, which he clearly remembered "interfered with full enjoyment of the long season of rest and the opportunities for social enjoyment within reach of us in a most hospitable and cultivated community." Poague felt well enough to exchange his new bay mare for a horse given to him by his father. Julia got Poague through the war, though after being stung by gravel during later engagements, she became skittish under fire, virtually "unmanageable in battle." Somehow man and horse survived the war, and Julia faithfully served the Poague family the rest of her days.[3]

Julia had her first exposure to fire during the Bristoe Station Campaign. On October 14, General A. P. Hill sent two brigades dashing into slaughter. Due to inadequate reconnaissance, Hill thought he had the opportunity to strike at the rear of the retreating 3d Corps. Thousands of Union men had crossed Broad Run and countless more waited on the riverbank, unaware of the approaching Confederate brigades. What Hill did not know, until the shooting began, was that three brigades of Major General G. K. Warren's 2d Corps were marching up to the area from the south. Their commanders quickly assembled the troops behind the railroad embankment of the Orange and Alexandria Railroad, effectively flanking the advancing Confederate brigades. Caught by a fierce enfilading fire, the Confederate generals had no choice but to attack. When the brigades charged across a field, however, the Union troops mowed them down. Over 1,300 Confederates were killed, wounded, or captured in a matter of minutes (Union casualties were approximately 600). The three Union brigades slipped across Broad Run that night, and the inconclusive Bristoe Station battle was over. There would be no repeat of the Second Battle of Manassas for General Lee.[4]

As always, Poague was present and fighting. In his memoir, he devoted only two paragraphs to the battle, emphasizing the flight of some Union soldiers when Poague's battalion surprised them with artillery shells: "such scampering and skeddaling was hardly ever seen." He gave less attention to the heavy losses of General John R. Cooke's and General W. W. Kirkland's brigades when they charged the Union troops protected by the railroad cut. Also, he did not describe the firing of his guns for two hours against a larger number of Union artillery pieces. He did mention that a few (five to be exact) of Colonel McIntosh's cannons were captured. He concluded, as other accounts did, with a story of his men chasing rabbits in the overgrown fields and stubby pine thickets: "Burying comrades and running rabbits at the same time. Such is war!"[5]

Rabbits were on John Worsham's mind, too. The 2d Brigade came to the battlefield too late to participate in any fighting. While lying down in a long straight line, preparing to attack, some men saw a rabbit running toward them. One of them caught it and a "wild yell burst from the men," destroying any element of surprise.[6] Robin Berkeley did not chase any rabbits, or at least he did not say so. His battery arrived at Bristoe Station around 5:00 P.M., too late for the battle. Robin noted, though, that General Hill had lost "five guns in McIntosh's Battalion by bad management." His critical view of Hill's performance was shared by many in the Army of Northern Virginia, including General Lee.[7]

The next several weeks brought two sharp defeats for the Army of Northern Virginia at Kelly's Ford and Rappahannock Station on November 7, then little more fighting until late November. On November 26, Meade's Army of the Potomac began to move. To prevent an attack on the Confederate right flank, the 2d Corps, under the temporary command of Jubal Early (Dick Ewell was sick), moved to Mine Run to stop them. On November 27, Major General Edward Johnson boldly led his single division into attack against six divisions of the Union 3d and 6th Corps scattered amid the piney woods surrounding Payne's Farm. John Worsham's 21st Virginia was in the thick of things again, sustaining four wounded in action that Worsham described as "general and heavy."[8] Nearby, Robin Berkeley's battery was not engaged. The unit was marching away from Payne's Farm on November 27, headed west toward Verdiersville. The battery was subsequently ordered to reverse direction and return to the fields near Payne's Farm. No fighting occurred on these days.[9]

For once, Poague did not take part in the battle. He did, however, see General Lee during those tense days in late November and thought he "looked more martial and imposing" than Poague had ever seen him. Another veteran, Lieutenant Colonel William W. Blackford, had a similar impression of Lee at this time. After Blackford made an early morning report to Lee, the general spoke firmly:

"If they don't attack us today we must attack them." Slapping his hand with a hairbrush, Lee again said: "We must attack them, sir! . . . You must exert yourselves."

The attack of Meade never took place; in fact, his army had begun to retreat. Lee did not attack either. Nevertheless, Blackford would never forget his meeting in November 1863 with General Lee, "his handsome face all aglow, and his eyes fairly flashing fire as he brandished his brush." With encounters like these, it is not surprising that the Army of Northern Virginia followed Lee to the bitter end in the muddy fields of Appomattox.[10]

After Mine Run, the Army of Northern Virginia went into winter quarters. John Worsham spent most of his time in camp near Mount Pisgah Church in Orange County. The men put up huts of wood or half wood and half tent, attended a church they had built, and in general found the campground "the most comfortable we had during the war." Worsham enjoyed the "sociability" of the camp and his hikes up Clark's Mountain, where he could see the Union tents in Culpeper County. He also tried to do the unusual for a man at this time—bathe every week! In his memoir, he describes in detail one winter day when he used an ax to cut a large hole in the ice, then "undressed, took a good bath, dressed, and . . . returned to camp." His only complaint was insufficient rations. For months the men lived on short rations, still carefully prepared by one of the 21st's black slave cooks, Archer or Ned or others unnamed. Worsham spoke for thousands of his Confederate veterans when he wrote, "None but the Confederate soldiers knows how they lived."[11]

For the month of December, Private Robin Berkeley of Kirkpatrick's Battery shared the camp at Mount Pisgah Church with Worsham's 21st Virginia. He, too, complained of short rations (his men sent their cook home), even on Christmas Day, when the meal "consisted of some soldier-bread and black rice and a piece of salted beef about two inches square." The mess drew lots for the beef; it was too small to divide. The only enjoyment came from some applejack that had been smuggled into camp. On December 31, however, the men got some "coffee, sugar and peaches," a rare treat.

On January 1, 1864, Nelson's Battalion was ordered to move almost due south to Frederick's Hall. Situated on the Virginia

Central Railroad between Gordonsville and Hanover Junction, it was much closer to Berkeley's home. It also meant that his battalion had to leave an established camp and erect a new one.[12] The men quickly fell to work clearing the ground, pitching tents, building a chimney, and constructing a stable. Although Robin did not get home as often as he had during the past winter, he did manage to secure a 7-day furlough in late January, a 48-hour leave in mid-February, and another 48-hour leave in late February. As a kindness to the men, officers turned 48-hour leaves into 3-day leaves by dating them the day after the men left. Of course, the men still had to pay a price for tardiness. When Robin returned twelve hours late from his 7-day furlough, his immediate superior, Lieutenant George Hobson, put him on the "broom squad" for four days. Robin did not hold this punishment against Hobson: "I would be perfectly willing to sweep camp a dozen mornings for one more day at home."

It is not surprising that Robin wanted to visit his large extended family. When at home, he saw numerous relatives; and when at camp, he wrote home regularly, including letters to his cousin and sweetheart, Nannie. Undoubtedly, this very closeness cast a pall over camp life for Robin, especially when the winter of 1863–64 was compared to the winter of 1862–63. In the earlier winter, wonderful dinners and parties with his family enlivened the long cold season. The later winter was broken up with frequent moves, including several difficult days in early February when his battery had been sent at night to Morton's Ford. For four nights they had no tents, while by day they made slow progress through mud. Morton's Ford proved to be a false alarm, so the battery was ordered to Orange Court House, where they set up another camp and then waited for their tents and baggage to follow.[13]

Given the additional rigors of this winter and the occasional pessimism expressed by Robin, it is not entirely surprising to read his gloomy prediction for the war. On February 28, after a day at church and a dinner with Uncle Landon, Robin confided to his diary the "great uncertainty of how this horrid and bloody war will end. It looks dark and very doubtful." The next day, Robin returned to camp and in his despair wrote, "Chances are I may never see home again. This horrid war is getting so bloody and so desperate."[14]

Although some readers may find Robin's fears justified, to others they might raise questions. Why was Robin so gloomy? After all, his battery had hardly been bloodied compared to what Poague's batteries had been through. Rank is not the issue here, because Worsham had been through plenty of tough battles. Some may argue that the difference lies in immediacy. Poague and Worsham were older men recalling their youth, and daily emotions are some of the hardest feelings to pinpoint. But Fred Fleet's letters did not display Robin's gloominess. The key differences are personality and circumstances. All the other writers are more upbeat, more sanguine than Robin Berkeley. Still, Robin is hardly a cynical pessimist; witness his description of the joyful evenings in the winter of 1862–63. What turned his doubt and worry into fear and foreboding was circumstance. He had seen plenty of evidence of war's hard hand, especially at Gettysburg. Little wonder that Robin feared that a grim fate was in store for his little-used artillery battery. It is equally understandable, then, that Fred Fleet would still ache for war, given that his unit had seen little action. Both Fred's wish and Robin's fears would soon be realized.

In the meantime, though, the two men went separate ways. Robin stayed in camp until April 23, except for a 3-day march to Chancellorsville in March. He passed his twenty-fourth birthday (March 27) in camp, his 2-year "met the Yankees in arms" anniversary (April 5), and a day (April 18) of "fasting and prayer" ordered by President Davis. He also grew closer to his messmates: "All these men were my friends; I loved them. They requited honorably my regards; we served and fought; we smiled and wept in concert." They also shared their fears: "Our anxiety is intense." When the battery finally moved out on April 23 and put the guns in position on the south bank of the Rapidan River, Robin could see "Yankee tents as far as the eye can reach." He wondered and he worried about the upcoming battle: "What a mighty host to keep back! Can we do it? We will try. Who of us will be left when peace comes?"[15]

For Lieutenant Fred Fleet, the fall finally brought relief from the boredom of Burton's Farm. Ordered to report to General Beauregard in Charleston, South Carolina, Wise's Brigade marched out on September 16 and rode the railroad to Charleston. General Wise's Brigade had orders to guard the land lying between the Ashley and Edisto rivers. General Beauregard reportedly told Wise that the section was critical to the defense of Charleston, though Fred wondered if Beauregard was "trying to tickle the old General's vanity by giving him what he supposes is the most dangerous position."[16]

At least, after three years of inactivity, the 26th Virginia finally found some action in Charleston. Unfortunately, the Christmas Day attack on the USS *Marblehead* ended in failure, with the loss to Wise's Brigade being three men killed or mortally wounded, nine men wounded, and two howitzers captured. The men were chased off by a small Union infantry force and the guns of the *Pawnee*—the same gunboat that John Worsham had fired at in 1861. The next engagement was a brief repulse of a Union attack on the Confederate line on February 10, 1864. The 26th Virginia had two men wounded—its first casualties in nearly three years of service.[17]

Ironically, the soldier in this study who most desired action by this stage of the war was not even there. Fred Fleet had gone home on furlough in early February, arriving at Green Mount on the same day that his regiment fought in Charleston. Fred spent his leave visiting family and friends, even finding time to go ice skating with Benny in what Benny called the "coldest weather since 1856 & 57."[18]

This was not the first time the Fleet brothers had been reunited. In December 1863, Benny had left for Charleston with a "box of clothes for the different soldiers," Fred's "old Black Trunk," and some "eatables." He left Richmond on Tuesday, December 15, and traveled by train and wagon to his brother's camp, arriving there on Friday, December 18. He found his brother "very well & looking very handsome, as fair as a lady & would be very like a lady but for his rank beard." Fred gave his brother the tour of the city, including the obligatory walk up the steps of St. Michael's steeple to look at Battery Wagner and Fort Sumter. The visit had to be cut short, however, when the 26th began its preparation for the intended attack on December 25. So Benny walked the five miles from camp to Charleston, bought a "pass" to walk around the city for twenty-five cents, and left on the northbound train on December 21.[19]

Fred's other highlight in Charleston was his reassignment to the headquarters staff. In November he was appointed Assistant Adjutant General of the 26th Virginia, serving on the small staff of an officer he admired, Colonel Powhatan Robertson Page. With the appointment came a temporary promotion to captain.[20] Yet the new job and temporary promotion probably meant little to Fred when he returned to his unit in late March 1864. He had just seen war's evil, unpredictable hand in the most unlikely of places—home.

There had been tension throughout his furlough, with Benny called on frequently to serve in the Home Guard. None of these calls really bothered Benny, who had wanted to fight since 1862. That winter he had been full of energy and enthusiasm, dancing till dawn to the lively tunes of "Arch the Fiddler" at a party with fifty-seven "ladies," staying overnight at the Ballard House in Richmond where he met "Generals Morgan, Stuart, A. Hill, Breckenridge, Capt. Wm. Boulware and a good many of the big guns," and itching to join Colonel Mosby's Rangers in the spring of 1864. Benny had also courted trouble for months, often scouting Union cavalry and hanging close to skirmishes with Union troops. It was not surprising, then, that he wanted to be part of the adventurous and dangerous Rangers.

Benny spent some of his time that winter getting ready to join Mosby. He sent a letter of introduction to Colonel Mosby, assembled the proper uniform, and scoured the countryside for just the right horse. Finally he found an 8-year-old Canadian that his father bought for $1,000. He proudly showed the horse to everyone, including his big brother Fred who was home on furlough. The plan was for both boys to leave for Richmond on March 2.[21]

The trip never materialized. On Wednesday (March 2), Benny went to scout the retreat of Colonel Ulric Dahlgren's cavalry from their surprise attack on Richmond. He was shot in the left arm, fled to the woods to hide, and there died from loss of blood. The next day his new horse found its way back to Green Mount, which alerted the family to Benny's absence. It was left to Benny's dog, Stuart, to find the lifeless body. An angry and distraught Fred Fleet personally (and unofficially) extended his own furlough to join the hunt for Dahlgren's unit. Confederate cavalry eventually trapped the Union raiders, capturing over 100 men and killing Dahlgren in a skirmish.[22]

For weeks afterward the shock of Benny's sudden, surprising death hung like a pall over the correspondence of Fred and his family. Just before leaving on the train for duty in Florida, Fred wrote to his father, "I am hourly reminded of him, not only by the crepe on my arm but by a great many little incidents which crowd upon me every day." It still haunted Fred a month later, when he wrote that "as each Wednesday comes around, wherever I am, on the dusty march or whirling along on the swift cars, I look back with a sad & melancholy feeling to Wednesday eight weeks ago, and the distressing circumstances connected with that day."[23]

Fred's family tragedy stood in sharp contrast to the experiences of Major William T. Poague, who regarded the season as the "only quiet winter of the war." His battery set up winter camp at Lindsay's Turnout, a spot on the Virginia Central Railroad three miles southwest of Gordonsville. The men built huts, stables, and a log church. There were services on Sundays, prayer meetings during the week, and special services presided over by visiting preachers. To top it off, Poague received a promotion to lieutenant colonel.[24] All might have been wonderful, except for Poague's winter assignment: president of a court-martial for the artillery of the 3d Corps. Fortunately, most of the cases involved "minor offences," but some involved desertion, and the sentence for that infraction was death. To Poague, this winter became the "most trying and least pleasant of all."

In April the pace began to quicken, capped by the review of Longstreet's Corps when it returned from Tennessee. Poague thought the review was as "imposing and inspiring" as any he had seen, but "no one thought it would be the last." The men knew they were at a material disadvantage but remained "hopeful and confident" nonetheless, their hopes resting in their commander, General Robert E. Lee. To help his children bridge the experiential gap between their time of peace and his time of war, Poague used a sports analogy: "You football boys, as you have trotted out on the field against an admittedly stronger team, can form some conception of the intense interest that filled the breasts of Lee's men as they marched in the direction of the Wilderness." [25]

For all the soldiers, the losses in the summer of 1863 and the insufficient rations in the winter of 1864 had been extremely disheartening. Yet for most of them, the hope for final victory rose with the temperature in the early spring of 1864. Historian Douglas Southall Freeman claims the "army approached the spring with confidence." He quotes an 1864 letter written by General Dodson Ramseur to reinforce his point: " 'I feel so hopeful about the coming campaign. I have never felt so encouraged before.' "[26]

NOTES

1. Worsham, *One of Jackson's Foot Cavalry*, 160–61.
2. Ibid., 161; Jones, *Christ in the Camp*, 312–52.
3. Poague, *Gunner with Stonewall*, 78–79.
4. William D. Henderson, *The Road to Bristoe Station: Campaigning with Lee and Meade, August 1–October 20, 1863* (Lynchburg, 1987), 163–91; Freeman, *Lee's Lieutenants*, 3:240–47.
5. Poague, *Gunner with Stonewall*, 79–80; Henderson, *Bristoe Station*, 177, 180, 185, 187, 191.
6. Worsham, *One of Jackson's Foot Cavalry*, 162.
7. Berkeley, *Diary*, October 14, 1863, 54; Henderson, *Bristoe Station*, 189–90.
8. Martin F. Graham and George F. Skoch, *Mine Run: A Campaign of Lost Opportunities, October 21, 1863–May 1, 1864* (Lynchburg, 1987), 9–29, 55–57; Worsham, *One of Jackson's Foot Cavalry*, 167.
9. Berkeley, *Diary*, November 27–30 and December 1–2, 1863, 62–63.
10. Poague, *Gunner with Stonewall*, 81; Blackford, *War Years with JEB Stuart*, 245–46.
11. Worsham, *One of Jackson's Foot Cavalry*, 170–77 (quotations on 175, 177, and 173).
12. Berkeley, *Diary*, entries from December 3 to 31, 1863, 63–64 (quotation on 64); January 1, 1864, 65; map, 70.
13. Ibid., January 5, 1864, 65; January 6–7, 1864, 65; January 12–27, 1864, 66; January 27, 1864, 66; February 14, 1864, 68; February 26, 1864, 69; February 5, 1864, 67; on visits home, January 28, 29, 30, 31, and February 1, 3, and 4, 1864, 66–67; letters home, March 28, April 14, 25, 26, 28, 29, and May 1, 1864, 69–73; letters to Nannie Berkeley, April 15, 19, and 28, 1864, 71–72; February 6–14, 1864, 67–68.
14. Ibid., February 28–29, 1864, 69.
15. Ibid., March 2, 3, and 27 and April 5 and 8, 1864, 69–71; April 1, 1864, 71, and April 23, 1864, 72.
16. Wiatt, *26th Virginia Infantry*, 13; Fleet, *Green Mount*, Fred Fleet to Pa, September 17, 1863, 267–69; Fred Fleet to Ma, September 20, 1863, 269–70; Wiatt, *26th Virginia Infantry*, 13–15; Fleet, *Green Mount*, Fred Fleet to Benny Fleet, September 28, 1863, 272.

17. Wiatt, *26th Virginia Infantry*, 15–16; Fleet, *Green Mount*, Fred Fleet to Pa, December 30, 1863, 293–95; Wiatt, *26th Virginia Infantry*, 17–18.

18. Fleet, *Green Mount*, Benny Fleet's journal, February 9–10, 1864, 307; February 18, 1864, 308 (ice skating); February 23, 24, 26, 27, and 28, 1864, 309–10 (Fred's visits with family and friends).

19. Ibid., December 14–23, 1863, 290–92.

20. Ibid., Pa and Ma to Fred Fleet, November 22, 1863, 282–83; Fred Fleet to Ma, December 5, 1863, 287–88; Fred Fleet to Pa, January 24, 1864, 303–4.

21. Ibid., Benny Fleet's journal, January 21–22, 1864, 302 (party); Benny Fleet to Fred Fleet, January 26, 1864, 305 (in Richmond); Benny Fleet's journal, February 23–24, 1864, 309 (will join Mosby); May 5, 1863, 225–26, June 20, 1863, 243, June 26–27, 1863, 246–47 (chasing Union troops); February 6, 1864, 309 (got uniform); February 23–24, 1864, 309 (letter of introduction from Mr. Halbach); January 30, 1864, 306 and February 22, 1864, 309 (trying to get a horse); February 29, 1864, 310 (got horse); February 26, 1864, 309 (brothers' departure).

22. Ibid., entry in Fleet family Bible, March 2, 1864, 310–12; editor's note, 312; Fred Fleet to Pa, March 9, 1864, 312; Long, *The Civil War Day by Day*, 471.

23. Fleet, *Green Mount*, Fred Fleet to Pa, March 21, 1864, 316; Fred Fleet to Lou Fleet, April 27, 1864, 324.

24. Poague, *Gunner with Stonewall*, 81–82.

25. Ibid., 82, 85–86.

26. Freeman, *Lee's Lieutenants*, 3:333. See also Gallagher, *The Confederate War*, 34–40.

Chapter Ten

"All Our Sore Trials"
Civilians Endure the Third Year of the War

As THE WAR moved into its third year, the civilians in this study demonstrated that circumstance, social situation, and personality remained the determinants of their responses to it. Each woman had her home and community occupied or visited by Union soldiers, and each felt the pain of loss directly as loved ones died in the war. Daily life became more confined and circumscribed, and news from the battlefields fluctuated from victory to defeat. But each woman managed to survive, helped by particular good fortune and an abiding faith in God.

The woman least depressed by the turmoil of war remained Tee Edmonds. On the material side, her family never went without food or clothing or shelter that year. In many ways, life had more romance than ever before. Moreover, Tee happened to be living in the heart of the Mosby Confederacy. Historian Jeffrey Wert notes that Mosby's Confederacy at its largest consisted of four counties—Fauquier, Fairfax, Loudoun, and Prince William—but that Mosby himself defined only a smaller region within those four counties as his "confederacy." Its center, according to Wert, was upper Fauquier County. Almost daily, some member of Mosby's Rangers stopped at Belle Grove, especially the handsome Matthew F. Magner of Mississippi. Tee also saw her brothers Bud and Syd fairly often, as the 6th Virginia Cavalry remained stationed in Virginia.[1]

When reading Tee's journals, the frequency and gaiety of soldiers' visits stands out. In just one month, May 1863, Tee had no fewer than ten visits with Matthew Magner. One pleasant evening included a walk to a friend's house, where they joined a group of young people. The couple returned by moonlight to Belle Grove.[2] Christmas Day found the Edmondses with a cake and many friends around, reminding Tee of the holidays of old. The party went on at neighboring Mount Bleak, lasting past midnight and rendering "nearly all hands top heavy from yesterday's nog and toddy." The gay season continued that winter with card playing until 2:00 A.M. on December 30, two gallons of apple toddy on January 9 (enough to make everyone "lively"), and a skating party at the ice pond with a group of soldiers in February. No wonder, then, that Tee could plainly admit to her diary that she had "become perfectly devoted to the society of the Rebels, too much so for my own happiness and too indifferent to females." She could see how extraordinary this time was, too. "I can look back when the war is over and recall some of the happiest moments of my life—yes, even amid the terrible war with all its sorrow and grief."[3]

The pain of war crept into Tee's world by degrees. In May 1863, Private William T. Parks charmed all with his violin playing. He returned to Belle Grove numerous times, but in January he was reported killed in action in a skirmish with Union troops in Prince William County. Next, Sergeant J. Calhoun Sparks and Sergeant William C. Mickler, who had first visited in May 1863, reportedly met with a similar fate in January 1864. Fortunately, the accounts of these deaths were false: Parks and Mickler survived the war, and Sparks fought on until Catlett's Station in 1864, when he was killed while scouting. Then it was the banjo-playing Private M. W. Flanney, who entertained everyone at Belle Grove on March 22, 1864, and died fighting at Catlett's Station in May. Tee found no romance in this death: "Oh! Will the anguish, trouble, and sorrow of war never cease."[4]

At last came casualties in the pride and joy of Salem, Company A of the 6th Virginia Cavalry. In the Battle of the Wilderness in May 1864, John O. Carr was killed. Then on May 19 the Edmondses awoke to find Private Gallaher from Company A leading brother Bud's horse. Bud had been shot in the cheek, and Syd took him to the Chimborazo Hospital in Richmond. Syd wrote that General J. E. B. Stuart had been killed and as many as ten men from Company A captured. When Tee talked to Uncle Abner and others she maintained her composure, but when she saw her Aunt May, she "choked with grief and emotion and burst out crying." The full horror of war had finally penetrated Belle Grove.

Bud slowly mended at the hospital, with Syd checking on him as often as possible. Bud lost an eye and needed a summer at home to regain his strength. By October, his old vitality had returned. He and his cousin, Isaac ("Cap") Settle, joined some of Mosby's Rangers on a mission to see how they liked Mosby's way of doing things.[5]

Sorrow came to the Buck household, too. The bad news came suddenly, with no advance warning. On June 21, 1863, General Dorsey Pender's division marched through town with "bands playing and colors flying." A rumor circulated that day that the cavalry had a battle in Upperville, but Lucy Buck wrote that she could "scarce believe it." However, the next morning not long after breakfast, "father walked in looking pale and excited," and after dinner "Ma" told Lucy that her beloved cousin, Walter Buck, had "fallen." What did it mean? Lucy wrote in her diary, "Oh—such a shock!—it seems as if my heart had stopped beating and my limbs [grew] stiff and cold." Was he dead? Or mortally wounded and in enemy hands? Still, Lucy tried to deny the veracity of the report, because "first news was always exaggerated." By the end of the day the tragic facts had been confirmed in a letter sent by another cousin, Horace Buck. Unfortunately, Horace had no details. Lucy's last sentences in the diary entry that day express her overwhelming grief: "This destroys the very last vestige of hope. Oh! I'm—so sick! So sad at heart!"

The next morning a "black great wagon" brought Walter's body to Bel Air. Lucy thought "how often we had watched for his coming as for a ray of sunshine." Now his soul rested with God, while his body lay in the coffin in the middle of the parlor. Lucy wrote, "Never shall I forget the sight—there lay the still white figure under the southern window, the attitude one of such perfect, majestic repose as seems to quiet and subdue my grief."

Lucy was far from reconciled to Walter's death, though she wrote, "Oh!—it was hard, hard to think of giving him up in his glorious flush of youth." Still, she tried to tell herself that Walter had died quickly, "nobly indicating the cause to which he has devoted his every energy for the last two years." But that was not enough, nor was the reading of the Ninetieth Psalm by Mr. Berry or the singing of hymns. After family and friends had carried him out to be buried, his coffin "seemed to cast a shadow over the house which is lying there still—it seemed so lonely and sad when one knew he had crossed the threshold never to recross it again."

As the details of Walter's death filtered in, the gloom at the household deepened. According to some observers, Walter died leading a charge, shot through the throat. Initially, his body was recovered by Union soldiers, who refused to release it. Before the Union forces retreated, they buried Walter in a shallow grave. It was left to another cousin, Will, to dig through the dirt, find Walter's naked body in a blanket, and bring it out of the ground. The Union soldiers had kept all his possessions: "Porte monnaie [purse], papers, boots, clothing, arms, the little ring which he had worn until it seemed almost a part of himself, and [they] even cut the buttons from his coat."[6]

The memories and mementos continued to drift in for weeks. When the family took a ride up to Mrs. Fox's on July 3, Walter was always on Lucy's mind. "Every foot of ground passed over in the morning, every rock and shrub and tree seemed in some way associated with him." They stopped by to visit Walter's parents on the way home, and "Aunt L. looked so badly," while Walter's little sister Gussie showed them "his account book, little bosom pin, lock of hair, tiny fiddle and keys, checquer board." Sometimes Gussie would sit still with "averted head while the tears flowed silently down her cheeks." Two days later, his sister Jacquie brought a daguerreotype of Walter. A week later a letter arrived from Walter's commanding officer, Colonel Marshall, who praised his patriotism and religious convictions. Just as life began returning to what passed for normalcy in wartime, in came cousin Dick with Walter's horse Belle and his "bloodstained" saddle. Lucy wrote in her diary, "poor dear, dear boy."[7]

The "cruel war," as Susan Caldwell often referred to it, had made itself at home at the Bucks. To survive, the Bucks clung to Bel Air and their extended family more tightly than ever. They had to rely on each other even more, because on June 9, 1863, the remaining slaves left. Shocked and dumbfounded, the family managed to operate the household with help from the slaves of relatives and friends. On June 11, for instance, "Aunt Eliza milked the cows for us and very soon Aunt Evelyne came down from the mountain to iron for us." However, "we girls assisted in ironing and getting dinner." The relentless demands of running a large household quickly caught up with the white women. Just two days later, Lucy wrote that there "were pies to make for tomorrow . . . and supper to get besides milking, and washing the children." In fact, Lucy, too tired to eat supper, had to summon the energy to put the children to bed, bring in wood and water for the night, and clean the kitchen. The reward proved to be a bath for the four novices: Ma, Lucy, Nellie, and Laura. Lucy wrote, "am still very, very footsore and weary."[8]

In time, though, Lucy and her sisters became more accustomed to the increased workload. In July, Lucy wrote that she had "worked very hard this warm morning." In January she mentioned bringing in the "wood and chips" for the fires, and another day in the month she noted that she did "not get through with my work as soon as usual." Her burdens were also eased because just three days after the slaves left in June, Lucie (a "white, mountain girl," according to the editor) came over from Uncle Tom Buck's house to help out. She stayed until December 24. Apparently both employee and employers were saddened; Lucy wrote, "we hated so to give her up and she cried bitterly." When her replacement came to Bel Air on January 2, Lucy eyed her warily, finding "Laura" to be a "delicate looking, unsophisticated individual. Hope she'll be able to do more than her appearance indicates." Also helping out the family was a new cook, Sallie, who arrived on July 29 with her two children. After that date, she is not mentioned.

What of the slaves who had left? Early reports were negative; when a cavalryman from Front Royal had been guarding Mahala, she had told him that "she wished she was back in her home, that 'twas a good one." Her children had been crying, and Lucy condemned their mother in her diary: "I feel sorry for them because they are the innocent sufferers by their mother's folly." As for Harriett, nothing had been heard, but life did not remain as desperate for Mahala and her children. In December news came from Harry Roy that Mahala was running a boardinghouse in Chambersburg, Pennsylvania, and Eliza Ann was living with her. Furthermore, Mahala had gotten married. Lucy discounted the story: "I've my doubts about it though the servants will all believe it and 'twill have the effect of inducing numbers to leave home."[9]

Other demands of war pressed in on the Bucks, however, preventing the luxury of self-pity over the increased workload at home. On a generally positive note, there was a steady stream of visitors, mostly soldiers, as the Army of Northern Virginia continued to use the Shenandoah Valley as a primary highway. On June 17, for instance, Longstreet's Corps marched through Front Royal, right by Bel Air. The Bucks had a "continuous stream of the weary, dusty, travel-worn fellows calling for milk, bread, water. . . . We set buckets of water down to the road from which the children supplied the thirsty, and those who came to the house were furnished with every drop of milk that could be spared." The Bucks even provided breakfast for some of the men. One in particular stood out to Lucy, a Private Macauley from the 4th Alabama Regiment. He had remembered the family from his brief stop at Bel Air for breakfast the previous fall, and he especially wanted to see Lucy. He came into the kitchen (after formally greeting her) and watched her bake bread. At the right moment, "he helped me prepare the oven, draw out the fire, etc, etc, very much as he might have helped me furl my parasol or tie my overshoe two years ago." After the work was done, Lucy invited Macauley into the parlor, where some "well-bred" gentlemen of the Washington Artillery were visiting with members of the family. The entire group sang songs and discussed "music and poetry and novels."

Not all visits from soldiers were so pleasant. One evening after A. P. Hill's 3d Corps had marched through town, Lucy was working in the kitchen when a drunken soldier came in and "commenced swearing." A frightened Lucy called to her father, who calmed the man down. In his newly sober state, the chastened artillery officer was "very lavish in presents and money to the children."[10]

Even worse were several incidents that occurred as Lee's Army of Northern Virginia streamed back down the Shenandoah Valley after the failure at Gettysburg. On July 21 the Bucks served "scores of soldiers all day," and when a squad approached near dark, Lucy had to tell them she could not give them supper without "help" around. A soldier replied " 'Ah, well—that's always the case, we can't expect you ladies to trouble yourselves in providing for us.' " Lucy consoled herself by judging that there are "unreasonable ones in every army."

The price of "unreason" climbed overnight. When soldiers came for milk the next morning, none was available: someone had stolen "everything except the jars and little Britania cream pitcher" from the dairy. In quick measure, though, some articles were recovered. Cousin Laura found a soldier "paying his respects to our large cream jar, which lay there half empty." He gave it to Laura when she demanded it back, then said he had just "found" it in a field below the house. Uncle Gilbert found a "missing crock and plate." Enough was restored to feed some soldiers, including Private Herbert with "eyes like liquid violet of sunshine" and a very important visitor, General Robert E. Lee.

Lee stopped by the house in the late afternoon of July 22, accompanied by his staff. He greeted each member of the Buck family in a "warm, fatherly manner," then politely introduced each member of his staff. He invited Lucy to sit and talk, and when she demurred, he insisted, making room on a bench for her to sit next to him. Lucy told him how much it pleased her to see him, the defender, "the Father of Our State." He replied, " 'Oh, no! my daughter. I only wish he were more worthy of being seen." Lee then asked Nellie and Laura to sing a song, and they did— the first time they had sung in a month since the death of Walter. The soldiers had to leave soon afterward, but, before departing, General Lee signed the girls' autograph books and urged them not to "'let any of those fine young Yankee officers carry [them] off." They said they "depended upon him to prevent such a possibility." Lucy seemed to be in heaven, writing of the "filial reverence" she now felt for Lee and the "air of dignity about his every movement."[11]

There was not time to absorb the full import of this visit, though, as the war continued apace. The next day a group of cavalrymen came to dinner, and a skirmish broke out near Green Hill between the forces of General Stuart and some Union cavalrymen. The following day another battle started south of the town and, as the firing grew close, "some of the bullets and shells passed near enough to whisper some confidential messages to us." The firing soon ceased, and some men bivouacked while others marched off. Two days later all the soldiers were gone, and Pa learned that the Confederate forces had been protecting the movement of the bulk of the Stonewall Corps.

Amid this disrupting movement of soldiers, other visitors stopped by. The war's travelers included not only soldiers and refugees but middle- and upper-class sojourners as well. On July 13, Governor William "Extra Billy" Smith came to see Pa "on business" and reassured him that the Army of Northern Virginia would not be trapped by rising river waters in Maryland. In March 1864 a Methodist minister named Hammond begged for lodging for the night, as his carriage had broken down. Although Lucy felt "terribly put out by the unexpected invasion," the Bucks found room for Hammond, his wife and daughter, her nurse, and a driver. Traveling with a coterie of helpers seemed de rigueur. George Burwell stopped by on a "bitter cold" night in late November 1863 with his wife, daughter, son, and niece, "attended" by "twelve servants, three white drivers, eleven horses and five or six conveyances." Somehow the Bucks managed to accommodate the large group in the style of "Virginia hospitality" that had been the prewar custom.[12]

As did the other two women in this study, Lucy endured too-frequent visits by unwanted guests: Union soldiers. Some soldiers came by for water after the battle near Front Royal in July 1863; a cavalry squad suddenly appeared in late October and searched the yard for a Confederate soldier, finding young John Taylor hiding under the "syringa bushes near the gate"; and a much larger group of Union cavalry descended upon Front Royal on January 3, 1864, a "clear, bright, and cold day." They took food and a horse, and so worried Lieutenant Green Samuels (home on furlough) that he dressed like a woman and made his escape "after dark."

The most dramatic and dangerous raid came on a cold, "beautiful" day in February 1864. Lucy had skated in the morning (a sport she had first tried the month before), and in the afternoon Union cavalry appeared without warning. They took one of the Bucks' two horses, but just as Father was about to secure the horse's return, the Union sergeant saw Charlie Buck and a friend, on horseback, watching them from a hill. A second group of cavalrymen captured Charlie and brought him into town on the charge of spying. Charlie had been wounded in the foot, and Lucy and her friend, Miss Lizzie, tried to obtain his release. The Union colonel would not budge, despite the entreaties and clever arguments of the young women. Lucy invited him to Bel Air to discuss the matter. He refused to commit to a visit, but he did return the horse to the Bucks. Later, Father went to see him about Charlie, and the colonel said he would release him after he crossed the river. As Lucy feared, the colonel did not keep his word. He took Charlie with him, and he remained a prisoner until the end of the war.[13]

Despite all the raids and surprise visitors and bad news, the Bucks went on with their daily routine, snatching pleasure wherever they could. In the fall of 1863 servants Horace and Uncle Gilbert went "up to the mountain to dig out potatoes," finding only ten bushels when twenty had been planted. They blamed the loss on "robbers and deserters." The next month found Lucy picking and roasting chestnuts, then enjoying a walk in "the most glorious type of autumn splendor I ever saw." A few weeks later she spent an evening playing "a series of memory games." The evening ended with friends following Lucy to her bedroom "where we had a merry time relating our experiences during the war." The next day the same group of young friends spent the afternoon walking and splashing each other in the river, and capped off the day with a round of games. Lucy also helped stage a benefit show to raise money for the soldiers, and joined a fishing party in late April.[14]

It is this very forbearance in hard times that clearly ties together the quite different situations of Lucy Buck and Susan Caldwell. Like Lucy, Susan had to find enjoyment and solace amid pain and disruption. For Susan, joy came from the accomplishments of her children and hearing of the safety and comfort of her husband Lycurgus. As with the two younger women, Susan had to endure repeated Union raids and occupations. Ironically, the raids were more feared than the occupations. The raids came without warning, and no one could predict their length or severity. For example, in late May 1863 some Union cavalry units patrolled the town on three separate occasions in just one weekend. On Friday night they chased some members of the "Black Horse

Cavalry" (4th Virginia Cavalry) who had stopped for bread; on Saturday afternoon a group of 150 men "arrested every citizen on the street" to question them about Confederate activity; and on Sunday morning a large squadron of 700 rode through town on the way to Waterloo, returning the same way before nightfall, yet this time they "did not disturb anyone."[15]

Little wonder, then, that Susan preferred the order of occupations, distasteful as they might be. Historian Daniel Sutherland describes the enforced coexistence of occupier and occupied in nearby Culpeper County as a "strained relationship." Two long occupations occurred in 1863: the first when General John Sedgwick's 6th Corps stayed in Warrenton from July 19 to September 21; and the second when the Union army moved around Fauquier and adjoining counties, jockeying for position in the Bristoe Campaign of October 1863.[16]

A fascinating underside of the Union occupation was the bartering, buying, selling, and speculating that took place between occupiers and occupied. The Caldwells' story begins with some sugar and trails off with losses, gains, accusations, and defenses. In July, Lycurgus sent a barrel of sugar to Jefferson, where John Finks was supposed to get it. Susan provided this information, then added: "If sugar *should fall* I think it would be well to buy another barrel. It would *sell* rapidly in Warrenton."

In her next letter she expanded this comment to a general discussion of her well-being and the salability of several perishables. She could not get bacon, butter, or cider vinegar for shipment to Lycurgus (for sale in Richmond), because "no one has any meat to sell. . . . Yankees [have] taken all their meat." Tobacco was another story. Finks advised Lycurgus to buy some and ship it to Warrenton, where it "commands $2 and $2.25 per pound." Susan, too, wanted in on the deal: "Buy some for me. I can get *Virginia* money for it." Apparently, Confederate money was already worthless in her area. Susan wanted to sell tobacco "for *money* which will be current with us here." As for sugar, it too sold well, but the sharp-eyed Susan argued that "it sells at too high a price in Richmond at this time to speculate on."

When the story is resumed in mid-September, it is near the end of the Union occupation, though Susan fears "the army will remain here for time indefinite." Meanwhile, the Caldwells and

Finks got on fairly well, primarily because John Finks ran the town commissary. Susan paid "government prices" for coffee (forty cents), sugar (thirteen cents), flour (four cents per pound), and dried fruit. Also, they had butter, wheat, corn, candles, and soap, and they bought salt, whiskey, and molasses from the Union army. They could have bought more: "If federal money was plentiful with me I could buy lots—but I cannot even buy it, the Confederate money goes begging." John Finks, however, knew how to get the "right" money; Susan called him "blessed," but others might use a different term to describe his ability to "buy groceries and a nice suit of clothes—he bought beautiful Cassimere at $2 per yard." Overall, Susan could honestly write in the same letter that the children were "*well fed* and *clothed*, in fact they have never felt the effects of *war* and *blockade*," which many other Southern families could not claim in September 1863.[17]

The Caldwells pressed their good fortune by engaging in some risky tobacco speculation in late 1863 and early 1864. Seeing the value of tobacco, Lycurgus raised $890—nearly double his annual salary—to buy "two cases smoking and one box chewing tobacco." He used $300 of his own money, plus the $90 he got for selling Susan's velvet bonnet in Richmond, and borrowed $500 from Joseph Finks. Lycurgus carried the tobacco to "Mr. Cooper's store" in Culpeper Courthouse in November, unbeknown to Joseph Finks or Susan Caldwell. Then a group of Union soldiers took it from Cooper's store. None of this greatly distressed Susan, perhaps because at first she had no idea how much he had invested. She asked, "How much money did you spend in tobacco?" Then she added, "do not be worried about it yourself—I have $100."[18]

Lycurgus showed worry and guilt in his long-overdue letter to Susan the next March (there is no explanation of where his letters went). He described his full involvement and why he had to leave the tobacco at Cooper's store: "[He] would not take it in store at all unless I assumed the risk against the Yankees." So, "if the tobacco is a total loss, I could not help it." He went on to defend his decision, saying that he believed Lee's army would soon be in Culpeper, and that he had "no idea Meade would allow the robbery of private stores in town." Then, in a final burst of defensiveness or, to his mind, reassurance for his anxious wife, he wrote, "I did what I thought was for the best for Mr. F & you and have no censure for myself."[19]

Susan got this letter in late April and showed little concern for the loss: "I am very sorry we lost the tobacco, but sudden acts of robbery go on daily." Lycurgus could not write it off so easily. In August 1864 he noted that the tobacco left Cooper's store before the Union army came. Late in the same month, Susan replied that there were "no signs of the tobacco yet. Please attend to it if you can fearing the Yankees." Lycurgus did work on the deal, as he wrote on August 28: "Tom Saunders promises to look for it." Two weeks later, though, he reported that J. B. Stofer never "called" for the tobacco, as he had thought earlier. Then, surprisingly, the tobacco arrived in Warrenton. The boxes were even "too large . . . to have at the house." Unfortunately, what the long-awaited tobacco actually meant to the family income is not known, because neither correspondent mentions it again. As with so much else in this "cruel war," other events crowded out one dangerous, complicated deal.[20]

For Susan, the reoccupation of Warrenton by the Union army in April 1864 proved to be more bothersome than the missing tobacco. Two Union officers, Colonels Taylor and Gardner, stayed with them, but showed themselves to be "very gentlemanly." In general, the residents of Warrenton "only treat those kindly where kindness has been extended to us by them." Of course, they traded with the enemy, selling pies and cakes to the soldiers, then using the money to buy coffee, shoes, cashmere, and other items.

This trading and peace came with a price: the impugning of the reputation of the women of Warrenton. In the same letter, Susan wrote, "I understand various rumors are afloat across the lines in regard to the Ladies of Warrenton. We are as *loyal* now as ever." As she succinctly stated, "we are in the midst of them and are in their power," but the women did have their pride and decency *and* patriotism, despite what Lycurgus might have heard. As she wrote in an earlier letter, "We would not yet have sold ourselves for sugar and coffee. We keep *true* to the South amid all our sore trials."[21]

Susan and the other women of Warrenton found out the hard way that "too friendly a relationship [with Union officers] could set local tongues wagging about cavorting with the enemy," according to historian George Rable. Daniel Sutherland argued that for these marked women, "the price of being suspected is severe." Fortunately for Susan, the only reprisal she experienced was gossip.[22]

Another trial for Susan was lack of domestic help. After the mass exodus of slaves in late May 1863, she retained only the ever-faithful Aunt Lucy and a 13-year-old girl she "hired" for $25 to help watch Lucy Lee. Unlike the Bucks, the Caldwell and Finks families seemed to have had an easier time coping with the additional chores, perhaps because there were more adult women (Susan, Frances Caldwell ["Grand Ma"], and Lucy Ann Caldwell Finks ["Sister"]) in the house to handle the work. Whatever the reason, the burdens of extra work are rarely mentioned; nor, for that matter, is much else mentioned about the remaining slaves. In a letter written in February 1864 to Lycurgus, however, Susan did cover both subjects: "My time is much occupied for all hands are compelled to do some part in housework." Susan continued to worry about the loyalty of Aunt Lucy, especially after she had heard from her son George in Washington in September 1863: "We cannot tell what she intends doing." But Aunt Lucy was still there the next May, and Susan finally seemed more confident that she would stay: "Aunt Lucy is with us yet—I hardly think she will go." Even Lycurgus commended Aunt Lucy in one of his letters to Susan, telling her to "remember me to Aunt Lucy, the faithful among the faithless."[23]

There were far greater trials for Susan, however, than those brought on by the flight of slaves. One recurring problem was lack of communication with her family in Charleston. She often asked Lycurgus to write to them. Probably she had more faith in the mail service between Richmond and Charleston than in the service between Warrenton and Charleston. Her faith was not misplaced, given the frequent Union occupation and raids of Warrenton. In June 1863, for example, she asked Lycurgus to "please write to Charleston and insist upon them writing to me— they must know I am very anxious to hear from them and also from Manley." In July she asked Lycurgus to write to her mother "and encourage her to keep up a good heart." She had heard of the Union forces near Charleston and told Lycurgus she could not "but feel uneasy. May God preserve the City and my loved ones in it."

In February 1864, Susan asked Lycurgus to write to her "Ma" for her; then at last she heard about her family from Lycurgus. The next month he wrote that her parents were living in Blackville, South Carolina, surviving "off the money for which they sold Jim." Susan's older brother, William, had been appointed steward of a hospital in Charleston, and her younger brother, James "Manley," had been moved from a line company (4th Tennessee Cavalry) to an engineer company. So far, Manley had been fortunate: "He has been in several hard fought battles under Genl Cheatam and has never been hurt." The "health of all your Carolina friends" was good, and Lycurgus had asked Susan's parents to write to him "every fortnight." More news came from Charleston the next week. Her parents and friends were still fine, although Manley wanted a "detail—anything rather than a private," and the $40 Lycurgus sent to Mrs. Jeffords never reached her.[24]

A greater and continuing trial for Susan was Lycurgus's absence. She reduced the number of times per letter she told him she missed and needed him in 1863 and 1864, perhaps because that made it easier for them both to endure the long separations. Even though Lycurgus was less than 100 miles away, the times apart were truly long. After his visit home in September 1862, Lycurgus did not get back home until March 1863, missing another Christmas at Bel Air. Little could the family know that the absences would grow longer, not shorter. Lycurgus's next visit did not take place for over a year, when he finally was able to go home in early April 1864. The year encompassed the long Union occupations and also some of Lycurgus's military adventures. Tragically, it also included the death of his mother. She died "on the Sabbath morn quietly and peacefully as an infant falls asleep." She had been weak from an unknown illness for a few days, but according to the doctor it "was no worse than . . . ten years ago." But it was worse, and "Grand Ma" knew it; "she feared she would not get up again." She was sixty years old when she died. Her son could not make it to her funeral, so her son-in-law, Joshua Finks, attended to all the arrangements.[25]

Throughout the long separations, Susan tried to keep up her "usual cheerful disposition," but in a particularly touching letter she asked Lycurgus how he managed to get by during their long periods apart. She wrote, "Tell me if you can keep your spirits up when separated so long from those you love." She knew someone else who was "desperate," their acquaintance Mr. Brooke. His wife told Susan that he was "crazy to see her—but is afraid to venture home. He writes love letters to her half dozen at a time." She ended with the plaint that had become a constant in her letters: "Oh! how I long for this cruel war to be over—I feel ten years older."[26]

Even Lycurgus began to lose some of his tough, proud, high-mindedness as the war dragged into its fourth year. In his longest letter in the collection, he wrote the usual war news and his analysis of the conflict so far, still fairly optimistic on the movements of Southern armies. But he also expressed great longing and loneliness: "I do not think I can consent to live separated another Presidential term." Perhaps, though, with the "talk of peace" in the Democratic Party in the North, there would be "peace in a few months." Then Lycurgus captured all his hopes and worries and powerlessness: "I sometimes think and think till I grow dizzy in thought. . . . It troubles me no little to think I am in no situation to help you and the children." Moreover, he knew (but would not admit) the price he was paying for his rebelliousness: "How many thousands now striving for political independence are laying the foundations of pecuniary servitude for all time to them individually?" He realized that he would be financially poorer after the war than before it and that he might even be in debt for the rest of his life.

Lycurgus also engaged in some daydreaming about life at home with his children, an exercise that rarely appeared in his brief, fact-filled letters. He pictured Lucy Lee "munching apples," Jessie "singing a lullaby," Frank "counting the goodies in his saving box," and Willie "bridling the colt." He added, "There is a misty rain falling and such days there is a racket at home I know, but to me now it would be sweet music." He wanted nothing more than to "pop in unawares and kiss right and left, and spend a month, yes a lifetime with you all." Lycurgus's unusually revealing letter made a huge impact on Susan. She replied: "I shall ever keep this letter of yours around about me and peruse its contents over and again." She added, "Miss you—you cannot miss me more—I yearn after you—I long to be near you."[27]

Yet as difficult as the long separations were, the most trying experiences for Susan remained her husband's occasional military duties. Lycurgus went out on maneuvers several times in 1864, including nineteen days in the field in May and twenty-six days in June. During his stint in May, Lycurgus fought in his second battle. The Home Guard had been called out to help defend Richmond (again), and at one point in an exchange of cannon fire, Lycurgus answered the call for noncommissioned officers to prepare to charge into the woods with General Archibald Gracie's brigade. But the call never came, and Sergeant Lycurgus Caldwell and his men were ordered back to the trenches. The Union forces then retreated, and Richmond was preserved. Lycurgus carefully made the case for his action: "You would not have me play sick or act cowardly I know, and I believe I shall not be hurt."[28]

Far more dangerous military action occurred in March 1864, when the Home Guard were called out to protect Richmond from bold Union cavalrymen under General Hugh Judson Kilpatrick and Colonel Ulric Dahlgren. Lycurgus's Home Guard went to the outer fortifications of the city. Hearing that the Union forces were retreating, Lycurgus's battalion flanked them, got into a lying position on one side of the road, and waited for the Union forces to come down the road. Despite the darkness and heavy rain the untested men kept their cool, and when the Union columns got "within 20 yards" of the "company on the right," the "boys poured in a beautiful volley from right to left which caused the enemy to rein up and fall back." However, a few Union soldiers got between the first and second lines of the Home Guard, and when the second line saw them, they opened fire. Fortunately, Lycurgus was not hit, and in the brief light of rifle fire he saw that the company's flag was "30 yards to the rear." As he wrote to Susan, "We in the front were in most danger from our own men." The major got the men regrouped by dressing on the flag (lining up by an imaginary line extending out from the flag), and soon Lycurgus's battalion was ordered to the rear, as the 8th and 56th Virginia Regiments took their place. The Home Guard continued to protect the perimeter for the next few days, but there were no further attacks. Richmond had been saved, and Lycurgus could finally write to Susan, "I know I did my whole duty as a soldier."[29]

Susan did not share Lycurgus's satisfaction. She could only write, "Oh, how can I be thankful enough to Almighty God for his preservation of your life during the severe trial you have passed through." Ironically, or perhaps fortunately, she knew nothing of Kilpatrick's raid "until it was over." But she knew enough of how close to death her husband had come and repeated an earlier plea: "Pray never enter the army, you are serving the country in your position." She angled for a promise from Lycurgus that he would "not expose" himself to danger if possible. Then she used her strongest weapons, sympathy and guilt: "You have a very dependent family. Think of it and keep your health that some day we may enjoy the society of each other as in bygone days." As Drew Faust analyzes the paradoxical feelings of some Confederate wives, "The absence of the loved one made him all the more desired and desirable; the absence of protection and of material and emotional support underlined the importance of these male responsibilities and generated resentment at their withdrawal."[30]

Another Virginia mother used guilt for the opposite reason: to stiffen the resolve of her oldest son, who was serving in Wise's Brigade stationed near Richmond. As the journal entries of Benny Fleet and the correspondence between Fred Fleet and his family accumulate during the war years, the powerful presence of Ma becomes even more visible. It is she, more than Pa, who keeps spirits up and holds things together as the war takes its toll on Green Mount.

In her letters to Fred, Ma expressed admiration for Confederate soldiers and an unstinting willingness to help the cause. When she saw a twice-wounded friend of the family's at church, she remarked that he "looks as if he had been through the wars." But that only increased his stature in "we ladies eyes." Indeed, "I expect Betty Pointer will marry him now in spite of her father's and sister's opposition, I know *I would*."[31] Another time the family gave food and drink to General Stuart's "horse artillery" as it passed though King and Queen County. Ma wrote to Fred, "There is one thing I want my children to remember when we are dead and gone, that their parents did not make money out of the soldiers, but gave with a free hand, whenever it was in their power."

Ma provided encouragement for Fred and censure when he complained about serving in the quiet section of Richmond. As she wrote in July 1863, "I can fully sympathize with your feelings about sitting in one place continually when you want to be up and doing, but remember it is your post—not your own choosing, but which has been assigned to you—where the Providence of God has placed you, read Phil. IV:11 and don't complain." As for fighting, Ma was not inalterably opposed to Fred seeing action. After the 26th Virginia Regiment had fired on some Union gunboats, she wrote, "How thankful I felt that you all were so mercifully preserved and aren't you glad you were not on furlough." Ma was also pleased when Fred received his promotion to captain and appointment as acting adjutant general in November 1863, though she asked directly, "Why do you think he (Colonel Page) selected you?" Then, to bolster his ego for being in Charleston instead of a "hot" spot like Tennessee, she said, "I am sure it will be an honour enough to tell your children's children that you engaged in the defense of Charleston."[32]

As much respect as Ma had for regular soldiers (whether in the front lines or not), she had an equal measure of scorn for shirkers, whiners, and cowards. In early June 1863, Green Mount experienced one of many false alarms about "Yankee invasion." In this instance, Captain William C. Fleet rode by Green Mount on July 1, saying that the "Yankees were coming on with 'cavalry, infantry and artillery.' " The next morning, Ma put herself at the gate, "and in the course of an hour I staid there I saw a number of the scaredest men I ever wish to see." She listed some of the local notables who came by in a great rush: "Mr. Boulwar, Dr. G. Fauntleroy and Mr. Stirling. Dr. F. pretty white and scared to death." She complained to Fred, "In all this I have not heard one word of the citizens turning out to meet them." As often happened, no Union forces showed. Ma lamented: "there are 23 *men* able to shoot Yankees within a radius of only two miles. Yet they all say it is not worth while for two or three to resist a large force." Later in the same month, she supported an even tougher stance toward cowards and those who did not support the "cause." She told Fred, "[I] agree with poor James Roane that the man who won't help now in this our last extremity, should not be allowed to live amongst us."[33]

Given Ma's feelings toward Confederate shirkers, one can easily imagine her views toward Union raiders. A group swept through King and Queen County in early May, taking ten horses and mules owned by the Fleets. Unfortunately, Ma's letter to Fred describing the raid has not been preserved, only Fred's curt response to Ma's description of one Yankee as a gentleman. Fred wrote, "Why he had boldness enough to fool you & made you reconcile two incompatible elements, viz: Yankee & gentleman, which he could not be, I think, at the same time."[34]

After the second raid in June 1864, Ma had abandoned any respect for Union soldiers. The raid began with General Philip Sheridan and his staff camping on the fields of Green Mount for three days (June 4–6). While they treated the Fleets with respect, they took "all of the cattle, sheep, hogs." Even worse, from Pa's perspective, all his field slaves ran off with the Union army. Their flight temporarily paralyzed Pa; Ma wrote to Fred, "you must not feel slighted at poor Pa's not writing, he says he has no heart nor eyes to write, his eyes are worse." Friends and neighbors, however, came through for the Fleets. Captain Wilson sent men and mules to help plow, three women were hired to help Ma, and five other slaves were offered to the family. Also, the Union troops left the corn at Old Hall, a few pigs, a chicken, a cow for milk for the children, and the vegetable garden.

After Sheridan and his staff left on Monday, the situation turned worse. On Tuesday (June 7), Union deserters descended upon Green Mount during Pa's absence. In the morning three deserters rested on the porch of the cabin of one of the few remaining slaves, Milly; then they "went to sleep under the apple tree." In the afternoon, four more deserters appeared and entered the big house. One walked into Ma's chamber and "commenced searching my wardrobe." Two others locked themselves in a room with Lou. Ma wrote, "Imagine my feelings! I don't know how many seconds passed not many—my mind was complete chaos." Then Lou ran out of the room screaming and clung tightly to her mother. One of the men pointed his gun at them, and Ma told him to shoot. He did not, and one took Lou's hand and told her "to hush." Ma ordered, "Take your hand off my child." The men then ordered Ma to lock Lou and herself in the chamber. She and Lou prayed, and Lou told Ma what had frightened her the most. One man had asked her how old she was, and when she replied that she was thirteen, another one said, "That's too young."

Despite these moments of terror, what the men really wanted was money, not women. They tried to break into Pa's desk, but refused the last three silver teaspoons Lou offered them. With the women locked in the chamber, the deserters searched the entire house. Finding nothing, they threatened the slaves, commanded young David (who showed up after they left the house) to fill their canteen, then "laid down under the apple trees to play cards till night." Their party ended in about an hour when a group of Home Guard rode up and arrested them. The next day, Pa returned home, and he and some other local men vowed that the prisoners "should never annoy another woman and *they never will*." Ma concurred, writing to Fred, "if I were a man I would never take a prisoner. I would consider it my duty to rid the world of all such monsters."[35] None of the Fleets or the editors of their papers record whether the threat was carried out or not.

The Fleets had had a horrible spring—first the sudden death of Benny, then Fred leaving to join his unit in Florida, and finally the major raid on Green Mount in June. But the war was not finished with them yet; the Union noose began to tighten around southeastern Virginia in the spring of 1864. Soon the Fleets' beloved eldest son would see the fighting he had craved, as this long war finally brought even the reserve units into the maelstrom.

NOTES

1. Edmonds, *Journals*, September 6, 1862, 111–12; Wert, *Mosby's Rangers*, 116–17.
2. Edmonds, *Journals*, May 1, 1863, 142; May 2, 1863, 142; May 3, 1863, 142; May 5, 1863, 143; May 6, 1863, 144; May 8, 1863, 144; May 20, 1863, 147; May 26, 1863, 149; May 27, 1863, 150; May 30, 1863, 150; May 27, 1863, 150.
3. Ibid., December 22, 1863, 176; December 25, 1863, 177; December 26, 1863, 177; December 30, 1863, 177; January 9, 1864, 178; February 19, 1864, 183; October 15, 1863, 173–74.

4. Ibid., May 1, 1863, 142; May 14, 1863, 146; May 15, 1863, 146; October 31, 1863, 175; May 10, 1863, 145; footnotes 12, 19, and 20, 258–59; March 22, 1864, 185; April 20, 1864, 192.

5. Ibid., May 9, 1864, 194–95; June 13, 1864, 199; May 27, 1864, 196; June 10, 1864, 197; October 7, 1864, 207.

6. Buck, *Diary*, June 21, 1863, 202; June 22, 1863, 203; June 23, 1863, 204–5.

7. Ibid., July 3, 1863, 209; July 5, 1863, 209; July 11, 1863, 212; and September 12, 1863, 226.

8. Ibid., June 11 and June 13, 1863, 195.

9. Ibid., July 10, 1863, 212; January 2–3, 1864, 242; editor's note, 240; June 12, 1863, 195; December 24, 1863, 239; January 2, 1864, 242; July 29, 1863, 223; July 3, 1863, 208; and December 11, 1863, 238.

10. Ibid., June 17, 1863, 199–201; June 20, 1863, 202.

11. Ibid., July 21, 1863, 216; July 22, 1863, 216–18.

12. Ibid., July 23, 1863, 219; July 24, 1863, 220–21; July 26, 1863, 223; July 13, 1863, 213; March 16, 1864, 250; November 30, 1863, 236–37.

13. Ibid., July 24, 1863, 221; October 27, 1863, 231; January 3, 1864, 243; February 20, 1864, 245–48.

14. Ibid., October 6, 1863, 229; October 19, 1863, 230; November 11, 1863, 233; November 12, 1863, 234; February 12, 1864, 244; April 30, 1864, 250.

15. Caldwell, *Letters*, Susan Caldwell to Lycurgus Caldwell, May 31, 1863, 189. The arrested citizens were released that same day.

16. Sutherland, *Seasons of War*, 285; Caldwell, *Letters*, editor's footnote no. 44, 196.

17. Caldwell, *Letters*, Susan Caldwell to Lycurgus Caldwell, July 13, 1863, 194; Susan Caldwell to Lycurgus Caldwell, July 19, 1863, 195–96; Susan Caldwell to Lycurgus Caldwell, September 12, 1863, 197. Sutherland writes of Culpeper County residents in September 1863: "Less threatening but no less painful are the material losses that alternately sadden and anger people." *Seasons of War*, 287.

18. Caldwell, *Letters*, Lycurgus Caldwell to Susan Caldwell, March 9, 1864, 210; Susan Caldwell to Lycurgus Caldwell, December 7, 1863, 205.

19. Ibid., Lycurgus Caldwell to Susan Caldwell, March 9, 1864, 210–11.

20. Ibid., Susan Caldwell to Lycurgus Caldwell, undated, est. April 1864, 217; Lycurgus Caldwell to Susan Caldwell, August 6, 1864, 231–32; Lycurgus Caldwell to Susan Caldwell, August 7, 1864, 233; Susan Caldwell to Lycurgus Caldwell, August 26, 1864, 235; Lycurgus Caldwell to Susan Caldwell, August 28, 1864, 237; Lycurgus Caldwell to Susan Caldwell, September 16, 1864, 238; Susan Caldwell to Lycurgus Caldwell, October 2, 1864, 240.

21. Ibid., Susan Caldwell to Lycurgus Caldwell, April 25, 1864, 221; Susan Caldwell to Lycurgus Caldwell, April 22, 1864, 218.

22. Rable, *Civil Wars*, 165; Sutherland, *Seasons of War*, 353.

23. Caldwell, *Letters*, Susan Caldwell to Lycurgus Caldwell, May 29, 1863, 188; Susan Caldwell to Lycurgus Caldwell, February 28, 1863,

180; Susan Caldwell to Lycurgus Caldwell, February 17, 1864, 209; Susan Caldwell to Lycurgus Caldwell, September 12, 1863, 198; Susan Caldwell to Lycurgus Caldwell, May 5, 1864, 223; Lycurgus Caldwell to Susan Caldwell, June 27, 1864, 229.

24. Ibid., Susan Caldwell to Lycurgus Caldwell, June 12, 1863, 190; Susan Caldwell to Lycurgus Caldwell, July 19, 1863, 196; Susan Caldwell to Lycurgus Caldwell, February 17, 1864, 209; Lycurgus Caldwell to Susan Caldwell, March 9, 1864, 210; Lycurgus Caldwell to Susan Caldwell, March 19, 1864, 213.

Jordan notes that slaves sold for as much as $3,000 in Virginia in 1864, the highest price of any Confederate state. Texas slaves were sold for $691 in the same year. The price the Jeffordses asked for their slave Jim probably lay between these two figures. See *Black Confederates and Afro-Yankees*, 40.

25. Caldwell, *Letters*, Susan Caldwell to Lycurgus Caldwell, September 30, 1862, 154–55; Lycurgus Caldwell to Susan Caldwell, March 16, 1864, 214; Susan Caldwell to Lycurgus Caldwell, April 19, 1864, 216; Susan Caldwell to Lycurgus Caldwell, November 27, 1863, 202–3. See also Faust, *Mothers of Invention*, chapter 5, "We Little Knew: Husbands and Wives," 114–38, for an analysis of the challenges faced by other separated couples.

26. Caldwell, *Letters*, Susan Caldwell to Lycurgus Caldwell, April 25, 1864, 221.

27. Ibid., Lycurgus Caldwell to Susan Caldwell, August 6, 1864, 231; Susan Caldwell to Lycurgus Caldwell, August 29, 1864, 237.

28. Ibid., Lycurgus Caldwell to Susan Caldwell, May 25, 1864, 226; Lycurgus Caldwell to Susan Caldwell, June 27, 1864, 228; Lycurgus Caldwell to Susan Caldwell, May 25, 1864, 226.

29. Ibid., Lycurgus Caldwell to Susan Caldwell, March 9, 1864, 212–13.

30. Ibid., Susan Caldwell to Lycurgus Caldwell, undated but probably March or April 1864, 217; Faust, *Mothers of Invention*, 137.

31. Fleet, *Green Mount,* Ma to Fred Fleet, January 18, 1863, 197.

32. Ibid., Ma to Fred Fleet, April 7, 1863, 216; Ma to Fred Fleet, July 26, 1863, 253; Ma to Fred Fleet, August 9, 1863, 259; Pa and Ma to Fred Fleet, November 22, 1863, 283. The Biblical passage she cited reads, "Not that I speak in respect of want; for I have learned, in whatsoever state I am, therewith to be content."

33. Ibid., Ma to Fred Fleet, June 3, 1863, 235–36; Ma to Fred Fleet, June 16, 1863, 241.

34. Ibid., Fred Fleet to Ma, May 23, 1863, 231.

35. Ibid., Ma and Pa to Fred Fleet, June 12, 1864, 328–32.

Chapter Eleven

"A Season of Slaughter"

From the Wilderness to Petersburg, May–October 1864

LIEUTENANT COLONEL WILLIAM T. POAGUE was troubled. As he rode along the Plank Road at first light on May 6, he found "nearly all the men were still asleep." Poague knew the Union troops were out there in the tangled woods of the Wilderness, as did an officer he talked to that morning. But the officer seemed unconcerned, assuring Poague that his men would be "relieved by fresh troops before daylight." When sunlight began to filter through the leaves of the trees, the sleeping Confederates were startled out of their slumber by the sudden attack of two Union assault forces. Major General Winfield S. Hancock's 2d Army Corps and General James S. Wadsworth's 4th Division (from the 5th Army Corps) hit the Confederate lines hard and fast, capturing men, equipment, and flags by the score in a matter of minutes. The second day of the horrific battle known simply as "The Wilderness" had begun very badly for the Army of Northern Virginia.[1]

Back in the clearing of Widow Tapp's field, Poague and his battalion waited nervously. All around them could be heard the pop and whine of musket fire, the screams and groans of wounded men, and the tumult of shouts. Nothing could be seen, however, as the early morning drama took place in the dense thickets of woods beyond the farms. Then Confederate soldiers began pouring out of the woods in pell-mell retreat, as the fast-moving brigades of Wadsworth and Hancock pushed on relentlessly toward the Orange Plank Road. As the remnants of the Army of Northern Virginia's 3d Corps brigades streamed down the road, Generals Robert E. Lee and A. P. Hill worked strenuously to restore order.[2]

With Longstreet's Corps still not up, only one group stood between the advancing Union columns and utter defeat: Lieutenant Colonel William T. Poague's battalion with twelve guns. His men began with a "slow fire to the front with short range shells," soon adding oblique fire across the road to the south, followed by steady fire toward the north. In his memoirs, Poague said little about this dramatic moment in the battle, but the historian of the Army of Northern Virginia's artillery, Jennings C. Wise, adds the color that Poague left out: "The gunners worked with almost superhuman energy, the muzzles belched their withering blasts, the twelve pieces blended their discharges in one continuous roar." Intently watching their defense was General Lee, and Wise hardly exaggerates when he states that "this single incident brought more of honor to the little colonel of artillery than most soldiers attain in a life of service." Any residue of shame from Lee's rebuke of Poague at Gettysburg vanished in the smoke of the battalion's guns in the Wilderness.[3]

Poague's battalion alone could not stop several Union divisions. Just as the Union troops prepared to envelop Poague's battalion, the Texas Brigade appeared on the Orange Plank Road, marching with a "swinging gait" toward the Union lines. Ordered to counterattack, the Texas Brigade (and others) gathered behind the slight rise on which Poague's guns sat. After General Lee and General John Gregg had a brief conversation, Gregg gave the order to march and Lee shouted to the men, "Texans always move them!" With a tremendous yell, the men marched on straight at the Union line. For the first time, General Lee rode with the lead brigade, obviously caught up in the excitement of the moment. A number of soldiers shouted, "Go back, General Lee, go back!" General Gregg and Lee's aide, Colonel Charles Venable, finally convinced him to withdraw and leave the direct assault to others.[4]

Poague watched this entire episode, and years later added his own careful recollections to the legends that had grown up around it. He wrote, "[Lee] . . . was perfectly composed, but his face expressed a kind of grim determination I had not observed either at Sharpsburg or Gettysburg. . . . [There] . . . was no rearing or plunging on the part of the horse and no waving of sword by General Lee as is represented in a painting of the scene."[5]

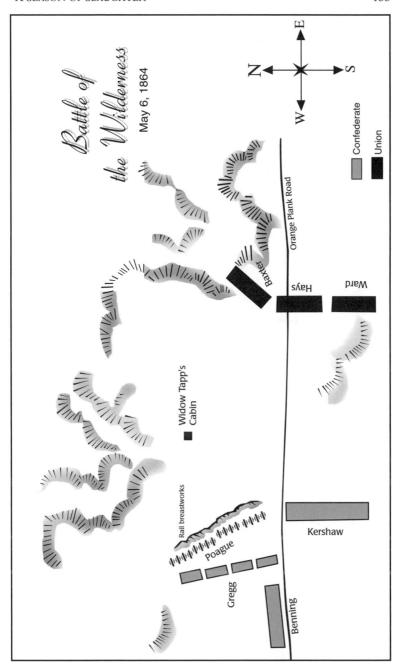

Battle of
the Wilderness
May 6, 1864

Confederate
Union

Orange Plank Road

Baxter

Hays

Ward

Widow Tapp's
Cabin

Rail breastworks

Poague

Gregg

Kershaw

Benning

Regardless of Lee's demeanor, all agree that the counterattack of the next two hours was General James Longstreet's show—and one of his finest. Throwing his brigades in columns at the jagged Union lines, his 1st Corps stopped the Union advance. With pinpoint firing from Poague's tired but inspired gunners, Longstreet's two divisions broke and partially destroyed almost five Union divisions. As one participant, William Royall, later wrote, the 1st Corps "had saved the Army of Northern Virginia from disaster."[6] The previous day's labors, however, had been performed by Lieutenant General Richard S. "Baldy" Ewell's 2d Corps. Sent by General Lee to erect a defensive line across the Orange Turnpike to prevent a westward movement of Major General Gouverneur Warren's 5th Corps, the Confederates worked feverishly on the western edge of Saunder's field in the sultry air of an unusually hot May morning.

In total, General Lee's Army of Northern Virginia numbered 65,000 men. It faced an old adversary, General Meade's Army of the Potomac, with 119,000 troops and a new general in charge of all the Union armies on hand to watch and lead, if necessary. Lieutenant General Ulysses S. Grant was fresh from several major victories in the West. Grant's immediate objective was to swing left (south) of Lee's Army of Northern Virginia and strike toward Richmond. Failing an easy progress toward the Confederacy's capital, Grant would attack Lee's army wherever it stood, "to hammer continuously against the armed forces of the enemy and his resources, until by mere attrition, if in no other way, there should be nothing left of him."[7]

It was as a direct result of Grant's goal that Sergeant John Worsham of the 21st Virginia, part of Brigadier General John M. Jones's Brigade under Major General Edward Johnson, came to be digging into the soft earth on Saunder's field on May 5. Holding the southern edge of a quickly built line, Jones's Brigade soon found out how weak the front right of their line was, as a quick and fierce attack on their front and right by General Joseph J. Bartlett's Brigade at 1:00 P.M. brought General Jones dashing up to the front from a meeting with General Early. As he rode up to lead his men, Jones was hit and instantly killed by a hail of bullets. This fire revealed the weakness of the right flank of Jones's

Brigade, which soon collapsed under the weight of Bartlett's forward advance and the shock of being leaderless.[8]

As Jones's Brigade fell back into the lines of its reserve (Cullen Battle's Brigade), one regiment stood its ground, the 21st Virginia. It then charged forward until it reached a "dense pine thicket" where the men rested until the 3d Brigade came on its left. Worsham went out ahead of his company, spotted a large group of Union soldiers in one part of the field, then ran back to one of the colonels in the 3d Regiment to inform him. The colonel gave the order to go forward, and "through the thicket we went . . . with a yell we were on them, front and flank! They gave ground and ran!" The 21st captured two Union cannons; and after another volley into a different Union force, the 21st hunkered down in the woods on the east side of the field. Gradually the 2d Brigade found its way back to the 21st and witnessed an old-fashioned fistfight between two soldiers, Union and Confederate, over possession of a gully. All firing ceased while the men slugged it out, the Reb eventually winning. The two exhausted men rolled into the gulley, and firing resumed. "Such is war!" exclaimed Worsham.[9]

After the fierce fighting of the afternoon, the 21st was allowed to rest for the night. It remained in place the next day (May 6), then on May 7 marched to the "flank of the extreme left of General Lee's line" and fired into a patch of woods by a ford. The 21st then returned to its previous spot on the line, and the company counted its losses: five wounded and one killed. For the brigade, the loss of General Jones, "a strict disciplinarian," was keenly felt.[10]

While the 21st Virginia rested in place on May 6, some of the fiercest fighting of the entire battle took place, involving thousands of men from the 1st Corps of the Army of Northern Virginia and the Union's 2d and 6th Army Corps. At one point in the day, friendly fire took the life of General Micah Jenkins of South Carolina and severely wounded General Longstreet (leaving General Lee temporarily in direct command of the 1st Corps).

When night fell over the charred and decimated Wilderness, over 28,000 men from both sides lay dead, dying, or wounded on that desolate ground. Private Robin Berkeley of Kirkpatrick's

Battery (in Nelson's Battalion) saw the carnage firsthand after his battery had camped near the rear of Ewell's 2d Corps on the first night of battle. When awakened at 4:00 A.M., Robin found "a big pile of amputated arms, hands, legs, and fingers within a foot or two of me." Once again the butcher's bill of battle had been high, but this time there would be no respite for the two huge armies. General Grant ordered his men to head south, trying once again to flank General Lee's Army of Northern Virginia.[11]

The tired legions of both major armies marched southeast a few miles and struck each other hard again, in a Union attempt to capture another tiny Virginia crossroads village, Spotsylvania Court House. The Army of the Potomac had left the Wilderness first, in an exhausting night march on May 7. The Confederate 1st Corps had marched south in a parallel line, and from May 8 until May 21 the armies would clash across open spaces and hastily erected fortifications for possession of this small piece of land.[12]

The biggest engagement of the thirteen days came on May 12, when General Hancock's entire 2d Corps attacked Confederate Major General Richard S. Ewell's lines stretched across the appropriately named "Bloody Angle." John Worsham had a frontline view of this dramatic attack; his 21st Virginia Regiment served as skirmishers for Ewell's 2d Corps at the salient. Carrying an order from the reserve of the regiment to the front on that damp, foggy morning, Worsham was startled to hear a cannon shot and "the screaming of a shell." He instinctively put his hands on his head "to see if it was on . . . [my] shoulder; the shell seemed to come so near me that it certainly took off my head." Relieved to find it in place, Worsham continued on to the front ranks, where he heard the sound of "40,000 men." He conveyed the news to his colonel, who immediately ordered in the skirmishers and the regiment to march to its left, so as to come around behind the breastworks other units had constructed. The regiment kept marching, past skirmishers, until it reached the rear and General Ewell. There the men heard the awful news: while they had been marching, their division, under Major General Edward Johnson, had been captured! Their fabled Stonewall Brigade, and Jones's and Steuart's Brigades, were no more. Now, only the 21st remained. Supplied with fresh ammunition, it was sent to aid in the counterattack on Hancock's 2d Corps. For two hours the men fired on the Union troops protected by the pens (small wooden forts) made the previous day by the Confederates, the blue troops "as thick as herrings in a barrel." The 21st was then ordered to the rear, where it rested, thankful that it had been initially ordered "out of the breastworks, even against our protest, and sent to the front on special service" (on May 11), thus allowing it to escape capture.[13]

Robin Berkeley of Kirkpatrick's Battery continued to experience little direct fighting, although on May 12 the battery remained in position all day without opportunity to fire back at the Union guns (Robin did not say why). Robin regarded the shelling as "the most terrible day I have ever lived." One reason for this judgment might be his witnessing of a close call for General Robert E. Lee and his staff. They had stopped for a moment near his gun, when two "scrapling shells" exploded in their midst. They were covered by smoke, but Robin could see that two horses were down. Then, "a second after, Old Mas' Bob rode out of the smoke on Traveller, amid the loud shouts of A. P. Hill's corps." Robin remarked, "The expression on his [Lee's] face as he rode out of that smoke has always remained firmly vised in my memory." Miraculously, the only casualties of the shelling were the two horses.[14]

The same could not be said for the armies. General Lee had lost 12,000 men in five days, and General Grant lost 9,000 on May 12 alone. Overall, the Union Army had 33,000 casualties from the Wilderness and Spotsylvania Court House, approximately 28 percent of its combat force. The Army of Northern Virginia had fewer casualties, 23,000, but they comprised a higher proportion of its combat force, approximately 33 percent.[15]

Both sides could claim an element of victory, and each charged the other with defeat. Lee had blunted two huge attacks by an army twice the size of his forces and maintained his defense of Richmond. Grant had demonstrated determination and tenacity by attacking a tough opponent two times in less than a week, despite enormous human losses. His large army inched closer to Richmond and, most important, his effort to win through sheer attrition had begun to take its toll on the Army of Northern Virginia. With the resolve of a prizefighter, Grant ordered his army to conduct another night march, on toward another tiny spot on the map, the North Anna River. None of the soldiers in this study had dramatic experiences in the fighting at North Anna River, but two of them, William Poague and Robin Berkeley, saw plenty of action in General Grant's last wasteful attempt to carry well-fortified breastworks with frontal assaults, the Battle of Cold Harbor.

After the Battle of North Anna River, Grant had continued his movement south. His army returned to the old ground where the Seven Days Battle had been waged in 1862. By June 2 the two armies faced each other across a 4-mile front, stretching from below Old Cold Harbor north to the Old Church Road. Grant had his entire army at his disposal, which gave him almost twice as many men as Lee. Sharp fighting for position had occurred on May 31, June 1, and June 2. With his entire army present, Grant was not about to sit idle. Consequently, he ordered an attack on the Confederate line to begin before dawn on June 3. It would be his greatest miscalculation.[16]

The grand assault across a 4-mile front would prove momentous for two Confederate artillerymen, too. For Lieutenant Colonel William T. Poague, the day began with a message to report to General Henry Heth, who commanded the extreme left of Lee's defenses. As Heth showed Poague where he wanted the guns, Union skirmishers fired at the two men. In Poague's words, "I suggested to him it would be very hazardous to try to get guns into position at that point after daylight. . . . I proposed to seek and find a point nearby, the approach to which would be less exposed." But Heth would have none of it: he wanted Poague's guns on the extreme left, especially since he had no cavalry. Poague reluctantly obeyed, but protested in his memoirs: "I ought to have been notified in time to get my guns up to Heth's line before daylight, as I learned afterwards other battalions had been put in position *under cover of darkness*."[17]

Poague's worst fears came true. He sent two batteries into position, but just as the men unlimbered the guns, they were hit by a "perfect hail of bullets" that killed or wounded all the officers and completely incapacitated the batteries. Somehow, Poague and a few men managed to move two of the guns to a different position, by hand. Then they were ready to fire upon any Union advances—but the advances never came. Instead, the artillerymen were fired upon all day by "small arms and shots from a battery on the extreme right." At one point during the day, two of Poague's men ran out to an injured officer, Lieutenant Kearny, and dragged him back to the thicket where the remaining members of the battery crouched. They dug a trench for Kearny, who said in reference to the torrent of small arms fire, "Well, boys, if this is to be my grave as probably it will, I feel so much more comfortable here than out there in the rain." Remarkably, Kearny survived, although he lost his "shattered leg."

Poague, too, survived. A bullet hit the bone on the tip of his left shoulder, turning his arm "almost black" down to his wrist. A piece of shell hit him on the right side of the chest. He was pulled from the field and sent to a hospital in Richmond. The hospital was too full to accept any more patients, so Poague told the ambulance driver to take him to the American Hotel. Somehow he got a room, then "the attention of a physician and the kindly care of Ned Alexander, a member of the Rockbridge Artillery." Together, the physician and Ned sewed up his wounds and nursed him through a subsequent bout with pneumonia.

For Poague, the battle made a huge impact—and not just because of his injuries. He gave it the longest description of any single battle in his 5-page memoir and included a hand-drawn map of the position of the battery on that fateful day. Of all the general officers he served under, it was Heth who drew his criticism. Poague stated that he never learned "who was chargeable with the failure" to place his battery in position at night. He faulted Heth's decision to keep four guns in the front of his marching column on May 5: "This is but one of the many examples of infantry officers' manner of handling artillery."[18]

For Robin Berkeley, a month of "marching and fighting all the time" with only one man in his company wounded ended abruptly on a hot June morning. At 6:00 A.M. on June 3 the Kirkpatrick Battery received orders. As it marched toward its destination, it had to cut a road and endure a "tremendous artillery fire" that killed or wounded the entire 13-man crew on the first gun. Somehow, the men got the five remaining guns in place and fired all day long, never losing their position, despite the heaviest losses of the war for the battery: eight men killed and forty wounded. As the men fell, Lieutenant Hobson silently cried as he walked the breastworks, giving orders "calmly and deliberately." In Robin's mess of six, he was the only one without a wound at the end of the day. Robin's good friend and breakfast companion on June 3, Edmund Anderson, died of wounds later that night. Berkeley wrote in his diary, "I little thought, when we separated this morning, that it was for the last time on earth."

Five more men from Robin's battery died from wounds by the next day. The dead included Chris Harris, a "noble and brave boy" whose father arrived at camp "only to find his boy dead on his country's altar." Another boy, John Christian of Lynchburg, had been with the battery only six weeks; he died instantly when a "shell took off his head." He was fifteen years old.[19] After three years of dutiful service, Robin and his battery had finally experienced the full horrors of war. For three years circumstances had generally kept his unit out of the heaviest fighting. Now, as the Army of Northern Virginia grew smaller, untested units began to see more and more action.

For the generals, the battle had been another strategic draw. Grant neither gained nor ceded territory, while Lee continued to protect Richmond. However, 7,000 Union soldiers had been killed, wounded, or captured in that brief, hopeless assault against well-fortified breastworks. Their deaths finally convinced Grant of the futility of direct assault against strong defensive lines, forcing him to devise other means to break Lee's lines or, at the very least, weaken his army through piecemeal attacks.[20] For Lee and Grant, the war of open field maneuvers had given way to small movements of corps and endless construction of defensive works. They would take these hard-learned lessons to their next engagement, Petersburg.

After the disaster at Cold Harbor, Grant ordered the Army of the Potomac to march south, then cut back due east, crossing the James River below City Point, and head straight toward Petersburg. If he could get the jump on Lee's Army of Northern Virginia, he might be able to cut off several Confederate rail lines: the Norfolk and Petersburg Railroad, the Petersburg and Weldon Railroad, and the South Side Railroad. If the supply links to Richmond could be severed, Grant could close on Richmond from the south. At the very least, his army of over 100,000 could threaten if not capture Petersburg and severely restrict Lee's ability to maneuver. On June 12 the army began to move, and by June 16 the entire huge force, including supply wagons, had crossed the James River.[21]

Lieutenant Fred Fleet's quiet postings in the war finally came to an end in Petersburg. Soon after he rejoined his unit in South Carolina, the 26th Virginia was ordered to return to Virginia. General Beauregard had called for several scattered brigades to report to him in Petersburg to help defend that city from General Butler's Army of the James. In two weeks of fighting in May, both armies tried flanking and attacking to gain the superior position. By May 21, Butler's army held a fortified position at Bermuda Hundred, unable to get out and unable to be dislodged by Beauregard's assaults.[22]

On the morning of May 20 the brigades of General Wise and General James Green Martin attacked a section of Butler's line. Fred served as a courier between the two brigades, and as he carried a message along the Confederate line, he was struck in the side by a minié ball. Fortunately, the bullet only grazed him, "making a wound about an inch and a half long a quarter of an inch deep." Fred wrote to his father that he thanked the Lord for protecting him from greater harm; if the ball had "passed half an inch to the right" it would have entered his left lung. The wound "bled but little," so Fred continued to carry messages. About fifteen minutes later he was hit again, this time just above the knee. The ball actually fell on his foot, so he considered it a "spent ball." Although in pain, he stayed in the field until ordered to have his wound "examined and dressed."

For the next month, Fred was in and out of the hospital. Fortunately, his cousin Bernard Todd lived in Petersburg, so Fred spent most of this recovery time at Todd's house, not in the hospital. On June 6 he wrote that "both wounds are as healthy now as similar ones ever are," and only the side wound caused him pain. The news was far worse for Second Lieutenant Thomas Miller, one of Fred's "dearest friends." Miller had been shot in the right arm, and the subsequent amputation of the arm was "imperfectly done." The severed stump hemorrhaged, and Miller, "one of the noblest fellows," died on May 30, 1864.[23]

Despite this tragedy, Fred found reasons for optimism. His wounds were healing and the Board of Physicians gave him a 30-

day furlough. Moreover, "Lee is stronger than when the fighting commenced & his men, as well as those of the gallant Beauregard are in the best possible trim." He remained cheerful even after receiving the news of the Union raids on Green Mount. He managed to get home in June, and somehow extended his furlough (never discussed in his letters) until late August. Considering his earlier desire to see action, it is ironic that Fred's long furlough occurred during the 26th Virginia's two biggest battles, Petersburg on June 15 and 16 and the Crater on July 30.

At the Battle of Petersburg, Fred's former teacher and first recruiter, Lieutenant Colonel James Councill, surrendered several companies of the 26th Virginia to the 13th New Hampshire Infantry Regiment. Fred's favorite commanding officer, Colonel Powhatan R. Page, was killed. Colonel John Thomas Goode then assumed command of Wise's Brigade (Wise had been given command of the entire military district outside Petersburg), and Captain William K. Perrin was placed in charge of the reduced 26th Virginia. Between the two battles, the 26th lost more than half its men.[24] When Fred returned to the 26th Virginia in late August, he found himself stationed on top of the Crater. The Crater had been filled with dirt and lime, but it must have been ghoulish to sleep over "the pits in which so many dead white and black Yankees are buried." In the evenings the two sides would hold a ceasefire so newspapers could be exchanged. Afterward, the men returned to their holes, when "the order to commence firing is again given, and the minies are whistling again."[25]

Fred's monotonous trench duty continued for the next two months. Bright spots were visits to cousin Bernard Todd's family, a church service in Petersburg, and the sweet music of Union bands from across the pockmarked ground that separated the two sides. Fred compared the Confederate trench duty to that of the soldiers at Sebastopol in the Crimean War ten years earlier: "The allied armies of England & France remained in the trenches before Sebastopol in a climate far colder than our own and certainly men fighting for liberty and right, dearer than life itself, can endure as many hardships as troops contending for political advancement and military honors have shown themselves able to bear." Fred closely followed the war news from elsewhere, commenting briefly on General Sherman's Atlanta Campaign, General Early's struggles in the Shenandoah Valley, and General Sheridan's scorched-earth policy in that same valley. Despite setbacks for the Confederacy, Fred saw positive signs. In mid-October he wrote to his mother, "Genl. Lee has been considerably reinforced lately, and you need not be surprised to hear of some move similar to that made in the summer of '62."[26]

For the indefatigable Lieutenant Colonel William T. Poague, the Petersburg siege proved to be the one time during the war when he and his men did little fighting. Granted a 30-day furlough to recover from the wounds sustained at Cold Harbor, Poague discovered that even his home was not safe from the war. The family was compelled to temporarily evacuate the house in Rockbridge County to avoid the sweep of General David Hunter's army through the Shenandoah Valley, so Poague rested at "Mr. Joplings's" farm in Franklin County. Unfortunately for Poague and posterity, when his mother heard that Hunter's cavalry were looking for William, she destroyed all his wartime letters. On July 6, Poague reported back to his battalion. His men moved to stop a Union attack on Richmond on July 28, but it turned out to be a diversion. By early August his battalion became entrenched at Dutch Gap, where it stayed until April 2, 1865. During this longest winter of the war, Poague ironically found that his "sojourn at Dutch Gap was more pleasant and comfortable than any previous seven months of army life."[27]

As the circle began to close around the entrenched Army of Northern Virginia that summer and fall, Confederate attention turned toward General Jubal Early's Second Valley Campaign. After a summer of horrendous fighting and enormous losses, the Confederates looked toward one offensive that could bring them new hope. Circumstances would find John Worsham and Robin Berkeley marching north in the summer of 1864 in an effort to revive the flagging fortunes of their cause.

NOTES

1. Poague, *Gunner with Stonewall*, 88–89; Gordon C. Rhea, *The Battle of the Wilderness, May 5–6, 1864* (Baton Rouge, 1994), 281–85.

2. Rhea, *The Battle of the Wilderness*, 284–93.

3. Poague, *Gunner with Stonewall*, 89; Rhea, *The Battle of the Wilderness*, 294; Wise, *The Long Arm of Lee*, 2:767.

4. Poague, *Gunner with Stonewall*, 90; Rhea, *The Battle of the Wilderness*, 300–301.

5. Poague, *Gunner with Stonewall*, 90–91.

6. Rhea, *The Battle of the Wilderness*, 302–16; William L. Royall, *Some Reminiscences* (New York, 1909), 32–33.

7. Rhea, *The Battle of the Wilderness*, 123–26, 34, 41–52; *OR*, vol. 36, pt. 1, 12–13 (Grant's report).

8. Rhea, *The Battle of the Wilderness*, 145–53.

9. Worsham, *One of Jackson's Foot Cavalry*, 180–81; Rhea, *The Battle of the Wilderness*, 154–57.

10. Worsham, *One of Jackson's Foot Cavalry*, 182–83.

11. Rhea, *The Battle of the Wilderness*, 354–67, 370–74, 389–97, 404–25, 435–36, and 440; Berkeley, *Diary*, May 5, 1864, 73–74.

12. Gordon C. Rhea, *The Battles for Spotsylvania Court House and the Road to Yellow Tavern* (Baton Rouge, 1997), 1–44.

13. Worsham, *One of Jackson's Foot Cavalry*, 188–93 (quotations on 189, 192, and 193); Rhea, *The Battles for Spotsylvania Court House*, 244–307.

14. Berkeley, *Diary*, May 12, 1864, 75–76.

15. Rhea, *The Battles for Spotsylvania Court House*, 324, 311, and 319.

16. Richard J. Sommers, "Cold Harbor," in *The Civil War Battlefield Guide*, ed. Frances H. Kennedy (Boston, 1990), 215–20.

17. Poague, *Gunner with Stonewall*, 96–97.

18. Ibid., 97–100, 87–88, and 96–100 (quotations on 99 and 88).

19. Berkeley, *Diary*, May 31, 1864, 78–79; June 3, 1864, 79–80; June 4, 1864, 80.

20. Sommers, "Cold Harbor," in *The Civil War Battlefield Guide*, 215–20.

21. Noah Andre Trudeau, *The Last Citadel: Petersburg, Virginia, June 1864–April 1865* (Boston, 1991), 21.

22. Wiatt, *26th Virginia Infantry*, 20–21; J. Tracy Power, *Lee's Miserables: Life in the Army of Northern Virginia from the Wilderness to Appomattox* (Chapel Hill, 1998), 81–83.

23. Fleet, *Green Mount*, Fred Fleet to Pa, May 22, 1864, 326; Fred Fleet to Pa and Ma, June 6, 1864, 327.

24. Ibid., Fred Fleet to Ma, June 23, 1864, 332; Fred Fleet to Pa, August 19, 1864, 332–33; Wiatt, *26th Virginia Infantry*, 22–30.

25. Fleet, *Green Mount*, Fred Fleet to Lou Fleet, September 2, 1864, 335–36.

26. Ibid., Fred Fleet to Ma, September 8, 1864, 337–38; Fred Fleet to Pa, September 13, 1864, 338; Fred Fleet to Pa, September 29, 1864, 342; Fred Fleet to Ma, October 11, 1864, 344.

27. Poague, *Gunner with Stonewall*, 101–5 (quotation on 105).

CHAPTER TWELVE

MISSED OPPORTUNITIES
The Second Valley Campaign, Summer and Fall 1864

THE SECOND VALLEY CAMPAIGN actually began with Lieutenant General Ulysses S. Grant. In March of 1864, Grant developed a grand plan to press the Confederacy on five fronts: Atlanta, Mobile, eastern Virginia near Petersburg, central Virginia (using Meade's Army of the Potomac), and western Virginia. He ordered General Franz Sigel to take an army of 10,000 men from West Virginia to Lynchburg and destroy the Virginia and Tennessee Railroad as he marched. General George Crook would lead a smaller force to Saltville, Wytheville, then Staunton. At best, they could destroy the Confederacy's salt and cut off its access to a major breadbasket. At the least, their activity would force General Robert E. Lee to leave Major General John C. Breckinridge's small army of 5,000 men in the valley, unable to assist him in the upcoming struggles against Grant.[1]

With help from General Gabriel Wharton's brigade and cadets from Virginia Military Institute, Breckinridge won a battle at New Market and stopped Crook's advance into southwest Virginia. Breckinridge then sent some of his army to help fight Grant in the east, before the men had to return to the west to protect Lynchburg. They came as part of the newly christened Army of the Valley, led by the crusty subordinate of Jackson and Lee, Lieutenant General Jubal Early. Early had two primary tasks: thwart any Union advances from the west toward Richmond, and keep the vital foodstuffs of the Shenandoah Valley in Confederate hands. To accomplish these missions he had 14,000 men by mid-July, including cavalry and two battalions of artillery (one battalion was Lieutenant Colonel William Nelson's).[2]

At first things went beautifully for Early. When the 2d Corps marched into Lynchburg on June 17, they were "cheered to an echo" and brought food and water by the ladies, according to John Worsham. As more troops poured into the city on the eighteenth, Major General David Hunter decided not to fight, but to retreat. He headed west, toward Liberty, then Salem, burning bridges and destroying depots as time allowed. Near Salem the lead elements of Hunter's cavalry fought a brief skirmish with General John McCausland's horsemen, before the main body of Hunter's army caught up and pushed on through New Castle into West Virginia. There Hunter waited in safety, never explaining to anyone's satisfaction why he tarried there so long. His refusal to fight did not bother John Worsham, however; near Big Lick (present-day Roanoke), "two beautiful young ladies and their maids" filled "two huge wash tubs" with ice water and brandy julep, giving him "the biggest julep treat" of his life.[3]

With no Hunter to worry about, Early turned north, marching his shoeless army by Natural Bridge, past the charred ruins of the Virginia Military Institute (burned in June by Hunter's army) and by Stonewall Jackson's grave, and into Staunton, covering 235 miles in eleven days, a feat worthy of his predecessor, Jackson. The march down the Valley resumed the next day, and they reached Martinsburg (by July 3) so quickly that the Union forces there left many stores behind. Worsham got hold of a box with "cakes, oranges, bananas, lemons, etc. and a bottle of wine," which he proceeded to eat until he could "eat no more." The next day, July 4, Early allowed all the men to have the "biggest Fourth of July picnic celebration" of the war, courtesy of the Union army. (F Company had "oranges, lemons, cakes, and candy, and a keg of lager beer.") Worsham took a fine pair of boots from the plunder, for helping a friend deliver a trunk.[4] Robin Berkeley's battery did not fare so well; they got "sugar, coffee, hardtack, molasses, etc." When one member of the battery, John McCorkle, attempted to carry a bucket full of molasses back to camp, his mule was spooked by a Union shell, and man and mule were covered in molasses.[5]

The gaiety and gluttony of July 4 passed into memory after four days of steady marching through a subdued Maryland countryside. On July 9, Early's Army of the Valley clashed with a much smaller army at a big railroad crossing three miles south of Frederick, the Monocacy Junction. Here the Baltimore and Ohio Railroad crossed the Monocacy River, and the Frederick Branch of the Baltimore and Ohio Railroad originated and crossed the Washington Road (present-day Georgetown Pike). Major General Lewis Wallace's main task was to slow the progress of Early's army, giving more time for reinforcements from Grant to arrive in Washington. Wallace had about 5,800 men under arms, both from the 8th Corps and from the 6th Corps (Army of the Potomac), recently arrived in Washington.[6]

For John Worsham of the 21st, it was a confusing day that ended with "the most exciting time" he had seen during the war. The morning began with General John Gordon's division in reserve, the men allowed the rare opportunity to watch the battle instead of fight it. Then in the early afternoon, Gordon sent the 2d Brigade off to the right, where they soon charged a fence and took the ground. Next, Gordon called for the 2d Brigade to retreat, then flank right. The men climbed a hill, pulled apart a fence so that Gordon and the brigade could pass through it, and then charged a surprised unit of Union reinforcements, catching them completely off guard. Although the men had been "perfectly wild when they came in light of the enemy's column," Gordon had held them in check long enough to stun the Union forces. That night, Worsham ate "a good supper out of . . . [the] Yankee haversack" he scrounged from the field, and F Company counted one man wounded and another man killed.[7]

Victory could be claimed by Kirkpatrick's Battery too, but the cost was significantly higher for that small group. Acting as gunner (his position since Cold Harbor), Robin fired for only twenty minutes, effectively driving the Union forces from his front. In that short time, though, Gardner and Page from the battery were killed by a single shell, a shell that passed over Robin while he was leaning over to aim the cannon. Just after the battle, Lieutenant George W. Hobson had a conversation with Robin's brother: "Those poor boys must be buried and their graves marked, if I have to go back." As he finished uttering the word "back," a minié ball hit him in the right shoulder, then "passing diagonally downward, stopped on his left hip." Hobson "sank from his horse," breathed for maybe ten minutes, then died. This was the same young officer who had tears on his cheeks as his men fell at Cold Harbor, and the same one who reluctantly gave Robin sweeping duty in winter camp—a "good fellow, a brave man, and a conscientious Christian."[8]

The soldiers of Early's Army of the Valley had no time to mourn their dead. The next day, July 10, they marched thirty miles in blistering heat; the following day, they marched all the way to the fine home of Francis Blair, Silver Springs, in Maryland. Some of them set up camp there, enjoying the "large lawn running down to a beautiful and cold spring fixed up with marble basins." But from nearby John Worsham could also see "fortifications . . . the most formidable looking I ever saw." The Union forces "had a full sweep of the ground for at least a mile in their front."[9]

As the tired men straggled in from the exhausting march, Early and his generals assessed the situation. Solid intelligence informed them that the entire Union 6th Corps had been sent to Washington as reinforcements, and further intelligence said that another corps either did or would soon arrive (it later proved incorrect). Early postponed a decision to attack until the morning of July 12. That morning, as he walked out over the Union lines, he made a fateful decision: he would retreat back to Virginia, losing an opportunity to attack Washington but saving a more important prize, his army. On the evening of the twelfth, the Army of the Valley began its retreat, despite grumbling from some men like Worsham who believed they should have attacked on the eleventh (even though they admitted that straggling prevented that). They left Silver Springs and marched two straight days and nights, "the most severe" pace ever experienced by Robin Berkeley, to reach the safety of Big Spring (just north of Leesburg, Virginia). There they rested for a day and a half before resuming their march toward the Shenandoah Valley.[10]

July 12 found the bulk of Early's army on the move toward Strasburg, with Major General Stephen Dodson Ramseur's division and Nelson's artillery battalion guarding the route from the north near Winchester. Ramseur had information that a division of infantry and a regiment of cavalry lurked just above the town, so he decided to find them and push them back up north. There soon ensued another of a thousand small battles in the Civil War but one that took an enormous toll on a single unit, Kirkpatrick's Battery.[11]

As Ramseur's division marched up the Valley Pike, approaching Stephenson's Depot on the Winchester and Potomac Railroad, the infantrymen could hear fighting between cavalry from both sides. Soon the infantry and artillery were engaged as well and, at a critical moment in the battle, part of Ramseur's left flank panicked and ran, leading to the capture of 267 soldiers and the loss of all the guns from Kirkpatrick's Battery.[12]

Robin strongly believed that General Ramseur made a "mistake which cost us at least a hundred men killed and two hundred wounded." Apparently, his battery had been in position on the right, ready to fire, when Ramseur ordered its men to cross the road and set up on the left. Just as they began to cross the road, some companies on the left ran, leaving Kirkpatrick's Battery undefended and open to capture. Robin retraced the steps of the battle just four days later and wrote, "We could have fired at least a dozen rounds of canister into the crowded ranks of the Yanks . . . and I believe the canister would have saved the day."[13]

Instead, the battery suffered major losses: four men killed, six men wounded, twenty-five horses killed, and four guns taken. One of the wounded men, Lieutenant Bayse, had his foot amputated that night. Another soldier, William Good, died from his wounds within a few days. A third, Frank Miller, age sixteen, had his right leg amputated above the knee; he had been in the battery for only five months. In early August, more tragedy hit the small battery. Lieutenant Bayse and Bolling Hewitt died because they disobeyed their doctors' orders to rest at the hospital in Mount Jackson, preferring instead to take a "hundred-mile trip in an ambulance over a rough pike" to reach their homes. That brought the total number of dead from that brief engagement of Kirkpatrick's Battery to seven, leaving Robin to lament, "Alas! How many boys we have buried since we left our winter quarters in Orange. Who will be the next to fall?"[14]

The only advantage the battery gained from the battle was inactivity at the next engagement for Early's Army of the Valley, the Second Battle of Kernstown on July 24. On July 21, General Early had marched his army out of Winchester, heading down the Valley Pike toward Strasburg. Major General Horatio Wright assumed that Early was moving south to eventually join General Lee, so he sent the 6th and 19th Corps back to Washington, leaving General George Crook with a small army of just under 10,000 to guard the Valley. Crook's cavalry skirmished with Early's horsemen on July 22 and July 23. When Early ascertained that he faced smaller numbers of just 10,000, he decided to move his entire army north, to attack Crook's token force at Kernstown and his full force near Winchester. Crook quickly saw what was happening and moved his army to Kernstown on July 24.[15]

The cavalry skirmishing lasted all morning, as the infantry divisions of both sides assembled for battle. The 21st Virginia, serving in General William Terry's Brigade, was used as skirmishers on the left flank of General John B. Gordon's divisions. Around noon, Gordon began his advance, and the 21st Virginia crossed the same field as it had in the First Battle of Kernstown in March 1862. This time, however, it would enjoy greater success. In quick movements it stormed two stone walls, pushing back the Union defenders and leaving a major "stamping with rage" because they had decided to storm the second wall on their own. The timing proved fortuitous, however, because at that very moment General John C. Breckinridge's small army attacked the Union left. With Gordon's divisions hitting the center hard and Breckinridge's men pushing in from the east, General Crook was forced to retreat. He kept moving on the Valley Pike toward Bunker Hill; then, after a brief rest, he found safety at Harpers Ferry. Worsham declared this "the most easily won battle of the war," as Early continued his string of successes that summer.[16]

As the Army of the Valley destroyed sections of the Baltimore and Ohio Railroad near Martinsburg and awaited the return of a bigger Union force, Early made a controversial decision. He ordered the cavalry under Generals John McCausland and Bradley Johnson to exact retribution from a Union town for the destruction of a number of houses in the Valley by Hunter's army. McCausland and Johnson rode to Chambersburg, Pennsylvania, on July 30 and demanded $100,000 in gold or $500,000 in U.S. currency as compensation. If the authorities refused, the town would be burned. The city fathers did refuse, and by the end of the day, Chambersburg lay in ruins. Neither Worsham nor Berkeley participated in this action, nor do they mention it in their memoirs.[17]

The war was turning uglier, and Early's men would soon regret their act of retaliation. Even as Early dominated the Valley, the siege of Petersburg began to take on the appearance of a stalemate in August. Accordingly, General Grant felt that he could and should press and destroy Early's Army of the Valley. Furthermore, it was time to destroy the war-sustaining productivity of the Valley as well, to hasten the end of this war. On August 5, Grant rode to the Union forces encamped near Frederick, now under the command of General David Hunter. Grant wanted Hunter to give field command to the fierce Major General Philip Sheridan. Not wishing to play second fiddle to Sheridan, Hunter asked to be relieved. On August 6, Sheridan arrived with thousands of soldiers, as Grant brought the newly named Army of the Shenandoah to its eventual strength of 48,000 men. Now, at last, the federal government would treat the Valley war seriously; it had a general, some veteran brigades, and superior numbers to carry out Grant's brutal mission.[18]

For nearly six weeks, however, there was no large battle between the two armies. Plagued by faulty intelligence, each general overestimated the size of the other's army. From August 6 through September 18 they marched their men around the northern reaches of the Valley, with Early in particular trying to make his force seem larger than it was. Throughout most of this time, Early was ably assisted by Major General Fitzhugh Lee, who had been sent to help him in mid-August. There were many small skirmishes during this period and after two of them, John Worsham had acquired a horse, poncho, blanket, saddle, a Colt "five-shooter, a sixteen-shot Winchester rifle, a saber, a nose bag for my horse and a bag of oats, also a canteen, six extra saddles, and a Yankee haversack filled with rations." He was made acting adjutant of the 21st Virginia Regiment on September 12. Robin Berkeley did not get promoted at this time, but he did write several letters about the enormous number of apples he ate, allowing him to "weigh more now that I ever did before in my life." On August 29 his battery was issued new guns made by the Tredegar

Iron Works, and in September they heard the dim news of the fall of Atlanta. The pessimistic Robin wrote, "The future looks dark and hopeless for the South."[19]

Little did Robin know that his gloomy prediction would hold true for the Army of the Valley too, as they faced the full might of General Sheridan's 40,000-man army for the first time on September 19 in a familiar spot, Winchester. Just two days before, General Grant had a brief conference with Sheridan and gave him the authority to fully engage Early in battle. When Early temporarily divided his army on September 18, Sheridan saw his chance. In the pre-dawn hours of September 19, Sheridan had his entire army closing in on Winchester.[20]

The initial fighting began at sunrise, with the Union cavalrymen attacking the lightly guarded Berryville Canyon (a 2-mile-long canyon through which the Berryville Pike passed). The overwhelmed skirmishers of General Ramseur fell back and, as brigades were rushed to stop the advance, Nelson's Battalion of artillery wheeled into action and began the yeoman's job it would do all day. Hearing of the attack, General Early sent General Rodes's and General Gordon's divisions to help Ramseur, so off marched Terry's Brigade, unafraid because, according to John Worsham, "we knew we could whip Sheridan easily."[21]

At first it seemed that might be true. Ramseur's division held its ground, as infantrymen fired volley after volley into advancing Union ranks while Nelson's Battalion kept up its deadly, steady barrage. Robin Berkeley wrote, "We would concentrate on the first [line] a very heavy artillery fire, which never failed to break it, and this [first line] falling back on their second line made that line give way, and the two routed lines going back on their third line made that line also give way."[22]

All day, Robin's battery maintained its fire despite losing at least ten men (three from Robin's gun). His battery alone fired 1,600 rounds, "about four times as much as we have ever used in a fight before." The battery became so undermanned that Robin served as "gunner, sergeant and lieutenant," while Colonel Nelson acted as chief of all artillery and Captain Kirkpatrick commanded Nelson's Battalion. At one point during the exhausting day a shell hit the middle horse of Robin's limber, or gun carriage, "right between the eyes," where it burst, spattering blood

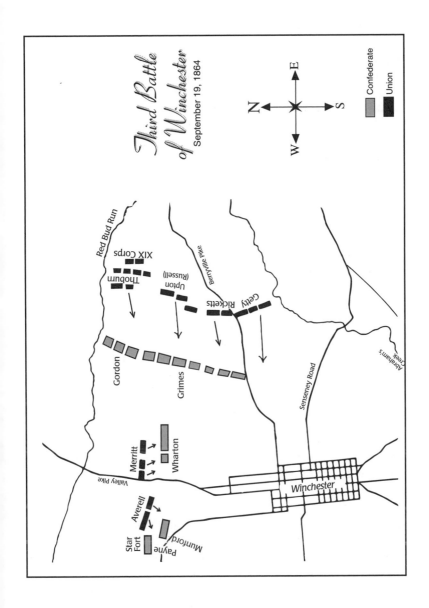

Third Battle of Winchester
September 19, 1864

and brains over Charlie Taliaferro, the horse driver. In a rare macabre moment, Robin wrote, "I could not help being amused at his appearance, yet it was an awful gruesome place to be amused." Taliaferro proved his steadiness, though, by calmly wiping off the gore with damp cotton. In Robin's view, "Soldiers are never made cooler, or braver, than Charles Taliaferro."[23]

While Nelson's Battalion helped save the day for Early's army, the 2d Brigade (now under the command of General William Terry and known officially as Terry's Brigade) under Major General John B. Gordon had arrived on the field and marched toward the sound of battle. They arrived just in time to turn back a Union advance on Early's left. Firing a volley, then finding the Union troops retreating, they pursued them "for three-quarters of a mile . . . [making] a clean sweep." Gordon's division soon linked up with General Rodes's division, and then Terry's Brigade "lay down to rest . . . we had been in action only about an hour, and we thought we had gained an easy victory."[24]

The scrappy veterans of many battles in and out of the Valley had not tangled with the likes of Philip Sheridan, however. All morning long he funneled fresh troops into the fight until they were stuck, even while retreating, thwarted by the disciplined fire and swift movements of Early's three divisions. Sheridan finally sent General Russell's seasoned division to counterattack, and it broke the Confederate surge by 1:00 P.M. Meanwhile, 3,000 cavalrymen under Generals Wesley Merritt and George Custer were making headway north of Winchester against John McCausland's and George Smith's 800 cavalry troops. By 1:30 P.M., General Averell had linked up with Merritt and Custer, and they were able to push back the much smaller force of Confederates until it rallied, with the aid of General Fitzhugh Lee and a brigade of his seasoned troops (General William Payne's), in a pine forest about a mile south of Stephenson's Depot.

With a combined force of nearly 5,000, the Union cavalry brigades formed a solid line of blue cantering down the Valley Pike, with bands playing and sabers flashing in the midafternoon sun. Lee may have felt his only hope lay in surprise and speed; greatly outnumbered, he ordered a charge. Payne's troopers used carbines and pistols against the Union swords, but the weight of numbers proved too much and the charge failed. After some fierce fighting, Lee called retreat. The victorious Union troops pressed on, only to be temporarily stopped by the shells from Lieutenant Colonel J. Floyd King's battalion and the effective fire of Colonel George Patton's brigade.[25]

Now it was time for Sheridan to throw in his last advantage: two divisions of infantry under his old friend, General George Crook. They made a fierce attack on General Gordon's left flank and front around 3:00 P.M., ultimately forcing Gordon to abandon the "Second Woods" and re-form a line with General Wharton's division on his left and General Rodes's division on his right. Sheridan ordered all his infantrymen to press forward, and by 5:00 P.M. they had pushed Early's army back into an "L" defensive line anchored on the Valley Pike. To help stop the steady Union advance, Early had recalled Colonel Patton's brigade and Lieutenant Colonel King's artillery battalion to aid General Wharton. That left Early's left flank only lightly guarded, and at just after 5:00 P.M., the Union cavalry had its moment of supreme glory (and revenge) when 5,000 Union horsemen galloped into Wharton's and Gordon's recently formed lines. Sheridan had used the superior numbers and force of men on 1,000-pound animals as a battering ram, and for this day, it proved tremendously effective.[26]

Some veterans broke and ran, while others, like John Worsham, tried to make a stand. Seeing no officers of the 21st present, Worsham boldly asked General Gordon where the line should be formed. His friend, W. S. Cumbia, held the flag while Gordon yelled, "Men, form on the colors of the 21st!" As the men dressed on Cumbia, Union sharpshooters plugged away at them. Then a Union brigade began advancing toward them, an unknown colonel told the 21st to fire, and Sergeant Worsham countermanded the order, telling them to hold their fire. He told the colonel the men should wait until the Union line drew closer, and just as he finished his sentence, a bullet struck him in the knee. Initially, "it did not hurt much," but in a few minutes Worsham felt so sick he had to lie down. Immediately it got worse: "I was so sick that I thought my time to die had come, and as I looked at my knee, I saw the blood running freely down my pants." Despite his pain and protests, two of his friends pulled him behind a large rock, then moved him again to a house in Winchester when a Union shell hit the rock.[27] Even as John Worsham sought shelter in Winchester, the relentless Union forces converged on Early's Army of the Valley. With the help of Ramseur's division, enough order was maintained to allow the bulk of Early's army to leave the field of battle with discipline, marching south down the Valley Pike toward the safety of Fisher's Hill.

It had been a tough day for all concerned. Early's small army had over 200 killed and 1,700 wounded, and add to that a large number (1,800) of "missing" (either captured, straggling, or deserted). The Army of the Valley had a casualty rate of 30 percent that day—one of the worst of the Civil War battles in the East. Most important, Early could not afford such huge losses, including the deaths of the rising star, Major General Robert E. Rodes, and the underused Colonel George Patton. Sheridan's Army of the Shenandoah had over twice as many killed and wounded: 697 and 3,983, respectively. That was expected, though, given that the Union army had been on the offensive much of the day. Even with the addition of 338 missing men, the Union had a casualty rate of only 12 percent, showing the ever-growing importance of larger numbers.[28]

By the end of this bloody day, much had changed not only for the two armies that counted their losses but also for both sides in this seemingly endless conflict. For the first time in the war, Union forces had scored a signal victory against a tough Valley army. No matter that the Union army was three times the size of the Confederate army, or that the cavalry of the Union was even more proportionally outsized than the Confederate cavalry, or that some participants and later scholars would question Sheridan's overall plan and management of the battle. The Union army had won, Early's army was in retreat down the Valley Pike, and Washingtonians were safer than ever.

The orderly retreat of the Army of the Valley was soon marred by another brief battle, known as Fisher's Hill. In order to hold on to this northern entrance to the Valley, Early spread his tired men along a 4-mile front stretching from Little North Mountain on his left (west) to the North Fork of the Shenandoah River on his right (east). Even worse, he lost the support of Major General John C. Breckinridge's troops, who were ordered to southwest Virginia to stop another Union foray. That left him with just under 12,000 soldiers, mainly infantry. To defend his long front, he ordered General Lunsford Lomax's brigades to serve as dismounted cavalry protecting the last mile on his left. He sent the rest of the cavalry into the Luray Valley, thus protecting his rear should he need to retreat farther up the Valley. Early set up a good defense along the ridges, hills, and man-made trenches, but Sheridan used his numbers to his advantage again, sending General George Crook's 8th Corps west, then rapidly back east, where they struck Lomax's dismounted cavalry hard at about 4:00 P.M. on September 22.[29]

Crook's unit quickly scattered the stunned and frightened cavalrymen and were about to engulf Robin's battery as well, when General Cullen Battle's brigade opened fire, allowing Kirkpatrick's Battery to bring out all but one gun. Unfortunately, it was John Hill Berkeley's gun, and he also lost his "horse, blankets, and all his clothes." Even worse, Robin's messmate, Frank Kinkle, was "shot about three inches above his right eye by a musket ball." He lived because his wool hat had absorbed most of the force of the bullet.[30]

Others were not so fortunate as Frank Kinkle. Lieutenant Colonel Sandie Pendleton (son of General Pendleton), who had such a tangled personal history with William T. Poague, received a mortal wound. Another twenty-nine Confederates would be killed and over 200 wounded by the end of the battle that saw Early's Army of the Valley in full retreat toward New Market. Almost 1,000 men were listed as missing, but only half that number were presumed captured. Although reports varied, Robin said that Nelson's Battalion lost three guns, King's Battalion one gun, and Braxton's Battalion nine guns. No wonder, then, that Robin wrote in his diary, "Surely the future looks gloomy and hopeless for the South just at present. May God help us."[31]

Robin was not the only person turning to God at that moment. General Early wrote a dire report of the situation on September 25, blaming numbers and his cavalry for the defeats: "The enemy's immense superiority in cavalry and the inefficiency of the greater part of mine has been the cause of *all* my disasters." He added: "My troops are very much shattered, the men very much exhausted, and many of them without shoes." Lee chastened Early, "You must do all in your power to invigorate your army . . . one victory will put all things right." To help Early, he sent General Joseph B. Kershaw's division, Breckinridge's division (if possible), and General Rosser's cavalry. Finally, he invoked the aid of a higher authority: "A Kind Providence will yet overrule everything for our good."[32]

As the Army of the Valley struggled to survive, John Worsham had a rough time getting home after his injury. First he had to endure a wild ambulance ride out of Winchester, at one point even flying over a stone wall to escape Union gunfire. He rode all night in the bumpy wagon and, after breakfast, asked the driver to remove his boot. As the driver did so, blood poured out of it. Worsham wisely left the boot off and the wound stopped bleeding. It was not until the ambulance got to Woodstock that a surgeon examined John's wound, cutting away his pants and dressing it. Worsham was then placed on a wagon and rode for two days until he reached Staunton, where the wound was dressed a second time. Then it was on to Charlottesville, where at last, four days after Worsham was shot, "the ball was taken out." From Charlottesville, Worsham was eventually moved to Richmond, where he spent the remainder of the war in the comfort of his parents' home. It was there he practiced his own therapy, using and bending his knee to prevent a complete stiffening of the joints. He regained full use of his leg and walked with only a trace of a limp for the next sixty years.[33]

For Robin Berkeley, the war continued on. He participated in the retreat up the Valley, making camp near Port Republic on September 25 and enjoying some captured beef and amateur cave exploring (of Weyer's Cave) on September 27. Then it was on to Waynesboro, where a kind farmer gave him and Tom Henderson dinner and some homemade soap. Then there was more marching around the Valley in the month of October, gradually moving north toward Strasburg. During that same month, Sheridan's Army of the Shenandoah put the torch to much of the upper Valley, destroying crops, livestock, barns, and mills. "The Burning" created a haze over the once-lush Valley, and in that smoke could be seen all the signs of true fratricidal conflict.[34]

Yet even as the smoke drifted from hamlet to hamlet, General Robert E. Lee and General Jubal Early planned one more gamble. Stalled in the trenches at Petersburg, Lee felt that a victory was needed to rejuvenate his army and his government's fortunes. When Kershaw's divisions (about 3,100 men) and Rosser's brigade of cavalry finally got to Early's depleted Army of the Valley, Lee encouraged Early to go on the offensive. Early and his generals then designed one of the boldest attacks of the entire war: a night march of General John B. Gordon's 2d Corps in front of Union lines, then a coordinated attack of Early's divisions on the spread-out Union lines near Cedar Creek. On a cool, moonlit night, October 18, Gordon's 2d Corps began its march.

Just before 5:00 A.M. on October 19, Kershaw's divisions hit the Union lines. Despite skirmishing the night before, the Union troops were caught off guard, reflecting the belief from the rawest private to the general in charge (who was in Winchester, returning from a conference in Washington) that Early's army was through for the season. That was not the case. In one of the most stunning advances of the war, Early's army pushed two Union corps three miles in just three hours, and it might have smashed the entire Army of the Shenandoah if the bulk of the famed 6th Corps had not held its ground.[35]

Robin Berkeley of Kirkpatrick's Battery was part of the great early morning success. He proudly noted that "twenty-two guns" and nearly 2,000 prisoners had been captured, but like the rest of the army—and historians since—he was baffled by the fact that by mid-morning, Early ordered the army to halt and regroup. Although everything from straggling to exhaustion to plundering has been blamed, historian Jeffrey Wert places the responsibility on the 7,500 cavalry troops of General Alfred Torbert. General Horatio Wright (commander of the 6th Corps) ordered Torbert to take his corps to the Union left, just above Middleton, at 9:00 A.M. There they skirmished with advance elements of General Gabriel Wharton's division. Detecting a well-armed and well-defended foe clustered behind four stone walls, Kershaw's division stopped at the northern outskirts of the little village.[36]

The only possible threat to this corps of cavalry was the 1,700 troopers under General Lunsford Lomax, but they were near Front Royal, trying to get in the rear of the Union army. As at Winchester and Fisher's Hill, cavalry, both Union and Confederate, would be Early's undoing. Although he continually chastised his men in his official reports, Early also never used them effectively.

Conversely, Sheridan used his numerically superior cavalry to great effect, either to close off attack routes or as shock troops for offensives.

For nearly six long hours, the bulk of Early's army stayed in place. Meanwhile, General Philip Sheridan raced the ten miles from Winchester to Cedar Creek on his magnificent black horse Rienzi, rallying stragglers and skulkers alike with his bold and confident manner. As he galloped along he shouted variations of his famous phrase, "Retreat—Hell! We'll be back in our camps tonight." When he reached his generals at Cedar Creek he assessed the tactical situation, then laid out his plan—a counterattack.

At 4:00 P.M. the counterattack began, and as artillery and muskets blazed across the entire front, the battered Confederates held firm. Then around 4:30 P.M., General George Custer's cavalry division charged into the Confederate left, defended by Colonel Edmund Pendleton's brigade of Louisianans (known as York's Brigade). Once again, thousands of fast-riding Union cavalry had hit a thin infantry brigade of Confederates on the left. Just as at Winchester, the brigade broke under the shock of an overwhelming number of men and horses.

In a virtual repeat of the debacle at Fisher's Hill, the collapse of one brigade led to the flight of another. A panic spread among these veterans and, to the horror of the senior officers, brigade after brigade began to break ranks and run. As generals forlornly tried to stop the fleeing men, only the artillery units stood firm, firing and then retreating in orderly fashion while making "the most strenuous efforts to rally the infantry," according to General Early.[37]

Robin Berkeley noted that his battery "kept back the Yanks until dark," even managing to cross Cedar Creek. Then, because of the lack of Confederate infantry support, Union cavalry rode unmolested among the retreating artillerymen, recapturing their twenty-two guns and taking another twenty-three guns. Robin made "several narrow escapes" that long night before temporarily leaving the battery, cutting through fields, then returning to the Valley Pike and happening upon part of Gordon's division. Robin finally found his battery again in the morning, camped at New Market. Just before he got there he ran into some old friends in the Hanover Cavalry, who encouraged him to take a "furlough" of a few weeks. But he told them that "General Early needed every man which he could get and many more than he had, and that if we did [not] stand to our guns, the Yanks might get to our homes before we did."[38]

Thus ended the dramatic gambles of the audacious Army of the Valley. The soldiers stayed around New Market for nearly two weeks, rebuilding and counting the losses. A couple of Robin's messmates returned from home after recovering from wounds received at Cold Harbor. On October 25, Robin recorded a remarkable fact: "I am the only man in our mess who has never had to leave his post of duty." The same could not be said for the 2,900 Confederate casualties at Cedar Creek (compared to 5,600 Union casualties). They included General Stephen Dodson Ramseur, killed while trying to rally troops in the late afternoon at Cedar Creek.[39]

The Confederates' defeat at Cedar Creek had ramifications beyond the nearly 10,000 families affected by the sacrifices of the men from both sides. It ended General Lee's last attempt to relieve Richmond by threatening Washington. It severely damaged General Early's reputation; the easy criticism was that his mentor Stonewall Jackson had won against superior numbers in 1862, so why couldn't he? But the Confederacy had been much stronger in 1862, and none of the generals Jackson defeated had the boldness and fire of Philip Sheridan. For the Union, Cedar Creek made Sheridan a hero and helped reelect Abraham Lincoln.

With Washington safe, the upper Shenandoah destroyed and under Union control, the siege of Petersburg unending, and General Sherman's army marching through Georgia, prospects looked bleak for the Confederacy. As the Union military circle began to close around the shrinking Confederacy, both sides prepared to move into quarters for what many believed would be the last winter of the war.

NOTES

1. Richard R. Duncan, *Lee's Endangered Left: The Civil War in Western Virginia, Spring of 1864* (Baton Rouge, 1998), 8–25; William C. Davis, *The Battle of New Market* (Baton Rouge, 1975), 20–21.

2. Duncan, *Lee's Endangered Left*, 34–110; Davis, *The Battle of New Market*, 22–54, 160–92; Freeman, *Lee's Lieutenants*, 3:525–27; Jeffrey D. Wert, *From Winchester to Cedar Creek: The Shenandoah Campaign of 1864* (New York, 1987), 6–8, 22–26; *OR*, vol. 37, 340, report of General Robert E. Lee, July 19, 1864.

3. Duncan, *Lee's Endangered Left*, 247–302; Freeman, *Lee's Lieutenants*, 3:524–57; Worsham, *One of Jackson's Foot Cavalry*, 205–6.

4. Worsham, *One of Jackson's Foot Cavalry*, 206–8 (quotations on 207–8); Berkeley, *Diary*, June 25, 1864, 84; June 27, 1864, 84.

5. Berkeley, *Diary*, July 4, 1864, 85. When the pessimistic Berkeley saw Jackson's grave, he "thought of the future and . . . [his] heart sank." He may have been cheered by a brief visit with big brother Tommy and Uncle Carter near Staunton on June 27.

6. Wert, *From Winchester to Cedar Creek*, 8.

7. Worsham, *One of Jackson's Foot Cavalry*, 211–15 (quotations on 214).

8. Berkeley, *Diary*, July 9, 1864, 86–87; February 5, 1864, 67.

9. Freeman, *Lee's Lieutenants*, 3:464–65; Berkeley, *Diary*, July 10–11, 1864, 89; Worsham, *One of Jackson's Foot Cavalry*, 217.

10. *OR*, vol. 37, pt. 1, 347–49 (Early's report); Freeman, *Lee's Lieutenants*, 3:566–67; Worsham, *One of Jackson's Foot Cavalry*, 218; Berkeley, *Diary*, July 14, 1864, 88; July 16, 1864, 89.

11. Jubal Early, *War Memoirs: Autobiographical Sketch and Narrative of the War between the States* (Bloomington, 1960), ed. Frank E. Vandiver, 397; Freeman, *Lee's Lieutenants*, 3:520; Berkeley, *Diary*, July 20, 1864, 89.

12. *OR*, vol. 37, pt. 1, 326–27 (Averell's report); Freeman, *Lee's Lieutenants*, 3:570.

13. Berkeley, *Diary*, July 24, 1864, 91–92.

14. Ibid., July 20, 1864, 89; July 24, 1864, 90–91; August 7, 1864, 91 (quotation); July 24, 1864, 91 (quotation).

15. Joseph W. A. Whitehorne, "Second Kernstown: July 24, 1864," in *The Civil War Battlefield Guide*, 239–40; Early, *War Memoirs*, 398–99; Berkeley, *Diary*, July 24, 1864, 90.

16. Whitehorne, "Second Kernstown," in *The Civil War Battlefield Guide*, 240–42; Worsham, *One of Jackson's Foot Cavalry*, 220–22.

17. Early, *War Memoirs*, 401–5; Wert, *From Winchester to Cedar Creek*, 8.

18. Wert, *From Winchester to Cedar Creek*, 9–22.

19. Ibid., 29–45; Freeman, *Lee's Lieutenants*, 3:574–77; James L. Nichols, *General Fitzhugh Lee: A Biography* (Lynchburg, 1989), 77; Worsham, *One of Jackson's Foot Cavalry*, 223–29 (quotation on 227); Berkeley, *Diary*, August 19, 1864, 93; September 1, 1864, 94; September 7, 1864, 95; August 29, 1864, 94; and September 8, 1864, 95.

20. Wert, *From Winchester to Cedar Creek*, 42–45; Freeman, *Lee's Lieutenants*, 3:576–77.

21. Wert, *From Winchester to Cedar Creek*, 46–54; Wise, *The Long Arm of Lee*, 2:884–85; Worsham, *One of Jackson's Foot Cavalry*, 232.

22. Wert, *From Winchester to Cedar Creek*, 48–51; Berkeley, *Diary*, September 19, 1864, 97.

23. Berkeley, *Diary*, September 19, 1864, 96–99 (quotations on 97 and 98).

24. Wise, *The Long Arm of Lee*, 2:885–88; Worsham, *One of Jackson's Foot Cavalry*, 232–33 (quotations on both pages).

25. Wert, *From Winchester to Cedar Creek*, 54–80; Nichols, *General Fitzhugh Lee*, 78.

26. Wert, *From Winchester to Cedar Creek*, 80–95.

27. Worsham, *One of Jackson's Foot Cavalry*, 234–35.

28. Wert, *From Winchester to Cedar Creek*, 95–98, 103.

29. Ibid., 104–7, 109–19, 120–21; Freeman, *Lee's Lieutenants*, 3:583–84.

30. Berkeley, *Diary*, September 22, 1864, 100.

31. Wert, *From Winchester to Cedar Creek*, 122–29 (Union losses were thirty-six killed, 414 wounded, six missing); Berkeley, *Diary*, September 22, 1864, 100–101.

32. General Jubal Early to General Robert E. Lee, September 25, 1864, in *OR*, vol. 43, pt. 1, 557–58; General Robert E. Lee to General Jubal Early, September 27, 1864, in *OR*, vol. 43, pt. 1, 558–59.

33. Worsham, *One of Jackson's Foot Cavalry*, 236–38; Worsham, *One of Jackson's Foot Cavalry* (Robertson edition), xxiv (footnote 34).

34. Berkeley, *Diary*, entries from September 23 to October 14, 1864, 101–5; Wert, *From Winchester to Cedar Creek*, 143–45 and 158–60.

35. Wert, *From Winchester to Cedar Creek*, 152–58 and 240.

36. Berkeley, *Diary*, October 19, 1864, 106; Wert, *From Winchester to Cedar Creek*, 197–220. Wert has an excellent analysis of the causes for Early's halt (and rest) in chapter 12, "The Sun of Middleton," 197–220, including a dissection of commonly held views since the battle.

37. Wert, *From Winchester to Cedar Creek*, 239–51, 221–25, 230–34, 235–37; Wise, *The Long Arm of Lee*, 2:891; *OR*, vol. 43, pt. 1, 563 (Early report).

38. Berkeley, *Diary*, October 19, 1864, 107–8; Wise, *The Long Arm of Lee*, 2:892.

39. Berkeley, *Diary*, entries for October 20 to November 9, 1864, 108–10 (quotation from October 25, 1864, entry, 108); Wert, *From Winchester to Cedar Creek*, 246.

Chapter Thirteen

The Longest Year and the Hardest Winter, 1864–65

WHETHER ANALYZING THE home front in the last year of the war or the harsh winter of 1864–65, most modern historians present a picture of hardship, deprivation, disillusionment, and despair. Drew Faust argues that "the patriotism women had so enthusiastically embraced in 1861 began to erode before seemingly endless—and increasingly purposeless—demands for sacrifice." She adds: "by the last months of the war many women, especially those of the middling and lower orders, were not just holding husbands and brothers back from service but were actively urging them to desert." In a much earlier work, Douglas Southall Freeman devotes several pages in *Lee's Lieutenants* to a depiction of the mounting woes of the Confederacy in the "ghastly winter," summarizing at one point: "The result of weakened command, lack of victory, loss of hope, hunger, and alarm on the home front was desertion." He then gives desertion figures supplied by the Confederate Bureau of Conscription, a "disputed" number of 100,000 from all the armies, 60,000 of them from Virginia alone.[1]

Other historians share Freeman's gloomy view. In *The Confederate Nation*, Emory Thomas presents a list of problems—desertion, inflation, tax resistance, shortages—that led to a "fragmented" Confederacy where "in ever growing numbers in 1864 the Confederates reconciled themselves to defeat and reunion with their Northern enemies."[2] Nowhere did problems seem worse than in the Confederate capital of Richmond. As the latest chronicler of Richmond, Ernest Furgurson, describes the times, "spies were underfoot, food was scarce, prices beyond reach, Grant closing in, Sherman rampaging through South Carolina."[3]

Nor were the problems confined to urban areas. For rural Culpeper County, after three years of war and a long winter (1863–64) of Union occupation, according to historian Daniel Sutherland, "some staunch Rebels, well-respected in the community . . . felt their allegiance weakening." Forty-two citizens signed a petition requesting exemption from 1863 and 1864 taxes. By February 1865, Sutherland argues, "This is not a season of hope. It is very nearly a time of despair."[4]

Finding similar distress among some citizens in Albemarle, Campbell, and Augusta Counties in 1864–65, historian William Blair also notes that "signs of disaffection on the home front and within the army can mask the significant portion who still hoped for independence despite losing confidence in their government." Historian J. Tracy Power finds considerable discontent and despair among soldiers in the Army of Northern Virginia in the last winter of the war, tempered by the belief of "numerous veterans . . . that most of Lee's soldiers were willing to fight for as long as necessary and as long as possible."[5]

When we turn to the individual rather than the nation, city, or county, a story closer to the arguments of Blair and Power emerges, replete with hardship and hope. Overall, we see scarcity and worry among the individuals in this study, but not utter despair over the war. The greater problems are personal rather than political and serve as a reminder that the rhythms of life move on regardless of war or peace. For the three women in this study, the last year of the war brought continual complaints about the war itself, and more personal problems than two of them could bear.

Lucy Buck found that she could not escape the war, regardless of where she lived. In early June 1864 she traveled to her Aunt Cattie and Uncle Larue's home, Bloomfield, near Berryville to gather provisions for the Front Royal Bucks and to tutor a young cousin, Walker Buck. Lucy ended up staying there for most of the summer, right in the path of two armies that were marching around northern Virginia. She had dinner with the Edmund Lees (finding them "intolerably stupid" but a "good sort of people"), the same family whose house burning by the Union army in July led General Early to destroy Chambersburg, Pennsylvania. She helped serve dinner to fifty Confederate soldiers on July 17, then had to watch in horror on August 10 when a small band of Union soldiers raided her aunt and uncle's garden and stole the livestock.[6]

The most terrifying moment of the raid came when a Union soldier demanded that Uncle Larue hand over the horse he was leading away from the house. Lucy described the scene: "He cocked his pistol and aimed at him vowing he would shoot him down." But the soldier did not fire, and young Will Larue convinced him that the horse was of little value because he was blind in one eye. The soldier finally rode off, "swearing that he would report him (Uncle Larue) to headquarters."

Another band of Union soldiers raided the farm on August 18, rifling through the family's personal belongings and looking for jewelry and money. This time Aunt Cattie Larue had a pistol pointed at her, but again no shot was fired. Throughout that long day, groups of Union soldiers would suddenly appear, some demanding food, others paying for food, and still others stealing food ("they got all the geese and turkeys save the old gobbler and a little wild turkey and nearly all the chickens and ducks"). Little wonder, then, that when Lucy finally returned to Bel Air on August 27 she was sick from some undiagnosed illness. Her exhaustion spoiled much of her precious time with her brother Alvin, who was home on furlough when she arrived at Bel Air. The illness might also account for the rare gap in her diary; she made no entries between September 21, 1864, and February 13, 1865.

When she resumed writing on February 13, Lucy noted that she was sick for two weeks around Christmas, but mainly "there was too much that . . . to record I had not the spirit to write." Her Aunt Lizzie died on November 15, just after all her farm and livestock (except the house) were either burned or destroyed. Her brother Irving never got a leave to come home and the Union cavalry passed by in December, somehow sparing Bel Air from the torch and sword. Given all these hardships, her explanation for her long silence is not surprising: "My diary was laid by. Those sad autumn days my heart was too sad."[7]

But even the serious, self-critical Lucy could find pleasure, even enjoyment, in the daily life of Bel Air. On February 20 she had a "lovely day. Reading, writing, sewing and as this is my week—housekeeping. Eating walnuts, too." A few days later she sat up late talking and laughing and singing with Charlie Brown and Wythe Cooke, "two fine young Rebels." The next night an even larger group gathered to dance and play games. Many of the same young people partied into the wee hours of the morning the next week, even as news filtered in that Rosser had been "badly defeated." Of course, a "solemn" sermon in church the following Sunday made her "feel like forswearing dancing for the rest of the war." The feelings of guilt soon passed, and she spent much of March 27 with her cousin Sam Buck, learning new songs and playing marbles.[8]

During this same period, Tee Edmonds was more bothered by affairs of the heart than affairs of the war. In June 1864 she spent considerable time with Private George Triplett, Company B, 43d Battalion Virginia Cavalry, originally from Round Hill, near Mount Vernon in Fairfax County. He was great fun, but temperamental and thin-skinned; when Tee teased him about her old boyfriends and showed him "an old ambrotype" of George Leech, Triplett snatched it from her "and tore it to pieces, thus hoping to destroy my peculiar love for Methodist ministers." They exchanged words, and he left in silence to rejoin his company. All was forgiven by the time he returned a few days later from a visit to his mother.[9]

Tee and George had met in the fall of 1863. He soon became a regular visitor to Belle Grove, and in April he and Tee had their first kiss. Tee viewed it as a familiar "make-up" kiss after an argument; George saw something more, for in May he told Tee "how attached he was to me and even inventing plans for our future life." Others told Tee that George "deeply, madly" loved her, but she did not believe it, nor did she encourage those feelings (in her mind). Not only did Tee consider George "young and inexperienced," but she still carried a torch for the reserved, mysterious Lieutenant Matthew Magner of Mississippi. When he visited Tee on June 16 she reported in her diary, "I have succeeded in breaking the ice of reserve between us and, if I can keep the resolution, I will break more than that before we part for our respective duties of life." Her efforts proved useless in the short run. The next week she held a "big julep" at her house and when Magner showed up, they talked very formally, and Tee wrote in frustration, "I treat him friendly, but the more I do so, the more distant he becomes."

Meanwhile, the effervescent George soon lavished his affection on another, Tee's cousin Wint. He sent her love notes, they had an argument and, repeating his old behavior, he rode off in anger "and got drunk, vowing his heart was broken." Fortunately for him, Wint let the incident go by, and George "repented the rash act and asked forgiveness."[10]

All this personal commotion occurred while the war washed over Fauquier County. As always, Mosby's Rangers would come and go from Belle Grove, bragging of their exploits, enjoying the company of young women, then riding off for adventure. In July, for instance, Lieutenant Magner was captured by Union soldiers. He escaped in less than a month and rode to Belle Grove on August 11 to tell his story. Two days later, Mosby's men made a successful raid on Union supplies, carrying off hundreds of prisoners, mules, and cattle. Tee wrote, "Hurrah for Mosby, my gallant Mosby, the guerrilla chief." Naturally, Union forces felt compelled to respond to such raids; in July they briefly occupied Paris. Sometimes Tee felt that the skirmishes between Mosby's Rangers and the Union cavalry were "more like play, though once in awhile exposed to danger."[11]

That danger included capture (Magner), injury (Mosby was shot in the stomach while visiting friends), and prolonged exposure to the elements (Syd and friends were frostbitten after a raid in January 1865). And the danger could reach the steps of Belle Grove, too. After escaping the wrath of Sheridan in September and October, much of upper Fauquier County was put to the torch for assisting Mosby's Rangers in late November 1864. Tee had a brief but dramatic journal entry for November 28: "The Yankees burned our barn!"[12] Fortunately, the loss of a barn was the only recorded damage to Belle Grove that November. Many neighbors were less fortunate—hundreds of barns, mills, and haystacks in Fauquier and Loudoun counties were burned, and countless animals were seized or slaughtered.[13]

The Edmondses had enough provisions in their larder to get them through the winter with nary a word about scarcity. The day after Christmas they had a "taffie pulling," and in January they had a rich feast of oysters washed down with "Rio caffee," both items taken from the Union army by some of the Rangers.[14] The young people even found occasions for fun in this cold, snowy, fourth year of the war. On December 29 they had a dance, and on February 10 they had a "delightful sleighing time" over the "foot and a half" of freshly fallen snow.

However, the war was never far away. In the early hours of the morning of February 20, the Edmonds family heard loud knocks at the door, and a band of Union soldiers entered the house searching for Confederates and special letters. The Edmondses were hiding Mr. O'Rear, who managed to escape detection by the soldiers. One of the young officers impressed Tee with his manners; she wrote, "were he a Reb, I should have immediately been *struck*." Others in the party were less courteous, snatching some of Tee's letters from her trunk. That same day, though, the family had its vengeance; their own Syd and other Rangers attacked the Union force, recapturing some Confederates and horses. Only one Ranger, John Iden, was wounded, but that wound proved to be fatal. He spent a short time at Belle Grove in convalescence before dying on March 12. As winter snows melted in March, good and bad war news drifted into Belle Grove, while Mosby's Rangers (with Mosby back in the saddle by the end of March) continued their depredations. Even though the Union forces were making "bold advances," Tee remained torn between her concerns for the Confederacy, her "soldiers," and her own busy social life.[15]

For Susan Caldwell of Warrenton, social life continued to focus almost exclusively on her family, with the war providing one more heavy burden for her to carry. Throughout the summer, fall, and winter of 1864–65 there was no mention of food shortages. In fact, Susan sent Lycurgus some sugar and coffee in August and encouraged him to "enjoy sugar and coffee daily—I know you can afford it." In late August, Mr. Finks and two of Susan's children went to the Finks farm in Front Royal, presumably to get some vegetables. And even as late as March 1865, Susan wrote of receiving apples and spring vegetables from a Mr. Bronaugh.[16]

If food was not a problem, Union raids were. On January 13, 1865, the 8th Illinois Cavalry rode into town and some troopers searched a few houses. They took Mr. Finks's "new cloth coat," four felt hats, and Susan's spool cotton. At Finks's store they stole

350 pounds of tobacco and all the money. The problem, as usual, was lack of discipline. The men left when a "Sergeant came in and sent them away." Neither the sergeant nor any of his superiors, however, would order the troopers to return the stolen property. Fortunately, that was the only Union raid on the Finks-Caldwell household in the last year of the war.

More important, Lycurgus continued to serve in the Home Guard of Richmond. In October 1864 his regiment was called out to help defend Richmond and evidently stayed in the field for a couple of weeks. Sometimes the two sides exchanged fire, but Lycurgus's regiment had become so accustomed to its sound that "we hardly turn over on our straw if a dozen shots are fired in our front." He proudly proclaimed that no one had deserted from his regiment: "It has the best name in the local brigade."[17]

Even as the losses mounted for the Confederacy, both Lycurgus and Susan held on to their desire for "independence." In October, Lycurgus wrote to Susan, "Our soldiers are tired and want peace—but they will not clamor for it from Lincoln. They will fight him to the bitter end." Even Susan, who repeatedly referred to the "cruel war" in her letters of all four years, could write as late as January 1865, "God grant it may end as we all most ardently desire. That we shall be an *Independent nation* and nothing else—We cannot go back into the Union no, no—the blood already shed in the cause would cry aloud for vengeance." Then, in March, after the last attempt at reconciliation had failed in a February meeting between Lincoln and Vice President Stephens of the Confederacy, Susan still kept the "cause" alive in her heart: "I want Independence and nothing else—I could not consent to go back with a people that has been bent on exterminating us."[18]

Looming much larger than any problems caused by the war was a personal tragedy that struck the Caldwells in September 1864. Their youngest child, Lucy Lee, contracted scarlet fever. It began with a fever and, after home treatments for a night and day, Susan called the doctor, who diagnosed scarlet fever. Jessie and Frank had suffered and survived the same disease, so Susan hoped that Lucy would do the same. But it did not happen that way. On the second day she had "violent spasms," did not recognize anyone, and then died. She was not yet three years old. The letters that follow Lucy's death are full of raw pain and anguish.

Here in a letter to Lycurgus is a glimpse of Susan's agony: "Oh! My *darling babe*—Mama's *heart aches all day and night for you. I feel at times my heart will break when I know I cannot get my baby back to me any more.*"[19]

Nothing but time helped ease the loss. Susan's mother wrote in a sympathetic letter, "I know well of how to feel for you, I have had to go through the same." She suggested that Susan turn to God for strength. Susan's son Frank and daughter Jessie tried to comfort her by sleeping with her, or hugging her, or just standing by her "when Mama's heart aches." Less helpful (to the modern reader) was the advice of her husband. When Lycurgus first heard the news, he wrote of God's will, and how he wished he "could speak peace to your sorrowing soul." But in his next letter he told her not to deepen her depression further by buying and wearing black clothes. After reading her full account of Lucy's illness, he wrote, "In writing one hereafter concerning the dear little departed one do not write as if addressing her, but me. It makes one appreciate that you may not be equal to the affliction put upon us." He then suggested that she strive to be a good teacher to the three remaining children, both for their sake and to help overcome her grief through the performance of the "duties of life."[20]

Ever the dutiful wife, Susan wrote on October 30, "I will try to do as you desire . . . I need self control and pray for it daily." But she also reminded Lycurgus that he had "never felt the deep keen anguish of a Mother's heart." This anguish led her to have painful dreams, to forget her daily prayers, and sometimes to want to "scream my existence away." She tried to see Lucy's death as part of God's greater plan, but she could not. On October 9 she wrote, "I feel at times that God will punish me yet more severely because I cannot gain power over my own rebellious heart to say *God's will be done*. Oh! How hard to be submissive." Time did begin to heal this wound, but in January Susan still mentioned her "rebellious heart"; and in March, as the weather grew warmer, all the memories of Lucy came flooding back, depressing her once more. She wrote, "*my baby I miss all the day . . .* why has the Good Lord thus punished me?"[21]

As for the four men in our study, there is sufficient information on the Confederate soldiers to describe their last winter of the war. Together they paint a picture of an essentially intact army struggling desperately to hold on for one more campaign. William Poague and Fred Fleet reflected the optimism still felt by many in the Army of Northern Virginia. Poague spent the long winter at Dutch Gap. Having fought mosquitoes in the summer, he survived mortar and other shells until January 1, 1865. (There were only two casualties in his battalion in five months of shelling.) The officers had placed the camp on a "gentle southern slope," and the men built huts from pine logs. They supplemented their meager rations with vegetables from nearby farms, fish from the river, and boxes from home. They held regular church services, and on Christmas Day 1864, Poague and some fellow officers ate a feast—oysters, fish, roast turkey, fruit—and drank too much eggnog. The host was a "noted bon vivant," Private Dick Shirley, who had a friend in the "blockade running ports."[22]

This is the one period of Poague's military service that is complemented by letters he sent home (letters that, thankfully, his mother did not burn). One consistent theme throughout these letters is the undying faith in the "cause" that he and his fellow soldiers felt. In October 1864 he wrote to his mother, "I think our prospects are unusually bright and hopeful. If the Lord of Hosts will bless us in future as I believe he has done in the past, our independence is certain." Even after Lincoln's reelection, which Poague knew meant the extension of the war, he wrote to his mother, "with the blessing of Providence in the four years to come as in the four that are past, we will maintain our independence." He was tired of war, but would rather fight on "than endure peaceful and quiet subjection to yankee rule." After the failure of the peace conference in early February 1865, his battalion unanimously passed resolutions "indignantly rejecting the offered terms, renewing their vows of devotion to the great cause of Southern independence." As late as March 17, Poague wrote to his mother, "The spirit of the great bulk of the army is most excellent." He felt the same, grounding himself in his steadfast belief in God: "He is a wise, a just, and merciful Being, that however the war may terminate, whatever may befall us, He will overrule all so that that shall be done which will be best for this people." More than anything, he felt compelled to do his duty, to "defend my country"—the "government of my choice, the religion of my choice, the graves of my fathers, property, friends, relatives, my mother and little brother. It means all that I love or value on earth."[23]

One can never know whether Poague's brave and fatalistic statements were designed to stiffen his mother's resolve or his own. Undoubtedly, some of Poague's encouraging words were aimed at his mother, who had to shoulder all the household burdens after the sudden death of her husband in November 1864. But his father's death hit William hard, too. Added to the grief over the death of his father were the deaths of Wilson Poague, Sandie Pendleton, John Massie, two cousins, and a friend, Abbie Chancellor. For Poague, 1864 had been "a year of more sorrow by far than any" of his young life. So even while he counseled his mother not to "allow yourself undue trouble about the unfavorable aspect of affairs," he too saw "clouds that darken the horizon of our country, clouds more threatening perhaps than any that have ever overshadowed us." Views like these would place Poague between two of historian William Blair's three groups of Confederates in the winter of 1864–65: "those with unflagging hopes for victory," "those who saw bleak prospects ahead but were willing to keep the faith as long as Lee led the army," and those who simply wanted peace. Ultimately, Poague found solace and strength in his faith in God and in his fidelity to his duty. As he told his mother, "if one does his duty he can leave the result with God, feeling sure that for himself all things will be done well and wisely."[24]

Not possessed of the sturdy religious faith and perdurable optimism of Poague, Lieutenant Fred Fleet sat in his occasionally flooded "bombproofs" that winter, alternating between hope, determination, resignation, and despair. In November, Colonel Goode asked him to be acting adjutant general (AAG), a position Fred reluctantly accepted. He preferred to be with his company and did not think Goode was the officer that Powhatan Page had been.[25]

Nevertheless, Fred took the job and remained in that slot even after his old commander, General Henry Wise, returned to head the brigade. He assumed that Wise would appoint his own AAG, but the man he did appoint never appeared in camp. Instead, Fred spent January to March of 1865 with General Wise, his son,

Dick, and Lieutenant Warwick. By February they had built a "frame house" for the general, a bombproof to work in, and tents for the other staff officers, complete with "brick chimneys." Somehow the Fleets managed to keep Fred supplied with food, even providing a turkey and a bottle of wine for General Wise, a box of "eatables" for General Robert E. Lee, and extra food for the regular soldiers. When possible, Fred visited his cousins Bernard Todd and Dick Bagby.[26]

Sometimes Fred felt optimistic and defiant. After Lincoln's reelection he feared the war would be "long," but he would stay "til its close," never wishing "to live and see the South subdued." He sounded a similar note in a December letter, complaining that "many are low-spirited at the signs of the time and the weak hearted all over the land are crying peace, but I still say the issue is in the hand of God, and it is our duty to strive against subjugation to the utmost, and never submit." Even after the fall of Fort Fisher on January 15, 1865, Fred saw hope, because the "blockade running at Wilmington was the leech which drew the richest blood from our treasury." Like Poague's battalion, Fred's brigade passed a resolution in February 1865 to fight the war "to the bitter end," a vote he hoped would help the brigade's reputation.[27]

At other times Fred questioned the war and its ultimate purpose. In December he wrote to his mother, "We are constantly living now on the line—scarcely a day passes without someone being killed or wounded in the Brigade." The day before it had been a "most excellent soldier, John Longest." But with so many other deaths occurring daily, Longest was undoubtedly missed more at home than in the field. Of this sentiment Fred wrote, "Such a war! It deadens the sensibilities and destroys the finer feelings of us all." On January 17 he grew reflective in a letter home, writing to his father, "When we look at the thing in the abstract does it not seem foolish that two nations should sit down and dig [trenches], and dig again and sit down for eight long months in front of each other?"

Still, Fred kept to his post, not even asking for leave in January 1865. His family stayed true to the Confederacy, too, with his mother still feeding soldiers who passed by and writing to Fred in January, "Don't let's give up *now*." They were more than willing to see the end of slavery; both Fred and his father wished it gone if it blocked chances for peace. As Fred put it in a December letter, "I say let the negroes go to the winds—we are not fighting for them, but for our independence and for our very lives." (That was easier for the Fleets to say than for some other white families, because the Fleets had already lost their slaves.) Even Fred's oldest sister remained loyal to the Confederacy, writing as late as April 3, 1865, after hearing of the fall of Richmond, "I hope it will not have a bad effect on our brave soldiers. I don't feel conquered one *bit*, not a single bit."[28]

One wonders if John Worsham had the same spirit as Lou Fleet, as he lay in his bed recuperating from his battle wound during the winter of 1864–65. He left no account of those months. Instead, he gave a history of the 21st Virginia and the 2d Corps from September 1864 through April 1865, not resuming his own personal story until his description of the fall of Richmond.[29]

Of all the soldiers in this study, only one had a truly awful time in the winter of 1864–65, Private Robin Berkeley of Kirkpatrick's Battery. Stuck with the remnants of the Army of the Valley, he moved camp five times in November and December before settling into a more permanent camp near Fisherville in mid-December. Here the men erected a hut for the mess and built stables for the horses. Robin spent Christmas Day in camp, looking pessimistically toward a future "dark, gloomy, bloody, and hopeless." Not sermons, nor letters from home, nor even a big snowfall cheered Robin. On January 1, 1865, he wrote, "Farewell, Old Year. Thou art gone, and with thee, many a noble and brave soldier. Who could count the vacant chairs in our southern homes, the bereaved and stricken fathers, mothers, sisters and wives?" The future appeared "gloomy, and almost hopeless." Even worse, Robin foresaw his own death: "I wonder if I shall live to see 1866. I do not believe I shall."[30] Like William Poague, though, faith and duty kept Robin going. In the same depressing January 1 entry he wrote, "May God give me grace to do my whole duty to Him, my fellow man and to my country."

Robin's only ray of sunshine in that bleak winter was a furlough to go home in January. He stayed there for sixteen days, visiting all his relatives (some several times). He found their belief in the cause and the possibility of victory surprising and unrealistic, writing, "I don't think our home people realize how near the end is on us, or what that end will most probably be." He had no doubt what the future would be—"dark, bloody and hopeless" (his favorite phrase that winter). He spent a terrible day at home on January 18, dreading the return to his unit. His only hope was that he would have the "courage, strength and grace, in this coming campaign, to do my whole duty to my God, my country, and my fellow man."

Robin returned to his battery on January 20, finding most of the men absent on "horse furlough" (take your horse home, feed and take care of it, and return to the unit in the spring). The weather for the rest of January did nothing to improve his mood; entries usually note "cold and damp." On February 3, Robin complained that he was doing the duties of the "lieutenant, the orderly sergeant, a corporal, and a gunner." Only Nelson's Battalion of artillery with six guns remained with Early; the other battalions had been sent on to Richmond.[31] February was enlivened by a brief trip home and a snowball fight on the eighteenth. Robin also continued to attend church and to correspond with his family. Rumors reached camp of Union forces gathering at Winchester for a march down the Valley, and on the third anniversary of the inauguration of President Jefferson Davis (February 22) that Robin had witnessed in Richmond, he wrote, "I don't think the future looks as promising as our President then painted it."[32]

This time the pessimistic Robin was right. Sheridan's cavalry left Winchester on February 27, moved down the Valley, and on a cold, sleet-filled March afternoon (the second) surrounded Early's small army of fewer than 1,500 near Waynesboro. Robin fired his gun "five or six times," but when Early's left flank collapsed, the entire army had to flee. They had only one avenue of escape, a "little narrow plank over the railroad bridge" (Virginia Central), making it easy for the Union cavalry to ride ahead of them and completely trap the fleeing army. Nearly 1,000 soldiers were captured, including thirty men from Robin's company. The Army of the Valley had fought its last battle; and though its commander, Early, escaped, the army was finished.[33]

Robin spent the next week marching toward Winchester. The prisoners were given few rations; the Union captors said they had lost the commissary wagons. The only food the prisoners got was from the local populace, and Robin wrote, "I never knew what it was to be hungry before." On March 8 he reached Stephenson's Depot (near his earlier fight), where he was shipped by boxcar to Baltimore and ultimately to Fort McHenry. Robin caught a terrible flu or virus and thought he would die, until revived by a glass of whiskey and a cup of coffee. He then was carried out to the island prison, Fort Delaware. There he would spend the last two months of the war, "watching the waves and the boats" on the river from his bunk window, looking away from the stack of coffins outside the hospital "dead-house," and thinking as he spent his twenty-fifth birthday (March 27) in prison, "The end of this long and bloody war is certainly drawing to a close and that very rapidly. And what an awful close it is going to be."[34]

NOTES

1. Faust, *Mothers of Invention*, 238 and 243; Freeman, *Lee's Lieutenants*, 3:622, 623, 624 (quotations from each page).

2. Thomas, *The Confederate Nation*, 284–85.

3. Ernest B. Furgurson, *Ashes of Glory: Richmond at War* (New York, 1998), 297.

4. Sutherland, *Seasons of War*, 367 and 371 (quotations from both pages).

5. Blair, *Virginia's Private War*, 130; Power, *Lee's Miserables*, 217–44 (quotation on 227).

6. Buck, *Diary*, June 7, 1864, 258; June 9, 1864, 259; June 27, 1864, 264; July 20, 1864, 268; July 17, 1864, 268; August 10, 1864, 270.

7. Ibid., August 10, 1864, 271; August 18, 1864, 274–77; August 20–September 9, 1864, entries, 278–82, scattered references to illness and Alvin; February 13, 1865, 287–89 (quotation on 287).

8. Ibid., February 20, 1865, 289–90; February 24, 1865, 290; February 25 and March 6, 1865, 291–92; March 10, 1865, 292–93; March 27, 1865, 294.

9. Edmonds, *Journals*, June 10, 1864, 197–98; June 11, 1864, 198; June 12, 1864, 198 (quotation); June 16, 1864, 199.

10. Ibid., September 7, 1863, 168; September 20, 1863, 169; September 26–27, 1863, 170; October 11–12, 1863, 172–73; October 14, 173, and numerous other visits between November 1863 and May 1864; April 25, 1864, 192; May 29, 1864, 196 (quotation from George); June 10, 1864, 197–98 (quotation from Tee); June 16, 1864, 199 (quotation from Tee); June 24, 1864, 200 (quotation); July 17, 1864, 201.

11. Ibid., July 19, 1864, 202; August 11, 1864, 204; August 13, 1864, 204–5; July 20–21, 1864, 202–3; June 16, 1864, 199.

12. Ibid., December 22, 1864, 210–11; October 29, 1864, 208; January 19, 1865, 212; November 28, 1864, 209.

13. Wert, *Mosby's Rangers*, 260–63.

14. Edmonds, *Journals*, December 26, 1864, 210; January 19, 1865, 212.

15. Ibid., December 29, 1864, 211; February 10, 1865, 213; February 20, 1865, 213–14 (quotation); February 27–March 5, 1865, 215–16; March 13, 1865, 217; war news: February 26, March 8, 21, 28, and 31, 1865, 215–18; social life: March 1, 9, 11, 13, 16, and 20, 1865, 215–18.

16. Caldwell, *Letters*, Susan Caldwell to Lycurgus Caldwell, August 14, 1864, 234; Susan Caldwell to Lycurgus Caldwell, August 29, 1864, 237.

17. Ibid., Susan Caldwell to Lycurgus Caldwell, January 15, 1865, 253–56; Susan Caldwell to Lycurgus Caldwell, October 2, 1864, 240; Susan Caldwell to Lycurgus Caldwell, January 15, 1865, 256; Lycurgus Caldwell to Susan Caldwell, October 26, 1864, 243–45.

18. Ibid., Lycurgus Caldwell to Susan Caldwell, October 26, 1864, 245; Susan Caldwell to Lycurgus Caldwell, undated (but reference to peace conference places it in early February 1865), 258; Susan Caldwell to Lycurgus Caldwell, March 26, 1865, 262.

19. Ibid., Susan Caldwell to Lycurgus Caldwell, October 9, 1864, 241–42.

20. Ibid., Mary Jeffords to Susan Caldwell, October 17, 1864, 242–43; Susan Caldwell to Lycurgus Caldwell, undated (but sometime in early October 1864), and October 16, 1864, 246–47; Lycurgus Caldwell to Susan Caldwell, September 16, 1864, 238–39; Lycurgus Caldwell to Susan Caldwell, September 27, 1864, 240; Lycurgus Caldwell to Susan Caldwell, October 26, 1864, 243.

21. Ibid., Susan Caldwell to Lycurgus Caldwell, October 30, 1864, 247–48; Susan Caldwell to Lycurgus Caldwell, October 9, 1864, 241; Susan Caldwell to Lycurgus Caldwell, October 16, 1864, 247; Susan Caldwell to Lycurgus Caldwell, October 30, 1864, 248; Susan Caldwell to Lycurgus Caldwell, January 15, 1865, 255; Susan Caldwell to Lycurgus Caldwell, March 26, 1865, 261.

22. Poague, *Gunner with Stonewall*, 105–9 (quotations on 109).

23. Ibid., William Poague to Elizabeth Poague, October 5, 1864, 139–40; William Poague to Elizabeth Poague, November 4, 1864, 142–43; William Poague to Elizabeth Poague, February 11, 1865, 148–49; William Poague to Elizabeth Poague, March 17, 1865, 153.

24. Ibid., William Poague to Elizabeth Poague, December 29, 1864, 144; Blair, *Virginia's Private War*, 131.

25. Fleet, *Green Mount*, Fred Fleet to Pa, November 10, 1864, 346.

26. Ibid., Fred Fleet to Pa, December 9, 1864, 349; Fred Fleet to Ma, February 9, 1865, 359; Ma to Fred Fleet, January 27, 1865, 357–58; Fred Fleet to Ma, February 2, 1865, 358–59; Fred Fleet to Lou Fleet, December 21, 1864, 350–51; Fred Fleet to Ma, December 31, 1864, 352; Fred Fleet to Ma, February 9, 1865, 359–60.

27. Ibid., Fred Fleet to Ma, September 8, 1864, 338; Fred Fleet to Lou Fleet, November 26, 1864, 348; Fred Fleet to Lou Fleet, December 21, 1864, 351–52; Fred Fleet to Ma, January 25, 1865, 357; Fred Fleet to Ma, February 2, 1865, 359.

28. Ibid., Fred Fleet to Ma, undated (but in December 1864, by references), 348; Fred Fleet to Pa, January 17, 1865, 353; Fred Fleet to Ma, January 23, 1865, 356; Ma to Fred Fleet, January 27, 1865, 357–58; Pa to Fred Fleet, January 19, 1865, 356; Fred Fleet to Pa, December 9, 1864, 349; Lou Fleet to Fred Fleet, April 3, 1865, 361. In January 1865, Pa hired ten blacks to work his land, at least two of whom were still somebody else's slaves. The highest-paid man would get $900, and the lowest-paid $600 (Pa to Fred Fleet, January 19, 1865, 354).

29. Worsham, *One of Jackson's Foot Cavalry*, 249–60.

30. Berkeley, *Diary*, November 14, 1864, 111; November 15, 1864, 111; November 17, 1864, 111; December 13, 1864, 112; December 14, 1864, 112–13; December 16, 1864, 113; December 20, 1864, 113; December 25, 1864, 113 (quotation); December 30, 1864, 114; December 31, 1864, 114; January 1, 1865, 114 (quotation).

31. Ibid., January 1, 1865, 114; January 4–20, 1865, 115–16; January 8, 1865, 115 (quotation); January 18, 1865, 116 (quotation); January 20, 1865, 116; January 21–February 3, 1865, 116–17; February 3, 1865, 117 (quotation); Wise, *The Long Arm of Lee*, 2:920.

32. Berkeley, *Diary*, February 7–10, 1865, 118; February 18, 1865, 119; February 12–21, 1865, 118–19; February 22, 1865, 119 (quotation).

33. Ibid., March 2, 1865, 121–22; *OR*, vol. 46, pt. 1, 502–17 (reports of the Battle of Waynesboro); Freeman, *Lee's Lieutenants*, 3:635–36; Charles C. Osborne, *Jubal: The Life and Times of General Jubel A. Early, CSA, Defender of the Lost Cause* (Baton Rouge, 1992), 386–92. On March 30, 1865, General Lee relieved General Early of command.

34. Berkeley, *Diary*, March 3–8, 1865, 124–26; March 6, 1865, 125 (quotation); March 9, 1865, 126; March 11, 1865, 127; March 12–31, 1865, 128–31; March 28, 1865, 131 (quotation); March 27, 1865, 131.

CHAPTER FOURTEEN

THE FINAL DAYS OF THE ARMY OF NORTHERN VIRGINIA, MARCH 25–APRIL 21, 1865

THE END OF the greatest war in American history came suddenly and swiftly for the Army of Northern Virginia. In February 1865, Robert E. Lee and other top generals plotted out one more strategic gamble: an attack on Grant's army, allowing General Joseph Johnston to unite with Lee's army around Richmond. Barring success there, some way would be found to link the two armies together for one united stand.[1]

The plan was never executed. The Confederate strategy began with a stunning early morning attack on Fort Stedman by General John B. Gordon's 2d Corps on March 25. The day ended with Union recapture of lost ground and a rapid rollback of Confederate forces around Richmond and Petersburg. In just fifteen days, Richmond and Petersburg would be evacuated, the Confederate government on the run to the south, and the Army of Northern Virginia surrendered by its proud commander at a little hamlet in southside Virginia, Appomattox Court House.

The defeats came quickly. First, nearly 5,000 Confederates were captured at the Battle of Five Forks (April 1). The next day, Union forces captured Sutherland Station of the Southside Railroad. The Army of Northern Virginia had not only lost a battle, but it also had lost nearly an entire division, its security on its right, and its southern rail lifeline. Lee now had no choice but to order a retreat from the lines around Petersburg and Richmond, setting the stage for the most dramatic chapter in the story of the final days of the Confederacy.[2]

While the Confederate right collapsed, General Lee tried to buy time to keep his army intact. That time was provided by the steady artillery fire of Lieutenant Colonel William T. Poague's three batteries guarding the Turnbull Home and the Washington Artillery guarding Forts Gregg and Whitworth. After firing for hours on April 2, Poague's position was flanked (through use of woods to cover an advance), and he escaped on his brother's horse, Josh, "a great jumper." Years later, Poague allowed himself a bit of boasting and a criticism of the infantry: "The artillery rendered signal service that day . . . not an infantryman was on our part of the line."[3]

After Poague and his batteries had retreated and reformed, Poague received a message to report his situation to General Lee. He found Lee "dignified, serene, self-possessed" as he planned the evacuation and night march. The general's only outward sign of stress was a "somewhat flushed" face. Witnessing this calm in the midst of chaos, Poague wrote, "nothing before had so impressed me with his towering greatness." Lee ordered Poague to march with General Cadmus Wilcox on the retreat west. They left the night of April 2 and reached Amelia Court House on April 4, the intended convergence site for the divided sections of the Army of Northern Virginia marching from Richmond and Petersburg.[4]

As the disparate elements of the Army of Northern Virginia slowly marched west, the citizens of Petersburg and Richmond prepared for the unthinkable: occupation. The Petersburg occupation on April 3 occurred with little fanfare, but the nighttime evacuation of Richmond that preceded Union occupation proved catastrophic. With the government headed west on a special train and the Army of Northern Virginia abandoning the defenses of Richmond, the thieves and revelers took over the streets on the night of April 2. Recovering from his wound at his parents' home in Richmond, Sergeant John Worsham saw a "flash of light" in his bedroom just before dawn, "accompanied immediately by a loud report with rumbling and shaking of the house, and a crash as if the front had fallen." Worsham knew that there had been a huge explosion, probably at "one of the magazines." Soon afterward his family heard that the city was burning, the fires started by retreating troops to prevent the Union from seizing the contents of the arsenals, magazines, and warehouses. Heavy smoke drifted out from the center of the city, carrying with it "chunks of fire" that hit Worsham's house but never succeeded in destroying it. By evening the Union troops had occupied the city and restored order, and the next day three Union officers interviewed Worsham at his home. Convinced that he was not a threat, they offered to station a guard at the house to protect it from looters! Thus began Worsham's new life back in the Union.[5]

As Worsham adjusted to Union occupation, the bulk of the Army of Northern Virginia finally made it to Amelia Court House, only to find that there were no rations. Troops went out foraging (in vain) on April 4, and on the fifth the army resumed its march, heading southwest to join the government now temporarily housed in Danville, Virginia. As they approached Jetersville, Major General Rooney Lee of the cavalry gave some awful news to his father, General Robert E. Lee: the Union army was rapidly approaching Burkeville, the intended destination of the Army of Northern Virginia. Lee faced the terrible choice of whether to fight his way to and at Burkeville, hoping to press on to Danville, or to conduct a forced night march to Farmville. From there, the army could march toward Danville or even ride on the Southside Railroad to Lynchburg, then march to Danville. Not knowing the terrain or the size or position of the Union cavalry and infantry, and having around 30,000 tired, hungry, and despondent men under his command, Lee gave the order to begin a march toward Farmville, twenty-three miles away.[6]

The night march tried everyone. The farm roads were in bad shape, the men were hungry, and the officers were perhaps the most tired of all, because according to Poague the officers "were strictly enjoined to be on the alert at all times and to see that the column was kept closed up." Since Friday, March 31, Poague had had only one period of uninterrupted sleep, a too-brief five hours on Tuesday at Amelia Court House. Poague's rare treat of a big meal at the home of his friend, the Reverend D. W. Shank, on April 5 may have been a mixed blessing, because that same night he had to stay awake for the entire march to Farmville. The next day he took a nap, only to find that his second-in-command, Captain Nathan Penick, did the same. Poague wrote, "The loss of sleep, especially in this closing campaign, was the severest suffering that I endured in the whole war." Fortunately for Poague and Penick, their column kept going when they did not, and they were able to catch up with it after a while.[7]

The next shattering defeat for the exhausted Army of Northern Virginia came at Sailor's Creek. Attacked by a large force of Union cavalry and two Union corps (2d and 6th), three Confederate corps took a severe beating. Of the three, only Gordon's 2d Corps was able to hold its position until nightfall. Still, Gordon suffered 1,700 casualties compared to 536 for the Union. Lieutenant General Richard Anderson's loss was much greater: 2,600 men, most of them captured (compared to 172 Union casualties). General Richard Ewell fared even worse, losing nearly his entire corps; 3,400 out of 3,600 were casualties, including six generals. For the day, the Union scored another of its lopsided victories in the final days of the war in Virginia. Their forces captured the field, destroyed hundreds of wagons, and captured over 5,000 men, at a cost of 1,148 Union casualties. Somehow General Wise's regiment fought its way out of the Union vise, but it was an angry Henry Wise who confronted General Lee the next morning. Wise's commanding officers, Bushrod Johnson and George Pickett, received ample criticism for their leadership that day.[8]

There was no time for critical evaluation, however, because Union forces kept pressing in on the Army of Northern Virginia. The following day the army marched on toward Farmville, and General William Mahone's division had two key assignments: to serve as a rear guard for General Gordon's 2d Corps as it wearily crossed the High Bridge and marched toward Farmville, and to burn the wagons and railroad bridges at High Bridge. Mahone's division performed the first task admirably, but failed in the second; the fires set by engineers were quenched by Union skirmishers.

Much to the dismay of Mahone and Gordon, the Union's 2d Corps quickly crossed the High Bridge, forcing Mahone to set up a defensive line by Cumberland Church, about four miles north of Farmville. This line saved Lieutenant Colonel William Poague's guns, which had been hurried up from Farmville on the morning of April 7 to protect the supply wagons from Union cavalry. Poague's battalion arrived at Cumberland Church first, not knowing it would be facing infantry and cavalry. As Poague's guns fired away, Mahone's lead brigade appeared and "without halting an instant [he] pushed it right through our guns and soon had the enemy on the run." Poague gave high praise to Mahone's men: "This performance of Mahone's men was as fine a piece of work as ever I saw." When Poague sought out Mahone to thank him for saving his batteries, he found Mahone "in a towering passion abusing and swearing at the Yankees, who he had just learned that morning captured his headquarters wagon and his cow." That sounds like the Mahone most commonly described, and though future years would find Poague and Mahone on opposite sides politically, Poague appreciated the good work done by Mahone's men that day. Together, Mahone's division and Poague's battalion held back the lead elements of the Union's 2d Corps, which allowed the exhausted survivors of the Army of Northern Virginia to continue their trek west to a Southside Railroad stop twenty-five miles away, Appomattox Station.[9]

The next evening, April 8, as elements of the army continued to straggle into the tiny village of Appomattox Station, the highest-ranking generals of the Army of Northern Virginia gathered around their commander for the last "council of war." Generals Longstreet, Pendleton, Lee, and Gordon were there, along with some staff officers. By the dim light of a "low-burning bivouac-fire," the men sat on blankets or saddles around Lee, arguing over the possible avenues to take. Should they accept General Grant's offer of surrender? What were the consequences of surrender? What were the consequences if they did not surrender? By all accounts, it was a sad meeting. General John B. Gordon later wrote, "If all that was said and felt at that meeting could be given it would make a volume of measureless pathos." Throughout the meeting General Lee kept his composure, finally deciding that the army would try to break out of the tightening Union vise in the early morning. Fitz Lee's cavalry and Gordon's infantry, supported by artillery under Colonel Thomas Carter, would attempt to cut a hole through Union lines, and Longstreet's men could then follow as the army tried to march to Lynchburg.[10]

The last movement of the Army of Northern Virginia began in the middle of a cool April night. At 1:00 A.M. on the ninth, reveille sounded. By 2:00 A.M. Poague's battalion had moved onto the road as scheduled, looking for General Longstreet and his corps, but there was no sign of them. Bewildered, Poague rode into Appomattox, found General Rooney Lee, and asked him where he could find General Longstreet. Lee replied, "I know nothing of his whereabouts." He then ordered Poague to "wait until daylight to see how things look," which for Poague and his tired men meant a few hours of blessed sleep.[11]

At sunrise a courier instructed Poague to position his battalion on the left of Gordon's 2d Corps (a division is a better term, given that Gordon had only 1,600 men). On the right were Fitz Lee and his cavalry, estimated at 2,400 men. Lee's cavalry and Gordon's infantry moved forward, capturing two guns and clearing the Lynchburg Road. Then, just as quickly as the planned maneuver had occurred, Union infantry began to appear to their right and rear, and later Union cavalry on their left. The infantry pushed back Lee's cavalry and by 8:00 A.M., Gordon found himself surrounded on three sides. It was at this moment that Colonel Charles Venable found Gordon, who said to him: "Tell General Lee I have fought my Corps to a frazzle, and I fear I can do nothing unless I am heavily supported by Longstreet's Corps."[12]

Longstreet had his own problem: General Meade's 2d and 6th Corps were closing in on his 1st Corps. A courier told Longstreet to report to Lee; and when Longstreet arrived, he received the report that Gordon was virtually trapped and the rations on the railroad probably captured. Lee believed that the Army must surrender and asked Longstreet his opinion. Longstreet asked, if the Army of Northern Virginia continued to fight, would it aid the Southern cause? Lee replied, "I think not." Longstreet answered: "Then your situation speaks for itself."[13]

After discussing the choices further with Generals Mahone and E. Porter Alexander, General Lee rode off to find General Grant, with whom he would discuss the terms of surrender. As Lee rode away, the fighting continued. Lieutenant Colonel William Poague sought out General Gordon to inquire about the infantry needed by one of his batteries for support. Poague found the general's face "pale" and his body under the sway of an "overpowering emotion." Gordon pointed to his front at a rider galloping hard toward the Union line, a white flag "streaming behind him." In a "tremulous voice" Gordon said, "That will stop them!"[14] Poague asked Gordon's staffers what this meant. "Surrender!" Of Gordon or Lee? "General Lee" was the terse reply.

Completely stunned, Poague remembered that "all at once my heart got to my throat and everything around me became dim and obscure." A "dazed" Poague rode back to his batteries, instructing them to cease firing and reassemble at the road. The dreaded end had come, suddenly and without warning.[15] As lower-ranking officers passed orders to cease and desist, General Lee met with General Ulysses S. Grant, and together they composed the generous terms that Lee, Longstreet, Mahone, and others had sought.

William Poague disbanded his battalion on April 11. He had planned a brief speech of praise for his men, but he found himself "dumb—so utterly and unexpectedly overcome that I broke down at the very start—and was able only to utter in broken tones: 'Men, Farewell!' "[16]

For the sensitive Robin Berkeley, the four months in Fort Delaware Prison passed agonizingly slowly. First came the rumors, then the hard news of Lee's surrender. On April 11, Robin wrote in his diary, "Surely the last twenty-four hours has been a day of the most intense mental anxiety I have ever experienced." Then, when the awful news had been confirmed, he wrote, "To think that all the blood and treasure, which the South has so unsparingly poured on the altar of our country, should have been shed in vain."

Within a few days, though, Robin's old sense of duty and loyalty to the "cause" returned. He refused to swear the oath of allegiance to the Union first offered to the men on April 26. He maintained this position after hearing of prominent Virginians who had taken the oath, after seeing sick friends get special releases, and even after some 600 of the 1,500 officers on the island took the oath on June 18. Finally, when he heard that "all our people at home are taking the oath," Robin signed it on June 19. The next day he was shipped out and, after a very slow trip south, reached Richmond "about sunset" on June 23. He had enough money for a "decent" supper and a room at the Powhatan Hotel. The next morning he rode the train to Noel's, then walked home. Ironically, the first person of the household to greet Robin was "Frank, a negro man." Then his father, his younger brother Carter, and soon the whole family were welcoming him home after "four years, one month and seven days" in the Army of Northern Virginia.[17]

For John Worsham, in his sickbed in his Richmond home guarded by Union soldiers, the news of the surrender came as a shock. When the first rumors hit town on April 9, "None of the Confederate people believed it." When the news was confirmed, all Worsham could say was, "What a blow!"[18]

There is no record of the reactions of Lycurgus and Susan Caldwell to the news. Susan's last letter is dated March 26, 1865. The editors of her letters assume that Lycurgus was captured along with the entire Richmond Home Guard under General Custis Lee at Sailor's Creek on April 6. Somehow Lycurgus made it home, undoubtedly to the unbridled joy of Susan and the children.[19]

Fred Fleet's homecoming was not as joyous. After surviving Sailor's Creek and surrendering at Appomattox, Fred wended his way back to Green Mount. When he got home, he found out that his father, only forty-eight years old, had died of erysipelas in March. His death left Fred in charge of the planting that spring.[20]

The news of Lee's surrender did not reach Front Royal as rapidly. On April 12, Lucy Buck wrote that a recently returned prisoner had said that the Confederate armies were in "fine spirits." The next day, however, the truth was finally learned in Front Royal: "Father came in suddenly pale and grave with the words, 'Well, I fear the die is cast—Lee has surrendered.' " Lucy tried to describe the depths of her despair: "To remember half the horrible ideas that filled my heart and brain would be impossible—the one thought—subjugation—all staked, all lost. Our dearest hopes dashed—our fondest dreams dispelled." She even felt "tempted to envy poor Aunt Bettie lying cold and still in her little cabin tonight." The next day she viewed Aunt Bettie's body, and on April 15 she made the last entry in her wartime diary, briefly describing the visitors and news on a rainy day that ended with a "bad headache" and a "nervous attack."[21]

Bad news somehow reached Paris a bit sooner. On April 7, Tee Edmonds wrote of the confirmation of the fall of Richmond and Petersburg and expected more bad news. She added, "Everyone is dying with the blues." On April 15 or a couple of days earlier she penned an entry for April 9: "A sorrowful day in the annals of history for us." Although Tee knew of Lee's surrender at Appomattox, for her and for many of the families of Mosby's Confederacy, the war was not yet over because Mosby had not surrendered. Furthermore, Syd and Cap had escaped with their cavalry friends before the fall of Richmond, so they had yet to surrender or be paroled.[22]

Tee, though, could not stay depressed for long. On April 15 she and some friends organized a dance for themselves to celebrate the wedding of some unnamed black servants. The young white people had "plenty of nice cake and cream besides frozen custard." As she summarized the day, "In lieu of all the bad news we have heard, I enjoyed myself very much." The next morning Tee had a "toddy" to wake herself up and dwelled on her biggest problem: "My heart of stone is slightly wounded again by Cupid's dangerous arrow." She added, " 'He' said he is in love and I am too. Oh! War, war, why do your changes separate us thus." (The author assumes that Tee refers to the enigmatic Matthew Magner.)

For a few more days the state of war continued in Fauquier County. On April 18, Mosby gave his famous reply to a Union request to surrender. "No! Never! Never will I surrender, neither myself or my command!" Tee loved this defiant statement, writing in her diary, "God bless *his noble, brave, unyielding Southern heart.*" But three days later, Mosby's Rangers disbanded. Addressing his Rangers one last time, Mosby said he "knew not where he was going, and there was no hope for the South, but if hostilities broke out again he hoped to meet them on the field of action." His men began crying, and he joined them. Tee added her praise: "We cherish thy great adoration for our cause and the love which we give thy fame shall be seared in our memory."[23]

With the disbandment of Mosby's Rangers, the war had truly ended for Tee. On John Wilkes Booth's assassination of Abraham Lincoln, she wrote, "God bless him for that brave act." Other than that political comment and the occasional mention of a returning soldier, her later diary entries are full of accounts of visits, travels, parties, and conversations. As important to Tee as the end of the war was the surprise return of Matthew Magner to Virginia on May 4. For Tee, the transition to peace and Union rule occurred seamlessly.[24]

NOTES

1. Freeman, *Lee's Lieutenants*, 3:642–46; Power, *Lee's Miserables*, 270.

    2. Freeman, *Lee's Lieutenants*, 3:668–74; Carmichael, *Lee's Young Artillerist*, 158–64.

    3. Poague, *Gunner with Stonewall*, 110–12 (quotation on 112); Wise, *The Long Arm of Lee*, 2:931–32.

    4. Poague, *Gunner with Stonewall*, 113–14.

    5. Freeman, *Lee's Lieutenants*, 3:685–86; Worsham, *One of Jackson's Foot Cavalry*, 260–64; Donald C. Pfanz, *Richard S. Ewell: A Soldier's Life* (Chapel Hill, 1998), 428. General Ewell's men set fire to four warehouses, and the wind carried the fire to the rest of the business district.

    6. Freeman, *Lee's Lieutenants*, 3:689–99.

    7. Poague, *Gunner with Stonewall*, 115–17.

    8. Christopher M. Calkins, "Sailor's Creek," in *The Civil War Battlefield Guide*, 278–81; Wise, *End of an Era*, 430–34.

    9. Freeman, *Lee's Lieutenants*, 3:714, 716–19; Poague, *Gunner with Stonewall*, 117–18 (quotations on 118).

    10. John B. Gordon, *Reminiscences of the Civil War* (New York, 1903), 434–36 (quotation on 435); Nichols, *General Fitzhugh Lee*, 86; Freeman, *Lee's Lieutenants*, 3:724–25.

    11. Poague, *Gunner with Stonewall*, 121–22 (quotation on 122).

    12. Ibid., 122; Nichols, *General Fitzhugh Lee*, 86; Freeman, *Lee's Lieutenants*, 3:726–29 (Gordon quoted on 729).

    13. Freeman, *Lee's Lieutenants*, 3:729–30; James Longstreet, *From Manassas to Appomattox: Memoirs of the Civil War in America* (Philadelphia, 1896), 624–25.

    14. Freeman, *Lee's Lieutenants*, 3:730; *Richmond Times-Dispatch*, March 28, 1965, on Mahone; E. P. Alexander, *Military Memoirs of a Confederate: A Critical Narrative* (New York, 1907), 604–6; Poague, *Gunner with Stonewall*, 123–24.

    15. Poague, *Gunner with Stonewall*, 124.

    16. Freeman, *Lee's Lieutenants*, 3:738–40; Poague, *Gunner with Stonewall*, 129.

    17. Berkeley, *Diary*, April 9–11,1865, 132–33; April 26, 1865, 135; April 30, 1865, 136; June 7–9, 1865, 139; June 18, 1865, 141; June 19, 1865, 142; June 20, 1865, 142; June 23, 1865, 143–44; June 24, 1865, 145.

    18. Worsham, *One of Jackson's Foot Cavalry*, 264.

    19. Caldwell, *Letters*, 262–63.

    20. Fleet, *Green Mount*, 362. Fred Fleet is listed as 2d Lieutenant, AAAG, in Wise's Brigade, in William G. Nine and Ronald Wilson, *The Appomattox Paroles, April 9–15, 1865* (Lynchburg, 1989), 100.

    21. Buck, *Diary*, April 12, 1865, 297; April 13, 1865, 297; April 14, 1865, 297–98; April 15, 1865, 298.

    22. Edmonds, *Journals*, April 7, 1865, 218–19; April 9, 1865, 132; April 15, 1865, 219.

    23. Ibid., April 15, 1865, 219; April 16, 1865, 220; April 18, 1865, 220; April 21, 1865, 221–22.

    24. Ibid., April 21, 1865, 222 (quotation); April 22, 24, 26, 27, and 30, 1865, 222–23; May 4, 1865, 224.

CHAPTER FIFTEEN

THE BUILDING YEARS, 1865–1885

WITH THE END of the war came the end of the diaries, letters, and memoirs of almost all the individuals in this study. Of the journal writers, only two, Tee Edmonds and Lucy Buck, kept up their journals. Tee stopped writing in 1867, while Lucy continued on—with some sizeable gaps—until her death in 1914. The Fleets held onto their correspondence from 1865 to 1900, but in the edited volume of their letters the contributions from Fred, the Civil War veteran, steadily decline after he moves West in 1868.

What, then, of the other four persons? What can truly be said about their later lives, let alone how the war continued to affect them? At first glance, very little. There is a sketchy historical record, compiled from family records, family lore, official records, and recorded statements. But there is enough material to allow us to divide their postwar lives into two phases. The first phase, the "building years," covers the twenty years after the war, when the seven men and women were busy finding work or starting families or sustaining a family enterprise—or all three. The second phase, the "reflective years," describes the last third of their lives, when their careers peaked, their children moved out, and they had time to remember "their war" and their youth. Given the paucity of sources for the postwar period, some careful extrapolation from bare facts is required to reveal patterns of behavior and thought. These patterns—and a few particulars of each person's life—are the primary concerns of this chapter and Chapter 16.

In the immediate aftermath of the war, the most pressing need for most veterans was to plant a crop or find employment. Fred Fleet helped to get a crop in the ground and managed it through the summer, before leaving to resume his education at the University of Virginia in the fall of 1865. Robin Berkeley may have wanted to go to school, but he was needed at home and stayed there through the fall of 1866. William Poague had finished college, so his immediate concern was to help his mother with the family farm in Rockbridge County. John Worsham was appointed tollkeeper at the bridge of his friend, Joseph Mayo.[1]

For the women of this study, there were no jobs to seek; they stayed where they were, either assisting in or running a household. Lucy helped out at Bel Air, happily greeting her brothers and cousins upon their return from the war.[2] We can only assume that Susan Caldwell had an overwhelming sense of relief when Lycurgus returned home, because we have no correspondence after March 1865. More is known about Tee's experiences because she continued to make diary entries for two more years.

During the first six months after the war, Tee described her feelings and visits with others, despite a case of the "blues for six long weary weeks" in May and June (recognition that wartime adventure had ended?). All summer long Union soldiers came and went from Paris, but they did not interfere with Tee's steady rounds of visiting. The mysterious Magner still came in and out of Tee's life; in August he rode up to Belle Grove "looking like *Methuselah.*" He ate dinner with the Edmondses, but then, while Tee was changing her riding habit, he suddenly left "just like his queer way." Tee did not dwell on the meaning of his quick departure; there was a camp meeting to attend in a couple of weeks, which would remind Tee of "the meetings of old, before the war."

In September the Edmondses' most faithful black servant, Aunt Letty, finally left them. Her son, Sam, had to move to Fairfax with his wife and five children because his wife had been let go by her employers. Aunt Letty felt she should go with them "rather than be a nuisance" to the Edmondses when she finally got very old. Off they went in their wagon, with Aunt Letty crying and Tee reflecting on "the miserable changes that four years have brought upon our happy country, changes that we cannot get used to." The next month Tee received more bad news: Matthew Magner was returning to Mississippi. He had one last serious talk with Tee: "I shall not paint here all he said, but keep it secretly enshrined on memory's tablet." One can only assume that he expressed his love for her but, at the same time, his reluctance to become engaged. She wrote, "Oh, Magner, Magner, why is it that both of us should suffer thus."[3]

After the sharp readjustment from war to peace in the first year after the war, the seven individuals slowly set about building new lives. Overall, their jobs and activities reflect the continuing power of class and gender. Each man eventually found a paying job, while each woman continued to either run a home or help run a home. The particular circumstances each person faced partially reflect problems created by the war: difficulty in finding steady employment in the postwar South, lack of "suitable" white men for white women of a "certain age" to marry, and personal trauma brought on by the war.

For the three middle-class women in this study, their gender continued to be the primary factor shaping their opportunities and choices. Little is known of Susan Caldwell's life, except that in the years after the war she had two more children and continued to raise her other children and manage the household. Her husband Lycurgus and the unsinkable John Finks started a new weekly newspaper in Warrenton in 1865, the *True Index*. Apparently Lycurgus was the principal publisher and editor; John Finks also owned a drugstore. The Finkses and Caldwells continued to live together in their old house on Smith Street.[4]

More is known about Tee Edmonds's life, at least until her diary ends in February 1867. She continued her social whirl, attending all-night dances, debates, and weddings. In September 1866 she received bad news: Matthew Magner had died of cholera in Mississippi. Tee seemed to have moved on from her long infatuation with him, only leaving this sad poem in her journal:

There is an end to every tie
On earth and every pleasure,
The dearest friend we have must die,
Our only earthly treasure.[5]

As usual, Tee had plenty of admirers. At her friend's wedding, she and her escort, Mr. Nulton, hit it off quite well. George Triplett continued to woo her, as did the persistent John Armistead Chappelear. In her last journal entry, Tee wrote that Chappelear "worries me again with the same old foretold story. I try to prevail on him to forget so unworthy a creature as me and bestow his affections on someone else—but without success."

Tee also continued to share the prejudices and callousness of her class toward black people. In September 1866 she attended a concert that featured white choirs and a "Yankee negro band": "I feel disgraced! . . . I regret that I ever mingled with such a crowd." She at least felt sorrow in February 1867 when the family turned out one of their oldest former slaves, Aunt Easter, who had to be sent to "the poor house to be taken care of, as we have no servant now to do for her as she requires." She and her niece "Wirt" drove Aunt Easter to Piedmont, where she then left for the "poor house." All three women cried at the parting.[6] Such partings, unfortunately, were commonplace during Reconstruction, when thousands of former slaves who stayed with their former masters were let go because of lack of funds or a desire to unload those persons who were no longer useful to the household.

Little is recorded about Tee after 1867. Her exciting "single" life finally ended on January 6, 1870, just seven days short of her thirty-first birthday. Her choice was determined by her head for finances and her concern for her family. She married her neighbor and longtime suitor, John Armistead Chappelear. He agreed to pay off the $30,000 mortgage on Belle Grove in return for the title to the property and Tee's hand. He remodeled the house and made the land productive, thus allowing Tee and their five children, in the words of the journal's editor, Nancy Chappelear Baird, to take "many wonderful trips." Baird also speculates that "Tee had a much more exciting life with Armistead than anticipated"[7] —but perhaps not the romantic life the young Tee had so avidly sought.

For Lucy Buck, there would be neither romance nor marriage. She lived on at Bel Air, suffering with her brother Alvin when three of his children died of cholera in one week, and burdened by the family's great financial distress when her uncle's large winery business collapsed in 1876, dragging down her father, her brother Irving, most of the family, and eventually Bel Air itself. Only through loans and promises was Irving able to keep Bel Air in the family and then only until 1897, when the home finally had to be sold.[8]

For unstated reasons, Lucy stopped keeping a diary from the end of the war until 1873. It is the only long gap in a remarkable run that stretches from 1862 until her death in 1918. When she resumed her diary on January 1, 1873, she wrote, "I seemed to have lived and suffered a century, and feel that a less noble and worthy being will transcribe a less noble and worthy record of her life than in old times." She continued in this gloomy vein: "I look upon the advent of each incoming year as the dawn of a new season of trial and sorrow."[9]

Part of Lucy's disappointment may have been personal, not familial or financial. Now thirty-two, she may have thought that her opportunities for marriage had slipped away. According to the historian of Front Royal, Laura Hale, it was rumored that Lucy "carried a torch for Walter Scott Roy." He is mentioned throughout her wartime diary, and he gave her a ring to keep as a forfeit when they played the game of philopena in January 1861. Roy survived the war, trained to become a doctor, and married a local girl, Mattie Scott. Lucy's 1862 prophecy had come true. That April she had accidentally broken Roy's ring. She wrote at the time, "So sorry! Can it be ominous! I could never bear the idea of breaking a ring. Now the wish will never be realized." Lucy and her unmarried sister Laura continued to help their parents run Bel Air, even after the financial disasters of the late 1870s. Lucy remained, in the words of Laura Virginia Hale, "charming, vivacious, and popular."[10]

As for the men in this study, the war did little to alter their class or social standing. Using Fred Bailey's categories from his work on Tennessee's Confederate veterans, each person in the study came from either the "slaveholding yeomen" or the "wealthy elite." With the arguable exception of Fred Fleet, all would return to their social groups after the war. What Bailey wrote of Tennessee's Confederate veterans largely holds true for these Virginians: "A continuity of class structure spanned the decades from the Old South to the New South. From birth to death, individuals in these classes were aware of their social status and most remained in their place."[11] Still, the men faced enormous difficulties in establishing a solid economic footing in the postwar impoverished South. They had the advantages of good family names and respectable prewar wealth, but those assets opened only a few doors. After a certain point, each man had to make it on his own.

Three of the men entered the field of teaching. William Poague first ran the family farm in the Falling Spring community. Later, he ran a school at Fancy Hill in Rockbridge County; then in 1880–81 he taught in Lynchburg. In 1884 he was appointed treasurer of Virginia Military Institute, a position he would hold for thirty years (until his death at age seventy-eight). Poague also found time to serve three sessions in the Virginia House of Delegates, from 1871 to 1873. He was a member of the Conservative Party.[12]

Robin Berkeley began teaching in 1866, but did not have the capital to found his own school until 1886. In the intervening twenty years he taught in homes, including those of William Beverley of Leesburg and C. J. Stovin of Orange County, and at the Loudoun School in Leesburg. Throughout these years he sent money home to help his parents run White House and to help pay for the education of his younger siblings. Finally, in 1886, Robin bought a farm near Orange Court House and started his own school. He ran the school for fourteen years, then closed it down and spent four years teaching at Locust Dale Academy in Madison County before retiring at the age of sixty-four in 1904. He continued to run his farm until 1914, when he sold it and bought a house in Orange.[13]

Fred Fleet returned to the University of Virginia in 1865 determined to be a doctor, but after struggling with medical courses he turned to his real love, the classics. Through the sale of the family ferry and annual crops, and taking advantage of deferred payments, Fred was able to graduate in 1867. He immediately found a teaching position at Judge John Coleman's Kenmore Academy in Fredericksburg.[14]

Fred taught a class of teenage girls, and he soon fell in love with one of his students. To make matters worse, the student was none other than Mary Coleman, the 16-year-old daughter of the judge who employed him. For the first time in his life, the 24-year-old Fred found himself "desperately, yes *madly* in love." At first he said nothing, until he heard that another teacher had also fallen in love with Mary. On Christmas Eve he "poured out . . .

[his] soul" to her at a party at the Presbyterian Church. Fred had thought that Mary "cared something" for him, but he could not have been more wrong. At first she was "dreadfully startled," then she told him that she did not love him and "could hold out no hope she ever would." Her response devastated Fred, the Civil War veteran. He did not leave his room for three days, and only "religion and the thought of you all at home" kept him going.

Somehow Fred managed to pull himself together for the next school term. Desperate for work elsewhere, he secured a teaching and administrative position at William Jewell College in Liberty, Missouri, in the summer of 1868.[15] He moved to Missouri and, except for visits home in the summer, never lived in Virginia again. He made a career out of teaching and school administration.

Fred stayed at William Jewell College for five years before accepting the presidency of the Baptist Female College in Lexington, Missouri, in 1873. He held that job for six years, then became chairman of the Department of Greek at the University of Missouri. This comfortable post allowed Fred to devote more time to his new family in Missouri and his original family in Virginia. But his ambition never died, and when he was not appointed president of the University of Missouri in 1889, he accepted the superintendent's job at Mexico Military Academy in Mexico, Missouri. The academy flourished until disaster struck in 1896 when it burned to the ground. Miraculously, Fred was offered the same job at Culver Military Academy in Indiana, and he held that position until his retirement in 1910.[16]

John Worsham also had a number of jobs after the war. After a brief stint as a tollkeeper at Mayo's Bridge, Worsham became a partner in a Richmond tobacco company. In the 1870s he tried his hand at milling in Scottsville (in Fluvanna County, near Charlottesville) before running a barge line on the James River and Kanawha Canal. In 1882 he sold out to the Richmond and Allegheny Railroad, then returned to Richmond to live and to work as an auditor for the Virginia State Insurance Company. When that company folded, Worsham became bookkeeper for his son's business, Richmond Press. He worked there until his death in 1920.[17]

Aside from work, another crucial aspect of the veterans' lives must be mentioned: marriage. Every man would eventually marry, two within six years after the war and two much later. While it is tempting to look for psychological explanations for the late marriages of Berkeley and Poague, both men may have waited until their forties because it took them nearly twenty years after the war to gain some measure of economic security. Unfortunately, the full story is not recorded. What is known is the barest of facts. The first to wed was John Worsham. In February 1871 he married Mary Bell Pilcher of Richmond. They would have four children, one of whom died in infancy. John was one of two Confederate veterans in this study to outlive his wife. Mary Worsham died in 1914, while John lived on until 1920, staying with his son George in those final years.[18]

Fred Fleet wed Belle Seddon of Fredericksburg in the same year that Worsham married. Belle's uncle was James A. Seddon, former Secretary of War in the Confederacy. The couple began courting in the summer of 1870 (while Fred was visiting friends and relatives in Virginia), became engaged that year, and married in Fredericksburg at the Seddon home, Little Snowden. The Fleets had eight children, only one of whom died in infancy. Most of the children lived long lives, though few matched their mother's longevity: she died in 1940 at age eighty-nine, surviving her husband by twenty-nine years.[19]

William Poague remained a bachelor until age forty-three. In December 1878 he married Sarah Josephine Moore of Fancy Hill in Rockbridge County. Sarah was thirty when she became his bride. They would have four children.[20]

The last Confederate veteran to marry was Robin Berkeley. Like Poague, he was forty-three years old. His bride, Anna "Nannie" Louisa Berkeley, was thirty-eight. She was his first cousin and had been his "sweetheart" since 1861. After twenty years of courtship, they finally married in August 1883. The Berkeleys had a son, Landon, who had to bury first his mother (1898), then his father (1918), before reaching the age of forty.[21]

For all four veterans, the war interrupted or delayed a social ritual but did not prevent it from taking place. In this central area of their lives—love and family—the veterans undoubtedly found solace and strength in the peace and joy that marriage and children brought them.

NOTES

1. Fleet, *Green Mount After the War*, editor's note, 12; Berkeley, *Diary*, xxii; J. M. Wharey to William T. Poague, October 19, 1865, in Poague, *Gunner with Stonewall*, 156–58; Worsham, *One of Jackson's Foot Cavalry* (Robertson edition), xxiv.

2. Buck, *Diary*, editor's note, 298.

3. Edmonds, *Journals*, May 10, 1865, 224; May 16, 1865, 224; May 29, 1865, 225 (a sample of visits in just one month); July 4, 1865, 225 ("blues"); May 5, 1865, 224; July 17, 1865, 229; August 2, 1865, 231 (quotations on Magner); August 20, 1865, 231; September 6, 1865, 232; October 2, 1865, 233.

4. Caldwell, *Letters*, 263. Unfortunately, the owner of the original Caldwell letters says that the postwar records are "fragile" and "scattered." Bell Gale Chevigny to John Selby, July 8, 1999 (letter in author's possession).

5. Edmonds, *Journals*, July 21, 1866, 240; January 15, 1866, 244; February 22 and March 1 and 3, 1866, 236; April 12, 1866, 238–39; December 12, 1866, 292; September 13, 1866, 241 (quotation).

6. Ibid., April 12, 1866, 237–38; February 17, 1867, 246; February 19, 1867, 246 (quotation); September 30, 1866, 242; February 14, 1867, 246 (quotation).

7. Ibid., editor's note, 273.

8. Buck, *Diary*, editor's notes, 298, 351–52; Lucy Buck diary, March 6, 1897, "Our last day at dear old Bel Air."

9. Lucy Buck diary, January 1, 1873; all original diaries are in the possession of Dr. William F. Buck.

10. Laura Virginia Hale, *On Chester Street: Presence of the Past, Patterns of the Future* (Stephens City, VA, 1985), 97; Buck, *Diary*, editor's note, 283, January 9, 1862, 19–20 (mentions ring received the year before); April 27, 1862, 55; Hale, *On Chester Street*, 97.

11. Bailey, *Class and Tennessee's Confederate Generation*, 13 and 135.

12. Poague, *Gunner with Stonewall*, xix; *Lexington Gazette*, September 9, 1914; *Rockbridge County News*, September 10, 1914.

13. Berkeley, *Diary*, xxii; H. R. Berkeley Account Book, 1866–1892, in H. R. Berkeley Collection, Virginia Historical Society.

14. Fleet, *Green Mount After the War*, 12; Fred Fleet to Mother, October 9, 1865, 12–14; Fred Fleet to Ma, October 26, 1865, 17; Fred Fleet to Ma, April 3, 1866, 19; Fred Fleet to Ma, December 23, 1866, 20–21; Walker Hawes to Fred Fleet, September 17, 1867, 29.

15. Ibid., Fred Fleet to Mother, January 11, 1868, 33; Mother to Fred Fleet, October 13, 1868, 35–36.

16. Ibid., 107 (editor's note) and Fred Fleet to Mother, August 28, 1873, 108; Evelyn Hill to Bessie Fleet, December 24, 1878, 183–84; Fred Fleet to Mother, February 24, 1879, 184, 198–99 (editor's note on Fred and family's summers at Green Mount); Fred Fleet to Mother, April 23, 1883, 203–4; Fred Fleet to Mother, June 7, 1889, 236, and David Fleet to

Mother, August 21, 1889, 236–37; Fred Fleet to Mother, May 5, 1891 ("My health is better than it has been for years."), 243; Lou Fleet to Bess Fleet, September 25, 1896, 252, and Fred Fleet to Mother, September 27, 1896, 252 (Fred's retirement from Culver Military Academy), 267.

17. Worsham, *One of Jackson's Foot Cavalry* (Robertson edition), xxv; *Richmond Times-Dispatch*, September 20, 1920.

18. Worsham, *One of Jackson's Foot Cavalry* (Robertson edition), xxv; *Richmond Times-Dispatch*, September 20, 1920.

19. Fleet, *Green Mount After the War*, editor's notes on 53 and 59; genealogy on 275. Belle was eight years younger than Fred.

20. Poague, *Gunner with Stonewall*, xix; *Lexington Gazette*, September 9, 1914; Sarah Josephine Moore was born on October 22, 1848, and died on October 12, 1916, according to the inscription on her tombstone in the Lexington Presbyterian Church cemetery.

21. Berkeley, *Diary*, xxii; gravestone of Nannie L. Berkeley, Graham Cemetery, Orange County, Virginia. Nannie was born on May 3, 1845.

CHAPTER SIXTEEN

THE REFLECTIVE YEARS, 1885–1921

TO SAY THAT reflection on the war experience began in 1885 for the subjects of this study is only partially true. For some, reflection began as soon as the war ended. For others, it never occurred (or there is no record). For most, though, their personal years of reflection, celebration, and memorialization mirrored those of their region and nation. Historians such as Paul Buck, Gerald Linderman, Nina Silber, Stuart McConnell, Charles Wilson, Larry Logue, and Gaines Foster have examined this national time of reconciliation and recognition at length, offering detailed histories of the major organizations and key participants as well as political and psychological reasons for this remarkable healing process. For this study, Gaines Foster's work on Southerners' embrace of the Lost Cause is particularly useful. From the late 1880s onward, "For the next twenty years or so, southerners celebrated the Confederacy as never before or since." Gerald Linderman has proven as helpful as Foster, arguing that the war the veterans would come to celebrate was not the war they thought they had fought at the time. By 1900, he argues, "Civil War veterans had become symbols of changelessness—but only by obliterating or amending an experience so convulsive of their values that it had for a time cut the cord of experience."[1]

In the main, those individuals who participated in Confederate memorial rituals did so during the peak years of such activity, from 1885 to 1915. Yet the meaning of the war for the seven men and women in this study does not fit easily into Linderman's schema. Whether their opinions were recorded in diaries, letters, or memoirs, none of these individuals took as dim a view of the war by 1864–65 as Linderman's subjects did. This difference may be entirely random, but a psychological factor may be at work as well. Some Civil War soldiers grew accustomed to war and adjusted their inherited values to accommodate its horrors. Moreover, with their strong religious faith and fierce attachment to home and family, they felt compelled to serve and to fight— and to keep up their spirits. Those who expressed considerable fear and gloom late in the war, like Robin Berkeley and Susan Caldwell, had similar sentiments early in the conflict. It was their character, not circumstances, that determined their attitude toward the war and its legacy.

For some of the individuals in this study, the war and its memory would become a major focus of the last third of their lives. Others would give it little attention, and the thoughts of still others we know nothing about. It is the last category that will be dealt with first.

There is no record of the thoughts of Tee Edmonds or Susan Caldwell after the war ended. It can be assumed that the war letters and journal were important either to these women or to their families, or else they would not have been preserved. Unfortunately, like the villagers of Chassignolles described so beautifully in Gillian Tindall's *Celestine*, the living memory of one's ancestors lasts, at most, for four generations, and "beyond the great-grandparent level oblivion begins to descend." That has already happened to Tee and Susan.[2]

Lucy Buck occupies a category alone. For her, the fifty years after the war brought much family sorrow and considerable personal disappointment as she labored to help her family survive illness, death, and financial ruin, without the help of a husband. As she grew older she became the emotional anchor of the family, though turning often to her ever-present journal to record her thoughts and her family's history, not to mention her own image of herself as a chronicler of a special time and place in history.[3]

With her sister Laura, Lucy continued to live in Front Royal after leaving their beloved Bel Air in 1897. They moved closer to town, living first at Bon Air, then moving later to a new house on Chester Street they dubbed Cozy Corner. With brother Willie living in town and many cousins nearby, the Buck sisters never wanted for company, and their house on Chester Street with its fine porch became a convenient gathering place. Lucy found time to join the Daughters of the Confederacy in 1905, and faithfully participated in the activities of the Warren Memorial Association.

She helped place flags on soldiers' graves and attended Memorial Day services and parades in Front Royal.[4]

Lucy retained her loyalties to the Confederacy and its postwar apostles, the Conservative Democrats. In 1885 she wrote that "the democratic ticket has been unanimously carried everywhere and [Fitzhugh] Lee is really to be our next governor. The Legislature also is ours, which is more than one could have possibly expected." In a similar vein, when she attended the Centennial parade in New York City in 1889, she proudly noted that "before General Gordon of Georgia came into sight, he was greatly applauded but it was nothing to the cheers that greeted dear old Fitzhugh [Lee] when he appeared at the head of the gray-coated Virginians. My heart beat with pride for them as they passed." Lucy exchanged words with a spectator, a "rampant Republican who undertook to make himself disagreeable in his remarks to me. But I considered the source, and let it pass."[5]

Lucy also thought of the war, noting in 1885 that she "read a little in my war diary." She may have had plans to write a book based on her diary; in 1874 she "commenced writing an article for publication" (it was never printed). One wonders what historical treasures were destroyed in 1897 when the family moved out of Bel Air. On two separate occasions Lucy wrote of burning old letters, some from the "West End garret" and others "belonging to the boys."[6]

Fortunately for posterity, the Fleets of Green Mount did not burn family letters from the war or the postwar period. The latter were collected into a second edited book, *Green Mount After the War*, and one finds the dual stories of Ma and her daughters struggling to keep Green Mount in the family, while her sons Fred and David seek their fortunes out West. Like the many "Confederate carpetbaggers" described by Daniel Sutherland, the Fleet brothers "operated on the vague notion that life in the North (or West, in their case) would provide better opportunities, a fresh chance in life, a new identity, a new home." For Fred, schools in Missouri gave him the "fresh chance" he needed after the debacle at Judge Coleman's school in Fredericksburg. His success in Missouri led to other opportunities in that state and in Indiana. It also supplied him with enough money to help out his mother, sisters, and brothers. His younger brother David attended

VMI, then moved West for new opportunities. David's first jobs were in teaching, but he grew tired of that occupation and moved to Montesanto in booming Washington Territory. He started working as a civil engineer for the Northern Pacific Railroad, but branched out into real estate and later into politics. For many years he served as county auditor. He ran as a Democrat in a solidly Republican county and remained a Democrat for his entire life. Fred's youngest brother, Will, attended Richmond College, then returned home to help run Green Mount and served as county judge and county attorney. Fred's sisters taught at Green Mount, in other schools, and in homes for the rest of their lives.[7]

For Fred, his time "in service" proved invaluable when he was asked to become superintendent of Mexico Military Academy and later Culver Military Academy. In fact, he was a superintendent for the last twenty-one years of his professional life. Ironically, as superintendent, Colonel Fleet wore the Federal uniform. As he wrote to his mother in 1890, "Would you recognize your son in the same uniform Sheridan wore when he came to visit you in '64?" Equally improbable was the parade of cadets he led in October 1897, down the streets of Chicago, right past President William McKinley (Republican and Union veteran), whom Fred met later at a reception.[8]

Still, Fred remained true to his Confederate past and his Democratic Party leanings. In summers at Green Mount, his favorite pastime was spending an entire day recounting war stories with his former black servant, Meredith Diggs. They would end the day with a big meal and naps on "old army blankets." As for the Democratic Party, Fred and the rest of his family consistently favored Conservatives, then Democrats over the years. A measure of Fred's total disgust with Republicanism came in 1881, when he changed the name of his new son from Henry Wise (in honor of his old commander) Fleet to Henry *Wyatt* Fleet. Fred abhorred the Wise name after his one-time bomb shelter mate, John S. Wise, joined the Republican Party in 1881.[9]

The two other areas where the war seems to have affected Fred Fleet and his family are education and careers. Fred's oldest daughter, Mary (b. 1873), married the commandant of cadets at Culver Military Academy, Major Leigh Robinson Gignilliat, himself a native of Georgia, educated at VMI and Trinity College.

Fleet's other daughter, Belle (b. 1876), married a former commandant of cadets at Mexico Military Academy, Major Kenneth Gordon Matherson of South Carolina. Matherson was educated at
the Citadel, Stanford, and Columbia. He later became president
of Georgia Tech, then president of Drexel Institute of Technol-
ogy. Each of Fleet's five sons attended either Mexico Military
Academy or Culver Military Academy. The oldest, John Seddon,
earned BA and MA degrees from the University of Virginia and
spent most of his professional life as headmaster at Culver Military Academy. Henry Wyatt served in the U.S. Army in the Phil-
ippines and France, and later was head of the Reserve Officers'
Training Corps (ROTC) at Amherst College. The youngest son,
Reginald Scott, served as an artillery officer in World War I. After the war he became a businessman.[10]

As these brief biographies illustrate, the military and the
South continued to play major roles in the lives of the children of
Fred and Belle Fleet. The fact that their daughters married military school administrators is largely a function of proximity, but
the fact that their father enjoyed working at such schools and
fostered a similar love in his children also hints at the strong influence that his time at the University of Virginia and four years
in the Army of Northern Virginia continued to hold on him—no
matter how far he traveled or lived away from Virginia.

Another veteran, Robin Berkeley, did not seek opportunity
outside of Virginia. Unfortunately, the only records he kept after
the war were an account book, a few letters, and miscellaneous
legal and financial items. The editor of his diary, William H.
Runge, notes that Berkeley rewrote his wartime diary in the early
1890s, based on an earlier version and many missing "notes." The
assumption is that Berkeley had original notes and perhaps a diary, which he later combined into a full 4-year diary. He wrote it
for his son, and it was not published until 1961.[11]

As for Robin's postwar activities, Runge has only this to say:
"In later years . . . [Berkeley] talked little of his war experiences."
But Robin does make it clear to the reader what the war meant to
him at its end—and probably still meant in 1890. His last diary
entry concludes: "It was not all passed through in vain. That there
is at the bottom of this fiery furnace of affliction, through which
we Southern people have all gone, some pure gold left us." He

asked, "God grant that I may never see another war, with all its horrors, blood and desolation." Yet war also brought forth "the noblest impulses of the human heart," and "noble friendships were formed, which, I trust, time will never blot out." Fittingly, there is a photograph of Robin and his cousins, John Hill and John Lewis, on a farm sometime after 1900. They had grown up together, fought a war together, and come together in their old age.[12]

The postwar views and activities of William Poague are better documented. A religious and serious man, Poague found himself in the 1880s and 1890s to be an authority of sorts on the Civil War, as letters from veterans and writers in the VMI archives attest. Of course, he was the treasurer at VMI and came to know well a future superintendent and historian, Jennings Cropper Wise (fourth son of John S. Wise), who wrote a 2-volume work on the role of the artillery of the Army of Northern Virginia. Poague also knew a young cadet, Monroe F. Cockrell, who would later (1950s) find a publisher for Poague's memoirs. And there is a wonderful photograph of Lieutenant Colonel William T. Poague, age seventy-eight, sitting ramrod-straight on a horse leading the famed Rockbridge artillery guns, "Matthew, Mark, Luke, and John," to their official retirement from use by VMI cadets in 1913.[13]

Poague wrote his memoirs in 1903, mainly from memory but also with the aid of wartime letters and published histories available at that time. His memory may have been fresh because of the questions he kept answering for the curious. Moreover, his voice sounds honest because he was writing for his children, not the public. In an account of an 1889 reunion of veterans of Pickett's division at Gettysburg, Poague recalls hugging a former Union officer and drinking beer with veterans from both sides. One of the Confederate veterans said to his former enemies, "If you all had this up here that hot day in July 1863, we would have stayed here." Poague reveals a little about his feelings at the end of his narrative. Writing of his farewell to his men at Appomattox, he states, "I speak truly when I say there has never been a day since, when I could dwell on that last scene without experiencing emotions of deepest grief and sorrow."[14]

John Worsham took an almost entirely different approach to the war after it ended. For Worsham, the war's meaning became a crucial part of his adult life. For years he helped with reunions of F Company, wrote articles for the Southern Historical Society Papers, and participated in ceremonies such as the dedication of General Lee's statue in Richmond in 1890. In the early 1890s he began writing his memoir, using a notebook he kept during the war, letters he had written in wartime, correspondence from fellow F Company veterans, and books and articles by other Confederate veterans. He finished his memoir in 1912, when it was published by the Neale Company of New York. It received some excellent reviews, but its greatest value has been to twentieth-century historians of the Civil War, who have ceaselessly plundered its riches.[15]

NOTES

1. Paul Buck, *The Road to Reunion, 1865–1900* (New York, 1937); Nina Silber, *The Romance of Reunion: Northerners and the South, 1865–1900* (Chapel Hill, 1993); Stuart McConnell, *Glorious Contentment: The Grand Army of the Republic, 1865–1900* (Chapel Hill, 1992); Charles Reagan Wilson, *Baptized in Blood: The Religion of the Lost Cause, 1865–1920* (Athens, 1980); Larry M. Logue, *To Appomattox and Beyond: The Civil War Soldier in War and Peace* (Chicago, 1996); Gaines Foster, *Ghosts of the Confederacy: Defeat, the Lost Cause, and the Emergence of the New South, 1865–1913* (New York, 1987), 6; Linderman, *Embattled Courage*, 297.

2. Gillian Tindall, *Celestine: Voices from a French Village* (New York, 1995), 149.

3. Buck, *Diary* (Buck edition), 2–3 and 298; Buck, *Diary* (Baer edition), 321–23.

4. Hale, *On Chester Street*, 98–99; Lucy Buck diaries: June 8, 1905 (settled at Cozy Corner); July 12, 1905 (joined Daughters of the Confederacy); August 25, 1902, and June 3, 1905 (Warren Memorial Association activities); May 23, 1902, June 2, 1906, and May 23, 1918 (Memorial Day services and parades).

5. Lucy Buck diaries: November 4, 1885, and April 30, 1889.

6. Ibid., July 2, 1885; January 5, 1874; February 27 and March 1, 1897.

7. Daniel T. Sutherland, *The Confederate Carpetbaggers* (Baton Rouge, 1988), 44; Fleet, *Green Mount After the War*, Fred Fleet to David Fleet, April 29, 1873, 103–4, and Fred Fleet to Mother, February 24, 1879, 184, for two examples of Fred helping with family expenses; David Fleet to Fred Fleet, September 6, 1875, 142; David Fleet to Fred Fleet, October 8, 1883, 205 (engineer); David Fleet to Mother, November 10, 1884, 209 (county auditor); Mother to Will Fleet, March 11, 1877, 160 (Richmond College); Mother to Florence Fleet, March 9, 1882, 197 (Will returns to Green Mount); Will's later career, editor's note, 270; on Fleet daughters,

see editor's notes, 267–70, and over 100 entries on their various teaching positions throughout the book.

8. Ibid., Fred Fleet to Mother, October 11, 1890, 239; Fred Fleet to Mother, October 17, 1897, 253.

9. Ibid., editor's note, 199; on Democratic politics, see Fred Fleet to Mother, July 18, 1869, 40; Lou Fleet to Fred Fleet, July 6, 1869, 39; Mother to Fred Fleet, January 31, 1870, 49; Mother to Will Fleet, March 11, 1877, 160; David Fleet to Mother, November 15, 1883, 206; Lillian Fleet to Mother, November 20, 1884, 210; Fred Fleet to Will Fleet, November 6, 1886, 213; Fred Fleet to Will Fleet, November 1888, 230; on changing Henry Wise to Henry Wyatt, see editor's note, 190.

10. Ibid., editor's notes, 236, 255, 267, and 275.

11. Henry Robinson Berkeley papers, Virginia Historical Society, account book, 1866–1892, and assorted items, 1866–1918; Berkeley, *Diary*, xxiii–xxiv.

12. Berkeley, *Diary*, June 24, 1865, 145–46; photograph on 87.

13. William T. Poague file, Virginia Military Institute, Jonathan W. Daniel to Colonel William T. Poague, August 22, 1905; Fitzhugh Lee to Colonel William T. Poague, July 30, 1894; Thomas Munford to Colonel William T. Poague, January 20, 1898; Poague, *Gunner with Stonewall*, vii–viii and xiv.

14. Poague, *Gunner with Stonewall*, x–xi, 77, and 129.

15. Worsham, *One of Jackson's Foot Cavalry* (Robertson edition), xxv–xxviii and xiii–xiv.

EPILOGUE
Character Endures

ALL THE AGING Confederates in this study survived to see a new century dawn, though the shadows lengthened around them. The first of the seven to go was also the youngest, Fred Fleet. He died in 1911 at age sixty-eight, one year after his retirement from Culver Military Academy. He did not live to see two of his sons fight for the United States in a war across the sea or to see his son Henry serve as colonel of the Reserve Officers Training Corps unit at Amherst College.[1] The next was Susan Caldwell, who died in 1913 at age eighty-six. She outlived her beloved Lycurgus by three years, ending her days in the house on Smith Street that had been her home since the dark days of the Civil War.[2]

The following year, the bell finally tolled for the indomitable William T. Poague. He worked to the end as treasurer of VMI, and the flag was flown at half-mast at his adopted college upon his death in September 1914. At age seventy-nine he still rode his horse to work each day, and "always met his friends with a smile, and perhaps a pleasantry." He lived to hear a reading of an ode to him at the annual Lee-Jackson Day dinner in 1913 and to lead the parade that marked the return of one of his artillery pieces to VMI on May 10, 1913 (the fiftieth anniversary of General Jackson's death). Although he suffered from the "infirmities which sapped his strength in old age," he became quite ill only in the last month of his life. He was survived by his wife of thirty-five years, Sarah, and three of his four children. Two of his sons, William Thomas Jr. and Henry G., would serve as officers in the American Expeditionary Force (AEF) fighting in France in the Great War, with William serving in the Field Artillery. Fittingly, Poague was buried in the same Lexington cemetery that held the remains of General Stonewall Jackson and many other Confederate veterans, both famous and anonymous.[3]

Robin Berkeley lived until 1918, the last year of the Great War. Like Fred Fleet's and William Poague's sons, Robin's son, Landon,

231

served in the AEF, holding the rank of captain in an engineering regiment. Robin did not live to see the safe and successful end of his son's military service; he died in Orange in January 1918 at age seventy-seven, just before his son's unit was shipped to France. He outlived his beloved wife, Nannie, by twenty years, leaving behind his only child, Landon, his detailed diary, a small inheritance from the sale of his farm in 1914, and, most important, his legacy of integrity, hard work, and fidelity to duty. A testimonial from St. Thomas Episcopal Church in Orange mentions these qualities exhibited by Robin, who "filled the position of Recorder with eminent fitness and unswerving devotion." A similar sentiment is inscribed on his tombstone: "A Confederate Soldier. Always faithful to his duty, however disagreeable, arduous or dangerous."[4]

Lucy Buck died the same year as Robin Berkeley, 1918. At age seventy-five, she was active up to her last week, tending to the house and family as well as to her diary. Her last entry was made on August 19, when she wrote, "I suffered a good deal all day, but had a quiet, restful day." She died on the twentieth, nursed in her final hours by her devoted sister Laura. Her legacy was her lifelong support for her family and friends and the rich treasure of her wartime diaries.[5]

John Worsham lived to see the end of the Great War. He was spry and mentally alert up to his death at age eighty-one, working into his seventies as a bookkeeper for his son's business, the Richmond Press. He died on September 19, 1920—fifty-six years to the day after he was wounded at the Battle of Winchester—at his son's home in Richmond and was buried in Hollywood Cemetery. He saw his book published to excellent reviews in 1912, including the compliment, "If Dickens had followed Stonewall Jackson, he would have written just such a book as this."[6]

Tee Edmonds Chappelear outlived all the other individuals in this study by one year, passing away in 1921 at age eighty-two. Her husband, John Armistead, died in 1916, but Tee had her five children to comfort her in her final years. Five of her siblings spent their lives in Fauquier County, with brother Bud marrying cousin Adeline Edmonds; sister Mary Payne remaining with her husband, Dr. Albin Payne; and Jack, Bettie, and Clem staying single all their lives. Brother Syd moved to Missouri, where he found success in business and politics. Brother Ches moved to Texas, where he died in an industrial accident. We know nothing of Tee's thoughts in her last years, because she did not leave a written record. But a 1910 newspaper clipping in Tee's diary for 1863–1867 contained an obituary for John Cone, a Norfolk businessman with an estate worth over one million dollars. This was the same John Cone who had stopped at Belle Grove in 1865 while serving with Mosby's Rangers, and who had written to Tee upon his return home to Norfolk in 1865. Had Tee been thinking of a path not taken? We shall never know.[7]

What can ultimately be said of these seven individuals? What ties them and their stories together? What distinguishes them from each other and from their contemporaries? On one level, there is remarkable continuity in all these lives. Everyone came through the war relatively unscathed (physically). Moreover, each remained in his or her social class, the women focused on the family and home, the men finding niches in education or, in John Worsham's case, in mercantile endeavors and eventually in bookkeeping. Only the Fleets, who had the greatest number of slaves and the most extensive estates before the war, could truly be described as economically crippled by it. Yet even they managed to scrape by afterward, with the sons finding employment in education or business and the daughters and mother turning their house into a boarding school to keep the family and property intact.

Most important for the arguments of this study, the war did not alter the characters of the seven people. Lucy Buck, Susan Caldwell, and Robin Berkeley began the war as worriers and ended it as the same. Fred Fleet and William Poague approached life seriously and purposefully both throughout and after the war. John Worsham's optimistic, practical spirit guided him for four years during the war and later helped him write a lively memoir. And Tee Edmonds always focused on matters of the heart.

The seven subjects also shared similarities in their sentiments for the "cause." Each had a firm belief in God and His "higher purposes" for their lives. Not a single one endorsed secession before 1861, but after Virginia seceded, they steadfastly supported what they considered to be the cause of "independence." Each backed the Confederacy to its end (though Susan Caldwell's support was at best begrudged) through military service or shelter or aid. Like most Virginians, they all came to place much of their hope in General Robert E. Lee, the fighting spirit of the Army of Northern Virginia, and President Jefferson Davis. By the end, they may have felt as Susan Caldwell did, that they had to keep fighting to honor the sacrifice of so many. So fight on they did, until the final surrender.

For the men, the war and military service provided both opportunity and a crash course in maturity. All performed ably throughout the war, and all received promotions in fact, if not in act. Fred Fleet had to learn patience above all else, as he essentially saw no action until the last year of the war. Robin Berkeley faced a similar challenge, except in his last year of service, when he saw enough fighting and hardship to last a lifetime. John Worsham and William Poague were two of the most experienced soldiers in the Army of Northern Virginia, between them serving in almost every major battle fought by that famed army. Poague, of course, had an even lengthier list of battle campaigns than Worsham, who missed the last eight months of the war because of his wound. Each represents a "type" that served both North and South: Berkeley, the bright but lowly private for four years; Worsham, the dependable and knowledgeable noncommissioned officer; Fleet, the classic staff officer, consigned by circumstances to the rear for most of the war; and Poague, the quiet warrior whose education and bearing gave him his commission, but whose bravery and leadership skills gave him steady advancement through the ranks. Each man "grew up" a bit, tested by hardship, death, and disease and chastened by loss and failure. Yet even as their emotions hardened, their souls appeared to seek a deeper meaning to war and life through close bonds with fellow soldiers and a stronger commitment to serve God.

For the women, the war shook their entire world, demanding that they face challenges they had never dreamed of. Each had to adapt to a heavier household workload as servants fled and hired help became scarce. Each saw brothers or, in Susan's case, a husband, leave home for service of one sort or another, perhaps never to return. For Susan the household responsibilities nearly doubled, as Lycurgus was away for four years (though Mr. and Mrs. Finks helped shoulder the load). Each experienced the ravages of war firsthand, through the deaths of loved ones, plunder of their homes, and destruction of their property. Yet each one "grew up" a bit during the war, too. Tee and Lucy learned how to be more helpful around the home and each finally became a pillar supporting her family. Susan did not think she could bear even a month apart from Lycurgus, yet somehow she managed to survive four years of separation, numerous Union occupations, and the loss of her youngest child.

While the war did not dramatically alter the class, character, or values of these individuals, it significantly changed them and their world. They lost a war, a "cause," a way of life, and nearly half the men of their generation. For the rest of their adult lives they moved in a new world, one whose poverty and stunted opportunities stemmed largely from the war they had supported to its end. For these people, the survivors of the worst conflict in American history, life would never be the same. Surely those millions who came of age at this time fit Karl Mannheim's criteria for a generation: experience with the "same historical problems," "consciousness" of their "common situation," and the use of this consciousness as the "basis of their group solidarity." Beginning in the 1880s, thousands of veterans met for annual reunions, hundreds of books and articles on the war were published, and both Northern and Southern communities established memorials, erected statues, and held special events for veterans and those who had died in the war. As Anne Rose has written of this generation, "The Civil War tended to dominate the Victorians' vision, as they wrote with lucidity and force of this key personal event." For those who knew them directly—their children, grandchildren, and in some instances great-grandchildren—they were, as the young boy Bruce Catton saw them, "a breed apart."[8]

They knew they were a "special" generation, and those who survived, North and South, carried that peculiar mixture of guilt and pride that many veterans of wars possess. They had fought and died by the hundreds of thousands for their inherited ideals and causes. If they demanded recognition, respect, and occasionally reverence for their actions, who can blame them? They had to justify their sacrifices—and their losses.

On an entirely different level, that of the individual, the subjects in this study have something else to offer. By closely following their stories, one finds that the standard historical interpretations of events are not shared by all the participants. The strongest example from the battlefield is Gettysburg. As discussed in Chapter 8, none of the soldiers here saw Gettysburg as the "high-water mark" of the Confederacy. Instead, they viewed it as just another big battle, albeit a lost battle, in a long series of major and minor conflicts.

Similarly, not one of the women and none of the families of the soldiers withdrew support for the "cause" nor urged their men to desert during the last winter of the war. To be fair, contemporaries and modern historians such as William Blair and J. Tracy Power have noted and analyzed the fact that some Confederates remained loyal and supportive to the absolute end. But a legion of other scholars have examined those last seven months, seeking to find internal reasons for the collapse of the Confederacy (beyond the obvious ones). While none can deny the desertion and loss of material that occurred, a key point of this study has been to focus on some of the soldiers and civilians who strongly supported the Confederacy from beginning to end. This study asks why they persisted instead of why they surrendered. Their persistence, after all, kept this most horrific of American wars grinding on for a fourth, terrible year.

Another aspect of the complexity of the war is illustrated by the very moments that each of the seven men and women found most memorable. For John Worsham, the skirmish at Williamsport in 1863 loomed larger than countless other battles he fought. For William Poague, the paralyzing fire endured by his men at Cold Harbor remained a fresh and painful memory for years. For Lucy Buck, the memory of the war would always be dominated by the death of her beloved cousin, Walter Buck. In the end, these seven people and their generation leave us three powerful legacies. First and foremost is a single nation, with freedom for all, black and white. Second is the very problem that got them into war, the color line. Finally, they gave us a model for understanding how ordinary people can rise to the demands of extraordinary circumstances.

Without glorifying their prejudices or ignoring their weaknesses, we can learn from our subjects' grit and determination. Both sides in the war sought victory, but only one side won. Then the two sides had to learn how to work together again. This singular Civil War generation fought between themselves and then patched up their wounds and built the foundation of the modern industrial state. They also struggled to find meaning in the horrible sacrifices of their war, a struggle that persists to this day. At the same time, many of them demonstrated courage, coolness, and compassion in the face of shock and horror. In these and many other ways, the Civil War generation offers lessons for our generation—and all the ones to follow.

NOTES

1. Fleet, *Green Mount After the War*, editor's notes, 267–74.

2. Caldwell, *Letters*, editor's notes, 10.

3. *Rockbridge County News*, September 10, 1914; *Register of Former Cadets of the VMI* (Lexington, 1989), William T. Poague Jr., 129, and Henry G. Poague, 130.

4. *Orange Observer*, January 18, 1918, and January 25, 1918; Berkeley papers, Virginia Historical Society, unidentified newspaper clippings dated March 9, 1918, sent to the *Southern Churchman*; Berkeley, *Diary*, editor's notes, xxii; gravestone of Henry Robinson Berkeley, Graham Cemetery, Orange County, Virginia.

5. Lucy Buck diary, August 15 and 19, 1918.

6. *Richmond Times-Dispatch*, September 20, 1920; Worsham, *One of Jackson's Foot Cavalry*, editor's notes, xx–xxii.

7. Edmonds, *Journals*, editor's notes, xxiii and 273; Amanda Virginia Edmonds papers, Virginia Historical Society, Edmonds's journal, April 29, 1863–February 6, 1867, clipping on page 199.

8. Mannheim, "The Problem of Generations," in *Essays on the Sociology of Knowledge*, 304 and 290; Anne C. Rose, *Victorian America and the Civil War* (Cambridge, 1992), 251.

BIBLIOGRAPHICAL ESSAY

This book rests on two legs: the Civil War-era records of seven young adults from Virginia, and selected works from the vast literature on the Civil War. The papers of Henry Robinson Berkeley and Amanda "Tee" Edmonds are housed in the Virginia Historical Society, Richmond. The letters, journal, and diaries of Lucy Buck, Susan Caldwell, and Alexander "Fred" Fleet are in private hands. William T. Poague's memoirs and letters are held by the Virginia Military Institute, Lexington. To aid readers, I used the published, edited versions of these original documents: Henry Robinson Berkeley, *Four Years in the Confederate Artillery: The Diary of Private Henry Robinson Berkeley*, edited by William H. Runge (1961; reprint 1991); Lucy Buck, *Sad Earth, Sweet Heaven: The Diary of Lucy Rebecca Buck during the War Between the States, December 25, 1861–April 15, 1865*, edited by William P. Buck (1992); Susan Caldwell, *"My Heart Is So Rebellious": The Caldwell Letters, 1861–1865*, edited by J. Michael Welton (1990); Amanda Virginia Edmonds, *Journals of Amanda Virginia Edmonds: Lass of the Mosby Confederacy, 1859–1867*, edited by Nancy Chappelear Baird (1984); Benjamin Robert Fleet, *Green Mount: A Virginia Plantation Family during the Civil War: Being the Journal of Benjamin Robert Fleet and Letters of His Family*, edited by Betsy Fleet and John D. P. Fuller (1962); Maria Louisa Wacker Fleet, *Green Mount After the War: The Correspondence of Maria Louisa Wacker Fleet and Her Family, 1865–1900*, edited by Betsy Fleet (1978); William Thomas Poague, *Gunner with Stonewall: Reminiscences of William Thomas Poague, A Memoir Written for His Children in 1903*, edited by Monroe F. Cockrell (1987); and John H. Worsham, *One of Jackson's Foot Cavalry* (1912; reprint, 1992).

A good starting point for studying motivation and morale among civilians and soldiers in the Civil War is James M. McPherson, *For Cause and Comrades: Why Men Fought in the Civil War* (1997). Further explorations of the subject are found in Reid Mitchell, *Civil War Soldiers: Their Expectations and Experiences*

(1988), and *The Vacant Chair: The Northern Soldier Leaves Home* (1993); Gary W. Gallagher, *The Confederate War: How Popular Will, Nationalism, and Military Strategy Could Not Stave Off Defeat* (1997); Gerald Linderman, *Embattled Courage: The Experience of Combat in the American Civil War* (1987); William A. Blair, *Virginia's Private War: Feeding Body and Soul in the Confederacy, 1861–1865* (1998); and two older studies by Bell Irwin Wiley, *The Life of Johnny Reb: The Common Soldier of the Confederacy* (1943, reprint 1991), and *The Life of Billy Yank: The Common Soldier of the Union* (1952). Several historians attempt to wrap some of these ideas into a generational context: Peter S. Carmichael, *Lee's Young Artillerist: William R. J. Pegram* (1995); James Lee Conrad, *The Young Lions: Confederate Cadets at War* (1997); Kevin Conley Ruffner, *Maryland's Blue and Gray: A Border State's Union and Confederate Junior Officer Corps* (1997); and John C. Waugh, *The Class of 1846: From West Point to Appomattox: Stonewall Jackson, George McClellan, and Their Brothers* (1994). The use of generations as an organizing concept is discussed by Karl Mannheim, "The Problem of Generations," in *Essays on the Sociology of Knowledge*, ed. Karl Mannheim (1959), 276–322; Julian Marias, *Generations: A Historical Method* (1970); Alan B. Spitzer, "The Historical Problems of Generations," *American Historical Review* 78 (December 1973): 1353–85; and William Strauss and Neil Howe, *Generations: The History of America's Future, 1584 to 2069* (1991).

The prologue and first chapter offer a picture of Virginia in the 1850s and the first days of war, relying heavily on two primary sources: *Eighth Census of the United States, 1860*, and articles from the *Richmond Daily Dispatch* in 1861 (a pro-Confederate newspaper). Background on the secession movement in Virginia is found in Henry T. Shanks, *The Secession Movement in Virginia, 1847–1861* (1934), and Daniel M. Crofts, *Reluctant Confederates: Upper South Unionists in the Secession Crisis* (1989). Some of the flavor of life in Virginia in the late 1850s can be found in *Weevils in the Wheat: Interviews with Virginia Ex-Slaves*, edited by Charles L. Perdue, Thomas E. Bardon, and Robert K. Phillips (1976); and John S. Wise, *The End of an Era* (1899). A succinct overview of Virginia during the war is provided by James I. Robertson Jr., *Civil War Virginia: Battleground for a Nation* (1991).

The war's effects on Southern white women have been revisited again in recent years, most notably by Drew Gilpin Faust, *Mothers of Invention: Women of the Slaveholding South in the American Civil War* (1996); George C. Rable, *Civil Wars: Women and the Crisis of Southern Nationalism* (1989); and *Divided Houses: Gender and the Civil War*, edited by Catherine Clinton and Nina Silber (1992). A broader study of white and black women in the antebellum South is Sally G. McMillen's *Southern Women: Black and White in the Old South* (1992). An exciting new work on white women and politics in Virginia is Elizabeth R. Varon's *We Mean to Be Counted: The Roles of White Women in Politics in Antebellum Virginia* (1998). The long-standing debate over the concept of "separate spheres" for men and women in nineteenth-century America is reviewed by Linda Kerber in her article, "Separate Spheres, Female Worlds, Woman's Place: The Rhetoric of Women's History," *Journal of American History* 75, no. 1 (June 1988): 9–39.

The Battle of Manassas is succinctly surveyed in William C. Davis, *Battle at Bull Run: A History of the First Major Campaign of the Civil War* (1977). Two books by James I. Robertson Jr. helped with Chapter Three and other chapters: *The Stonewall Brigade* (1963), and *Stonewall Jackson: The Man, the Soldier, and the Legend* (1997).

The troubles of the Confederacy in its first winter are covered in Emory M. Thomas, *The Confederate Nation, 1861–1865* (1979), and William C. Davis, *Jefferson Davis: The Man and His Hour* (1991). The funeral of Obadiah Jennings is described in Craig Simpson, *A Good Southerner: The Life of Henry A. Wise of Virginia* (1985); Alfred Hoyt Bill, *The Beleaguered City: Richmond, 1861–1865* (1946); and Sallie Brock Putnam, *Richmond during the War: Four Years of Personal Observation* (1867; reprint 1983). Two volumes of the extensive Virginia Regimental Histories Series were needed in Chapter Four and elsewhere: Susan A. Riggs, *21st Virginia Infantry* (1991), and Robert Driver Jr., *The 1st and 2nd Rockbridge Artillery* (1987). For essential facts on the war, students can always rely on E. B. and Barbara Long, *The Civil War Day by Day: An Almanac, 1861–1865* (1971). The often cited one-volume history of the war is James M. McPherson's *Battle Cry of Freedom: The Civil War Era* (1988). To begin to understand the war from the perspective of slave and free blacks, see Ervin L. Jordan Jr., *Black Confederates and Afro-Yankees in Civil War Virginia* (1995).

Stonewall Jackson's Valley Campaign is ably analyzed in Robert Gaither Tanner, *Stonewall in the Valley* (1976); Robert K. Krick, *Conquering the Valley: Stonewall Jackson at Port Republic* (1996); and two books by James I. Robertson Jr., mentioned earlier. The best study of the Peninsula Campaign is Stephen W. Sears, *To the Gates of Richmond: The Peninsula Campaign* (1992). Two well-known sources helped in Chapter Five and other military history chapters: *The War of the Rebellion: A Compilation of the Official Records of the Union and Confederate Armies*, 128 vols. (1880–1901), and Douglas Southall Freeman, *Lee's Lieutenants: A Study in Command*, 3 vols. (1942–1944).

Chapter Six relies on some excellent battle histories to provide context for the actions of the soldiers in the study. Robert K. Krick's superb account, *Stonewall Jackson at Cedar Mountain* (1990), makes sense of this chaotic battle. John J. Hennessey brings similar clarity to the second battle fought at Manassas in *Return to Bull Run: The Campaign and Battle of Second Manassas* (1993). The Battle of Antietam is sensitively handled by Stephen W. Sears in *Landscape Turned Red: The Battle of Antietam* (1983). Two recent analyses of the Battle of Fredericksburg are found in Daniel T. Sutherland, *Fredericksburg and Chancellorsville: The Dare Mark Campaign* (1998), and Gary W. Gallagher, ed., *The Fredericksburg Campaign: Decision on the Rappahannock* (1995). Insight into the staff and command of the Army of Northern Virginia is provided by J. Boone Bartholomees Jr., *Buff Facings and Gilt Buttons: Staff and Headquarters Operations in the Army of Northern Virginia, 1861–1865* (1998). The first major religious revival in the Army of Northern Virginia is lovingly described by one of its leaders, J. William Jones, in *Christ in the Camp, or Religion in Lee's Army* (1887). Readers can find a full analysis of religious life in the Confederate armies in Steven E. Woodworth, *While God Is Marching On: The Religious World of Civil War Soldiers* (2001).

The activities of Colonel John Mosby's Rangers figure prominently in any discussion of Tee Edmonds's life during the war. A good introduction to Mosby and his exploits is Jeffrey D. Wert, *Mosby's Rangers* (1990); see also Paul Ashdown and Edward Caudill, *The Mosby Myth: A Confederate Hero in Life and Legend*

(2002). Two of Tee's brothers served in one of Mosby's units, described in Michael P. Musick, *6th Virginia Cavalry* (1990). Civilians living in the "frontier zone" between Union and Confederate armies were tremendously vulnerable. See Stephen V. Ash, *When the Yankees Came: Conflict and Chaos in the Occupied South, 1861– 1865* (1995).

Chapter Eight focuses on two major battles of 1863, Chancellorsville and Gettysburg. Robert E. Lee's greatest battlefield victory is given thorough examination by Ernest B. Furgurson, *Chancellorsville, 1863: The Souls of the Brave* (1992), and Stephen W. Sears, *Chancellorsville* (1997). The literature on the Battle of Gettysburg is overwhelming, but for this study three books proved useful: Carol Reardon, *Pickett's Charge in History and Memory* (1997); Lesley Gordon, *General George E. Pickett in Life and Legend* (1998); and George R. Stewart, *Pickett's Charge: A Microhistory of the Final Attack at Gettysburg, July 3, 1863* (1959, reprint 1980). For those with an insatiable appetite for knowledge of this battle, see three books edited by Gary W. Gallagher: *The First Day at Gettysburg: Essays on Confederate and Union Leadership* (1992), *The Second Day at Gettysburg: Essays on Confederate and Union Leadership* (1993), and *The Third Day at Gettysburg and Beyond* (1994).

The limited fighting and strains on the home front are the subjects of Chapters Nine and Ten. The battles in Virginia in the fall of 1863 are succinctly covered in William D. Henderson, *The Road to Bristoe Station: Campaigning with Lee and Meade, August 1– October 20, 1863* (1987), and Martin F. Graham and George F. Skoch, *Mine Run: A Campaign of Lost Opportunities, October 21, 1863–May 1, 1864* (1987). The movement and fighting of Fred Fleet's unit, the 26th Virginia, is described in Alex L. Wiatt, *26th Virginia Infantry* (1984). The stress of occupation on civilians in one Virginia county is masterfully analyzed by Daniel T. Sutherland in *Seasons of War: The Ordeal of a Confederate Community, 1861–65* (1995). Also of help are the works of Drew Faust and George Rable mentioned earlier.

The great battles of 1864 have become the domain of historian Gordon C. Rhea. He makes sense of the bloodiest campaign of the war in three prize-winning books: *The Battle of the Wilderness, May 5–6, 1864* (1994), *The Battles for Spotsylvania Court House and the Road to Yellow Tavern* (1997), and *To the North Anna River: Grant and Lee, May 13–25, 1864* (2000). For brief synopses of these and all major battles of the Civil War, see *The Civil War Battlefield Guide*, edited by Frances H. Kennedy (1990). On the struggle for control of Petersburg, see Noah Andre Trudeau, *The Last Citadel: Petersburg, Virginia, June 1864–April 1865* (1991). The condition of Lee's army in its last year is brilliantly probed by J. Tracy Power in *Lee's Miserables: Life in the Army of Northern Virginia from the Wilderness to Appomattox* (1998).

The starting point for studying Jubal Early's Second Valley Campaign is Jeffrey D. Wert, *From Winchester to Cedar Creek: The Shenandoah Campaign of 1864* (1987). For particular aspects of the fighting that year, see Richard R. Duncan, *Lee's Endangered Left: The War in Western Virginia, Spring of 1864* (1998); and William C. Davis, *The Battle of New Market* (1975). Two biographies proved useful: Charles C. Osborne, *Jubal: The Life and Times of General Jubal A. Early, CSA, Defender of the Lost Cause* (1992), and James L. Nichols, *General Fitzhugh Lee: A Biography* (1989). On the role of the artillery in battles, Jennings Cropper Wise's two-volume study, *The Long Arm of Lee, or The History of the Artillery of the Army of Northern Virginia* (1915; reprint 1991), helped in Chapter Twelve and other chapters.

The works of William Blair, J. Tracy Power, and Douglas Southall Freeman, all previously mentioned, provided crucial context for understanding the mood of Virginia in the waning months of the war. The final days of the Army of Northern Virginia are poignantly described by some key participants in E. P. Alexander, *Military Memoirs of a Confederate: A Critical Narrative* (1907); John B. Gordon, *Reminiscences of the Civil War* (1903); and James Longstreet, *From Manassas to Appomattox: Memoirs of the Civil War in America* (1896). Detailed lists of soldiers paroled at Appomattox are found in William G. Nine and Ronald Wilson, *The Appomattox Paroles, April 9–15, 1865* (1989).

The last three chapters outline the postwar lives of the seven individuals in the book. Several studies of this era were particularly useful: Fred A. Bailey, *Class and Tennessee's Confederate Generation* (1987); Paul Buck, *The Road to Reunion, 1865–1900* (1937); Gaines Foster, *Ghosts of the Confederacy: Defeat, the Lost Cause, and the Emergence of the New South, 1865–1913* (1987); Larry M. Logue, *To Appomattox and Beyond: The Civil War Soldier in War and Peace* (1996); Anne C. Rose, *Victorian America and the Civil War* (1992);

Nina Silber, *The Romance of Reunion: Northerners and the South, 1865–1900* (1993); Daniel T. Sutherland, *The Confederate Carpetbaggers* (1988); and Charles Reagan Wilson, *Baptized in Blood: The Religion of the Lost Cause, 1865–1920* (1980). Laura Virginia Hale helped place Lucy Buck in her postwar community in *On Chester Street: Presence of the Past, Patterns of the Future* (1985). Finally, anyone interested in writing social history should read Gillian Tindall, *Celestine: Voices from a French Village* (1995). Tindall combines the scrupulousness of a historian with the eloquence of a novelist.

INDEX